Routledge Philosophy GuideBook to

Leibniz and the *Monadology*

'written with great clarity and elegance and with an effective use of examples ... an excellent guide to a difficult work for undergraduates and graduate students.'
Nicholas Jolley, Syracuse University

Leibniz is a major figure in western philosophy and, with Descartes and Spinoza, one of the most influential philosophers of the Rationalist School. This Routledge Philosophy GuideBook guides the reader through the complexities of Leibniz's most famous work and the fullest statement of his mature philosophical thought, the *Monadology*. Anthony Savile clearly identifies the intellectual assumptions that underlie Leibniz's thought and locates the text within Leibniz's larger philosophical project.

Leibniz and the Monadology is a clear and engaging introduction to one of the finest systematic thinkers of the modern era. It is essential reading for all students coming to Leibniz for the first time.

Anthony Savile is Professor of Philosophy at King's College London.

**Routledge
Philosophy
GuideBooks**

Edited by Tim Crane and Jonathan Wolff
University College London

LONDON AND NEW YORK

Routledge Philosophy GuideBook to

Leibniz and the *Monadology*

ROUTLEDGE

■ Anthony Savile

First published 2000
by Routledge
11 New Fetter Lane, London EC4P 4EE

Simultaneously published in the USA and Canada
by Routledge
29 West 35th Street, New York, NY 1000

Routledge is an imprint of the Taylor & Francis Group

Typeset in Times and Gill Sans by Taylor & Francis Books Ltd
Printed and bound in Great Britain by Clays Ltd, St Ives plc

British Library Cataloguing in Publication Data
A catalogue record for this book is available from the British Library

Library of Congress Cataloging in Publication Data
Savile, Anthony.
Routledge philosophy guidebook to Leibniz and the Monadology
p. cm.– (Routledge philosophy guidebooks)
Includes bibliographical references and index.
1. Leibniz, Gottfried Wilhelm, Freiherr von, 1646-1716. 2. Monadology.
I. Leibniz, Gottfried Wilhelm, Freiherr von, 1646-1716. Monadology. 2000.
II. Title. III. Series.
B2599.M8 S28 2000
193–dc21   00-027144

ISBN 0–415–16575–X (hbk)
ISBN 0–415–16576–8 (pbk)

Contents

Introduction

Gottfried Wilhelm Leibniz was born into an academic family in Leipzig in 1646, just before the end of the Thirty Years War. His father was Professor of Moral Philosophy there and his mother the daughter of a local Professor of Law. Descartes had died in 1650 before Leibniz was 4, and he was younger by 12 years than Spinoza and by 14 than Locke. By the time he was 20, he had precociously completed his own legal studies and written a doctoral thesis on the subject of hard cases at law (*De casibus perplexis in jure*). Turning down the offer of a university post before the age of 21, he preferred to enter public service in the courts of German principalities and within a few years of completing his studies had become Counsellor at the Supreme Court of the Elector of Mainz. After a period spent in Paris on diplomatic mission (between 1672 and 1676), he accepted an appointment as librarian in the service of the then Duke of Brunswick, Johann-Frederick. Then, in 1685, when that gentleman was succeeded by his brother Ernst-August, Leibniz became the official historian of the House of Brunswick, the duties of which post occupied him on and off until his death in 1716.

During his court years, in what we would think of as significant civil service or even ministerial positions, Leibniz cultivated an extraordinarily wide range of intellectual interests, writing on international law, on theology, political theory, physics, geology and mathematics quite apart from on logic and philosophy. He discovered the differential and integral calculus at the age of 30 during his Paris years, independently of, though some nine years later than, Newton. He also pursued practical interests of political, scientific and academic importance. While in Paris he was engaged in a vain attempt to interest Louis XIV in a scheme for the military conquest of Egypt, largely with a view to diverting the French armies away from northern Europe and securing peace there. That militaristic idea bore no fruit until the much later Napoleonic campaign of 1798–99. Then he worked, this time successfully, to secure the promotion in 1692 of the House of Hanover to Electoral status – that is, to the Electoral College of the Holy Roman Empire, the members of which chose the Emperor from among their number. He concerned himself intensively with the engineering and modernization of the silver mines in the Harz mountains. He was instrumental in the foundation of the Academy of Sciences in Berlin, to the life presidency of which he was elected in 1701. Then, too, at various times he was in a position to give close political advice to Ernst-August of Hanover, to his successor Georg-Ludwig, who was to become George I of England, to the Emperor Charles VI and to Peter the Great, for whom he prepared plans for the political, scientific and economic development of Russia and for the foundation of a scientific academy in St Petersburg.

In the course of his official duties Leibniz travelled extensively in Europe, in France, in Austria, in Italy and briefly in England, and was able to meet and correspond with many of the leading intellectual figures of his day. In Paris he had contact with philosophers such as Arnauld and Malebranche and studied at length with the mathematician Christiaan Huygens; in London, where he was elected Fellow of the Royal Society in 1673, he met the eminent natural scientists Robert Boyle and Henry Oldenburg, Secretary to the Royal Society, and Christopher Wren, geometer and architect of London after the

1666 Great Fire. Through Oldenburg he also engaged an indirect and somewhat one-sided correspondence with the Cambridge recluse Isaac Newton. On passing through Holland in 1676, he encountered the microscopist van Leeuwenhoek and had four intense days of discussion with Spinoza.

The long span of Leibniz's intellectual life and his early involvement with philosophy made for engagement with a wide variety of philosophical traditions and issues. Early studies at home exposed him to the thought of the Scholastics; during his university years he was something of a materialist, influenced by the atomism of Bacon and Gassendi. In his mid-20s and early 30s, becoming disenchanted with the intellectual prospects for materialist thought, he turned towards the sort of immaterialism that came to shape his mature thinking after the decade between 1675 and 1685 when he was more narrowly concerned with mathematics than with philosophy. It is this anti-materialism that is epitomized in the *Monadology* itself and which I discuss in detail in this book.

Although Leibniz produced a prodigious quantity of philosophical writing very little of it was published during his lifetime; indeed, very little was intended for publication. For the most part, excepting occasional articles that appeared in the Leipzig *Acta Eruditorum* and the Paris-based *Journal des Sçavants*, his philosophical thoughts were prepared for individual scholars he had met, or with whom he corresponded, and were never presented as a worked-out system. The fullest attempts to expound his metaphysics systematically are to be found in the 1686 *Discourse on Metaphysics*, the *New System and Explanation of the New System* of 1695, and 'On the Ultimate Origination of Things' of 1697, but it was not until the last period of his life that he found the time and the impetus to set down the whole, which he did in two condensed papers written in French during a visit to Vienna. The more popular and less taxing of these was the *Principles of Nature and Grace Founded on Reason*, which he prepared for Prince Eugène of Savoy, and the second, which he had been asked to write by the counsellor of the Duke of Orleans, Nicolas Remond, but never sent off, was the *Principles of Philosophy* or, as he called it, *Elucidation Concerning Monads* – the subject of the present study. The title by which that work is known today, *Monadology*, was not one that Leibniz ever gave it, but was invented by the work's first editor, Heinrich Kohler, who published it in a German translation under that title in 1720.

Although systematic presentation of his thought was not set down by Leibniz until two years before his death, many of its main ideas guide the course of two major pieces of writing that occupied the later period of his philosophical endeavours. The first of these was the *Essays on Theodicy: Of God's Goodness, Man's Freedom and the Origin of Evil*, which, as the work's subtitle intimates, is concerned largely to show how the existence of a perfect God is compatible with the evil that we find in his creation and how the pre-ordained course of events that he chose to create is compatible with human freedom. This work was the only book-length work by Leibniz that was published during his lifetime (in 1710) and it arose in part out of conversations he had at the court at Hanover with the Electress Sophia (grand-daughter of James I and wife of Ernst-August of Brunswick) and her daughter Sophie Charlotte, who later became Queen of Prussia. It is a work that is in large part polemical in nature, seeking to correct theologico-philosophical errors that Leibniz found in Bayle's influential *Dictionary* and in much contemporary theology and Cartesian-inspired philosophy. At the end of sections in the manuscript of the *Monadology*, Leibniz makes frequent reference to passages of his *Theodicy* so that readers should have ready access to the fuller treatment of material presented so succinctly in the later work. When one follows up these references one cannot but be astonished by the breadth and depth of Leibniz's learning as much by the way in which argument with his theological adversaries is conducted on carefully thought through principles.

The other extensive work of Leibniz's maturity was a commentary on Locke's *Essay Concerning Human Understanding* (1690), which had been translated into French by Pierre Coste in 1701 and had found an early and enthusiastic welcome on the continent of Europe. Leibniz presents his commentary as a dialogue between a Lockean, Philalethes, and his own spokesman, Theophilus, often setting out Philalethes' position in Locke's own words and commenting extensively on aspects of it that particularly interested him. Here too we find Leibniz's rejection of much of Locke's empiricism stemming from the metaphysics that finds its fullest expression in the *Monadology*. To students whose introduction to philosophy is often through the medium of Locke's *Essay*, it can be of the greatest interest to see how Locke's often amateur-seeming musings are sympathetically but judiciously and acutely reviewed by a contemporary mind of the very first order. As it happened, Leibniz delayed the publication of his *New Essays on Human Understanding*, which were substantially complete in 1704, in order to give Locke a chance to respond to his observations and criticisms. Locke, however, died in 1704 before he had had occasion to do so, and Leibniz's work was consequently set on one side and was not to see the public light before 1765. At several places in my discussion of difficult passages of the *Monadology* I have found it helpful to consult the *New Essays*, and indications of the passages that bear most closely on topics discussed are given in the footnotes.

The *Monadology* itself consists of ninety numbered sections. Because the writing is so dense, it has been necessary to make frequent cross-references to passages of the work, and to avoid repetitiously quoting from the text I use Leibniz's numbering system to do so. The Appendix gives a full version of the *Monadology*. Readers may find it useful to have worked through that from start to finish before embarking on the commentary, and then to return to it *ad libitum* to confront my interpretative suggestions with the text itself.

The impersonal style of the *Monadology* gives the reader only a slight impression of Leibniz the man. Evidently he is not one to waste words and equally evidently he is confident of the power of his intellect to achieve a unified understanding of the complex world around him. In the later passages of the work one is impressed by his curiosity in and wonder at the variety of Nature and struck, too, by the very deep and entirely unsentimental piety of his Lutheran religious convictions. He had the reputation of being somewhat cantankerous with and dismissive of opponents, but in his other writings, particularly the *New Essays*, he comes across as a kindly, courteous, modest and sometimes even quite humorous person. At the end of his life he had fallen out of favour with Georg-Ludwig, the third ruler of the House of Brunswick he was to serve. Georg-Ludwig had removed to London in 1714 as George I on the death of Queen Anne and refused

Leibniz's request to be allowed to accompany him there. So Leibniz stayed in Hanover to become rather a figure of fun or amused contempt in a provincial and philistine backwater of European culture. He was, however, one of that culture's greatest luminaries, and one whom it would have been a great privilege to meet.

It cannot be said that Leibniz had great philosophical influence on his contemporaries, in part no doubt because of the very restricted circulation of his writings on the subject. The way in which he became a recognized figure of importance, particularly in Germany in the second half of the eighteenth century, was through the development of his speculative and metaphysical views as elaborated by Johann Christian Wolff (1679–1754), whose work was standardly studied in German universities throughout much of the eighteenth century. Notably, Wolff's Leibnizianism made a deep impact on Kant, in whose *Critique of Pure Reason* (1781) Leibniz himself came to figure as one of the main targets of Kant's anti-metaphysical programme. In particular, Kant saw Leibniz as pretending to *a priori* knowledge of the world as it is in itself and presented his own claim that the only knowledge we can have is of the world as it appears in our experience as sharply opposed to the Leibnizian vision. In the English-speaking world Leibniz's philosophy made little impact until Bertrand Russell's book on his thought appeared in 1901, partly one may surmise on account of the strongly anti-speculative cast of Hume's influential *Enquiry Concerning Human Understanding* (1747). If we hold up Leibniz's *Monadology* to Hume's hostile questions – 'Does it contain any abstract reasoning concerning quantity or number?' 'Does it contain any experimental reasoning concerning matter of fact and existence?' – we shall certainly answer 'No' on both counts. Hume's advice was famously: 'Commit it then to the flames: for it can contain nothing but sophistry and illusion.' For many years that advice must have seemed only common sense.

Happily, though, we did not commit the *Monadology* to the flames, and the flourishing state of Leibniz studies today shows that his thought has survived even the extreme empiricism of the Vienna Circle in the 1930s, which would have viewed its principal doctrines as unverifiable and hence utterly meaningless. Although not in evidence in the *Monadology* itself, one of Leibniz's preoccupations was with the philosophy of logic and language, and the twentieth-century's concern for those topics has discovered in what he had to say about them a treasure house of good sense and wisdom which can be detached from the less appealing of his metaphysical speculations. Then, more recent writers who have been interested in the metaphysics of possibility and necessity have found inspiration in the Leibnizian image of possible worlds, and that too has helped to keep his name alive for us.

If we consider the *Monadology* itself we shall scarcely find metaphysical theses there that have great appeal for thinkers of our own day, but because the anti-metaphysical animus of the past no longer exercizes the influence that it used to we are better able than before to admire the depth, the consistency and the ingenuity of Leibniz's mind as he struggles to uncover the world's intelligible structure. Even when we decline to accept the metaphysical vision that he proclaims, as we come to appreciate how the detail of that vision responds to what struck him as irresistible intellectual pressures we shall carry away from our reading an admiration for a philosophical integrity that we should be proud to equal and which we may well hold up to ourselves as an exemplary model.

Because the *Monadology* is so complex a work any commentary is bound to pose difficulties of its own for the uninitiated reader approaching it from without in the hope of discovering reasonably quickly what this particular eighteenth-century metaphysical construction is like. Trying to mirror the system accurately and to pursue its intricacies as far as they go, the commentator and guide risks multiplying the obstacles to understanding as he multiplies the pages that he takes to do it. To forestall any such discomfort, or at least to minimize it, I end this introduction by offering a brief and simplified outline of the story that follows. Readers who prefer to dispense with such aids to orientation should move on straightway; those who are uncertain whether what lies ahead is for them may be helped to decide whether or not to undertake the journey by taking a swift tour of the terrain that lies ahead.

Leibniz's overall philosophical ambition is none other than to provide us with a lucid understanding of the world in which we live and of our place in it. It is at once a philosophical and a theological exercize, philosophical because it aims to present his teachings as answerable to reason alone, and theological because reason leads us to recognize that an understanding of the world and of ourselves can be achieved only if we adopt God's own perspective on things and see their course as answering to the through-and-through rational plan for the world he creates.

Seeing things in this light forces us to ask at the very first step what methodological assumptions govern Leibniz's reflections, and Chapter 1 addresses that task. Leibniz himself announces two Great Principles from which everything else is presented as flowing. It is no surprise that the first of these should be the Principle of Contradiction, which sets the boundaries within which any power of reasoning must be exercized, be it the power of an infinite god or that of a puny finite creature like man. Metaphysical truths, or truths of reasoning, will be those whose opposite is a contradiction, and much of the philosophical system that Leibniz recommends has the character it does because, in his view, far more than we might initially expect can be shown to be fixed in this *a priori* way. Leaving it open for the time being just what comes to be held in place by this very first principle, we might suppose that the range of possibilities it permits is bound to be so enormous that philosophy should despair of providing any substantive understanding of our situation or guidance as to what to make of it. That is, if the philosopher relies on reason to see how things must be, the Principle of Contradiction may enable him to grasp something of what cannot be the case, but when it comes to discerning how matters substantially lie, there he must pass on the baton to the natural scientist or at least the observer who draws on skills other than those of philosophy itself. So one might think.

That, however, is not how Leibniz views the situation, for to his mind the philosopher has a second principle which he can legitimately call in aid, and this is the Principle of Sufficient Reason. This principle serves to assure him that whatever is not ruled out as a contradiction can only come to pass provided there is a reason why it should be so and not otherwise. So, while there may be very many ways in which we could imagine the world as being which would not involve us in any outright logical incoherence, just because so many of them would present it as entirely topsy-turvy and downright unreasonable Leibniz will say that they too can be ruled out from the start as ways for it to be. Putting it somewhat crudely, we can say that making the assumption that we have to explore the world with the help of reason, we are bound to take it as a methodological principle that the world lies open to our understanding. In consequence the world must be thought of as conforming to the requirement that it be fully explicable. The point at which this principle yields high returns is the point at which we come to see how very narrow are the limits within which this demand can be satisfied. Just because those limits turn out to be narrow ones, we find Leibniz's rationalistic strain of philosophy delivering remarkably precise results.

As one first encounters this second principle, a natural reaction is to suppose that all sorts of different dispensations that the world might have displayed would be envisageable as perfectly reasonable and comprehensible. If the laws of nature had been rather different, then maybe life itself would not have been possible, or the universe might have enjoyed a completely cyclical arrangement, oscillating between one Big Bang and another, with Big Crunches in the intervals between. Strange though such scenarios may seem, less so to ours maybe than to eighteenth-century minds that had never come across the speculations of hard-nosed cosmologists, we are inclined to think that each one is intelligible enough and that considerations of 'sufficient reason' can hardly be brought to bear in a way that makes our own familiar world privileged vis-à-vis those others any more than the Principle of Contradiction itself rules them out. Leibniz, however, would think that such a response is short-sighted and that it just rests on a failure to see just where his second principle in fact leads.

The demands of understanding could not be satisfied if something that we explain in terms of a further thing just leads to the same demand for explanation arising again. Chains of explanation cannot be left open like this, because then, from the point of view of understanding, nothing will have been achieved. The wheels will just be turning idly. So if the exercise of understanding is to reveal the nature of things to us in a way that is at all satisfactory, it can do so only if the explanations it offers us come to a halt, and that will be achieved only when we see the original source of earth-bound things to lie outside the world itself – to wit, in the decisions and decrees of a necessarily existing extramundane intelligence, God.

The details of Leibniz's proofs of God's existence occupy Chapter 2 and will not detain us here, though it is worth noting that today's speculations on this subject are much more likely to draw on Leibniz's own thought about it than on anything else that the literature has to offer. What is of importance here is to appreciate how it is that the appeal to God gives the Principle of Sufficient Reason real bite. So far it might seem as if the only point that is served by pursuing questions of understanding beyond the realm of the actual world is to stop a threat of regress. Explanations cannot be pushed further back, because we have arrived at a point at which, existing of necessity, God, or the ultimate reason for things, could itself have no further reason. It must simply be.

Of course, just to say that the final reason for everything can only be provided by appeal to God may be found gratifying theologically, but it hardly seems to solve the problem we set out with. Appeal to God's decrees might ultimately account for whatever happens, but it would scarcely seem to be something one could use to come to see why the world that exists should be chosen in preference to any other. Couldn't one even say that there would need to be a reason for God's choosing one way rather than another? If so, the regress of explanations looks set to start up again, outside the world this time rather than within it. Leibniz takes himself to have an answer to this question. God exists of necessity, and of necessity is omnipotent and omniscient; and of his very nature he is benevolent as well. So, the Principle of Sufficient Reason leads us to see that in his choice of a world at the moment of creation God will have been guided by a desire for the best (thus displaying his benevolence), and exercizing his omniscience will be sure to have identified that best correctly, and in virtue of his omnipotence will have realized it flawlessly. Sufficient Reason thus brings us to acknowledge that the actual world around us has the configuration that it does because it was selected by God from among the alternatives that presented themselves on account of its being the very best of the various possibilities that there were. This choice, lying rooted as it does in God's essential nature, can require no further explanation.

Again it may seem that even when Sufficient Reason is seconded in this way by the Principle of the Best, which guides God's choice, the result is still pretty meagre. Isn't a world the best just in virtue of it having pleased God to bring it into existence? Wouldn't any world that God may have cared to create be just like any other on that score? Leibniz's answer is certainly 'No', for, as he sees it, the idea of the best, to which God is responsive, has a very specific content. As he conceived of it, the good that God seeks to maximize is one that embodies as much variety as possible in its content subject to that variety being achieved though economy of means, that is, in accordance with the greatest possible degree of order. Hence if we seek to explain some fact about the natural world, such as, say, the distribution of certain species of lavender in Norfolk at the turn of the twenty-first century, at the end of the day we shall find ourselves saying that a world displaying that feature was chosen to exist in preference to all the other possible dispensations just because that was the world that permitted the simplest possible ordering of things together with the richest possible variety. Anything else would have fallen short either in the scale of variety or in the scale of order, to the detriment overall of the whole. Norfolk's actual distribution of lavender is integral to our world's being the best world possible – and hence to its coming to exist at all. So, too, with any other contingent truth, or fact, about the world.

To characterize God's conception of the good in terms of variety and order is only to tell half of the story. God himself is the very epitome of the good, and so it will turn out that the variety and order he elects will necessarily find their place in a world of creatures that somehow reflect God's own nature in a finite way, creatures that themselves are capable of limited knowledge, of exercizing limited power and displaying limited benevolence in their actions. This refinement of Leibniz's idea of the good will have its place later on when the moral dimension of his metaphysic becomes prominent, but for the moment I shall set it aside and ask what can be said about the metaphysical nature of a world that satisfies Sufficient Reason through answering to the Principle of the Best. It is at this point that the Principle of Contradiction comes into its own.

Whatever God creates in the pursuit of the best cannot but be something real, an infinity of real things to be sure, since anything less would impose unreasonable limitations on the variety that his creation would display. Now for Leibniz what is real can only be something that possesses a true unity, for to exist and to be one this or that are, he believes, the very same thing. What is more, those things that enjoy real unity cannot be complex, for if they were they would be liable to come apart, to dissolve and disintegrate, and thus lose the unity which is essentially theirs. So, as Leibniz sees it, the world that God creates must ultimately be a world of indissoluble simple things, elementary substances, or as he likes to call them 'monads'. Of course, everything we find and observe in the world around us is complex in one way or another, but unless these complexes are made up of real simples they could not themselves exist. The Principle of Contradiction alone forces this metaphysical stance upon us.

Chapter 3 introduces these monadic simples and discusses the nature Leibniz sees them as inevitably having. Because of their truly unitary character they cannot be physically divisible, and so must not be thought of as material atoms however minute their extension might be. Such things would in theory always be further divisible, hence not be simple. Then, because monads can not be even minimally extended in space they can not naturally perish or be generated, for decay and generation can only take place where there is a dissolution of the complex into its simpler elements or a combination of more simple things into an aggregate. Exempt from generation and corruption, monads must therefore be eternal, unless, by way of miracle, God should add to the stock of those he originally created once time's clock has begun to tick, or decree at some time that some should cease to be. However, while that is not ruled out as a pure impossibility, since we know God's creation to be flawless we can justly infer that he will have no reason to alter his original decree. Application of Sufficient Reason therefore assures us that miracles will not occur and that the original decree will never be modified by later additions or subtractions.

In Chapter 4 we see that there is more to be said about the monadic elements of things apart from that they are simple, extensionless and eternal. Even though they have no parts they must none the less have properties. Failing that they would not exist at all. Then whatever universe God might have created will have contained simples whose properties change. Otherwise there could be no time, which is required for their development. Further, we can see that all simples must have different properties from one another, for unless they do they would not be distinct individuals at all. Also, the changes that they undergo must take place gradually, and do so in fulfilment of the monads' own natures, since their simplicity precludes there being any causal inter-actions between them by way of a transmission or exchange of parts and properties. Lastly, since the complex wholes that come into exis-tence depend for their nature on that of the simples that make them up, the character of these simples alone must be capable of explaining all the observed and observable features of the grosser world.

This last demand must seem something of a mystery given the rather negative claims about monadic nature so far detailed. If anything the mystery is compounded by the more positive informa-tion Leibniz provides about it, which is the subject of Chapter 5. It is as if by elimination that we arrive at the insight that the properties that monads possess are to be thought of as nothing other than their perceptions and their desires or appetitions. So the individual monad's nature will ultimately consist in such things as its perceiving that the cat is on the mat and desiring that the cat be off the mat, or it may perceive that it is angry at the cat's still being on the mat and then come to desire that it should not be upset by such trivialities. (The examples emphasize that in their perceptual and appetitive represen-tations monads' thoughts extend both to their own perpetually changing states and to the composites that they and other monads enter into.) What is fundamental to this rather more developed picture of monadic nature is that we are to see that the ultimate constituents of the world have to be minds and that everything else that exists must be understood as a complex of one sort or another built up out of such simple mental elements. Once Leibniz has persuaded himself and his readers that the elements of any world which God could create can not be extended physical things, there is little alternative in the metaphysics that he can envisage but that they should be minds. Here we see Leibniz espousing a form of idealism that is very different in character from the slightly later empiricist vision of British thinkers such as Berkeley or Hume and different too in its ontological commitments from the metaphysics of the other major continental figures of his own time, Descartes and Spinoza. It is instructive to see how these differences arise.

Eighteenth-century British idealists did indeed hold, like Leibniz, that the only substances that existed apart from God himself must be minds, but they did so for reasons that were fundamentally determined by their theory of knowledge rather than their metaphysics. Following their continental predecessors (Leibniz included, but principally Descartes), both Berkeley and Hume held that the true objects of our acquaintance could only be our own perceptions, or ideas. Apart from them we could not justify other claims about what else the world might contain. Given that what we say about the world needs at the end of the day to be answerable to what we observe, the physical aspect of the natural world needs to be constructed out of these immediately given perceptual ideas. Naturally enough, perceptions or ideas seem to require subjects whose perceptions and ideas they are, and what could those subjects be other than minds? Here we have the heart of classic British idealism.[1] The root of Leibniz's comparable commitment to the primary existence of minds is, however, not epistemological. As we have seen, it is rooted in his metaphysics. For him, the only true existences must be simple substances because anything else will be divisible into parts, and so lack a true unity that alone would make it genuinely real. Minds are the only truly unitary substances that can be envisaged, so whatever it is that exists has to be understood in their terms. Contrasting Leibniz with Berkeley (d. 1753) and Hume (d. 1776), it is fair enough to say that whereas for them the external and material world is to be explained away, for Leibniz it demands to be explained.

The philosophy of Leibniz's continental peers Descartes (d. 1650) and Spinoza (d.1677), like that of Leibniz himself, was directed by metaphysical rather than epistemological concerns, though neither philosopher was drawn to the idealism that Leibniz thought us bound

---

1 In Hume's case, unlike Berkeley's, though the belief that there are minds, or subjects, or selves that possess the perceptions and ideas is more a natural belief of which we cannot rid ourselves rather than one that is rationally defensible. See the Appendix to his *Treatise on Human Nature*.

to embrace. For Descartes, substances might be either mental or physical, and for him each has as much claim to reality as the other. For Spinoza, the Principle of Contradiction alone leads to a view in which there can only be one substance, which we can call God or Nature as we will, and, indivisible though that is, it is neither a peculiarly mental thing nor a physical one, but presents itself to us as the neutral subject of both physical and mental states.

We shall soon enough come to Leibniz's way of constructing the physical world out of monadic simples. First, however, we should consider the universe of simples God that comes to create under the Principle of the Best. This is the topic of Chapter 6. What confronts God at the crucial moment of his creative choice has to be conceived of as an array of possibilities, or complete worlds, among which he selects one for existence in preference to all others. These possibilities are given independently of his will. That only comes into play as one of these possibilities recommends itself to him for selection in preference to all others. However, that these alternatives are genuine possibilities does depend on God's existence, since were he (*per impossibile*) not to exist there would be no way in which any of them could become actual, and to be possible is nothing other than to be capable of being that. Leibniz occasionally speaks of possibles striving for existence, but when he does so that can only mean that they vie with one another for God's creative attention. They could not bypass that, since under Sufficient Reason there would then be no explanation available of how they might do so. Apart from God's will in the matter, the best that is possible has no better claim on existence than the worst.

Not just any set of possibilities makes up a possible world. First, of course, we know we have to do only with sets of possible substances, minds of one kind or another furnished with the perceptions and desires that are theirs. Then, each one of these is completely determinate in terms of the properties (the perceptions and desires) that it has. It is part of Leibniz's understanding of the Principle of Contradiction that every proposition is either true or false, so that as far as possible substances go there is no room for vagueness of indeterminacy in God's view of their intrinsic characters. Further, a set of possibles only makes up a world if it is a complete set, by which is meant that no further elements could be added to it without inconsistency, or without diminishing the richness of its mixture of variety and order.

At first sight, these restrictions may look arbitrary, or at least puzzling. How could it make sense to think that there are collections of substances that could not be augmented without inconsistency, as Leibniz believed? And even if there are such sets, why should God not be able to select a segment of a world for creation rather than a replete whole? The somewhat speculative answer I propose to the first of these two questions, encouraged by Leibniz himself, is that the idea of a complete world is fundamentally that of a maximally varied and ordered set of monads that can co-exist with one another under a given set of natural laws. What distinguishes one world from another is just that their members operate in accordance with different laws (different laws that ultimately govern the flow of their simple elements' perceptions and desires), and that itself imposes restrictions on the monads that could be added into any given collection of elements. A monad from one possible world develops in accordance with the laws of its world, and having those as part of its nature, its very identity even, is what would make it impossible for it to join in with other monads developing under different laws had God selected them for existence. That is the source of the inadmissibility of some possible substances into other possible arrays.

To say this does no more than explain why worlds could not be augmented in ways not compatible with the laws that govern them. It does not explain at all why under a given set of laws there should be a maximal set of possibles. Why should its size not be without an upper limit? Here the crucial consideration that must move Leibniz is that after a certain point the only additions that could be made to a set of possible substances would be ones that threatened either the variety or the degree of order that it enjoys. Further simples could be introduced to the situation only at the expense of others or of some loss of order. So the idea of a world, as a maximal set of compossible substances, must itself involve these normative notions. And it is their centrality to the issue that provides the answer to the second question I asked. For given that to create what he does God chooses for the sake of the best, when it comes to comparing one set of possibles for creation with another the only ones that could be of any interest to him would be maximal sets. Anything less would be a less than best choice of candidates in the race, and this applies as much to possible sets of things that God ultimately decides not to create as to the one set that he in fact lights on when his final decision is made. The universe we end up with, then, must be the finest of all the fully replete sets of possible monads that there could be. Thus while there is no absolute impossibility for God to have chosen less than a fully replete world, when he makes the comparisons among worlds the only alternatives that could have any appeal for him are between worlds that are replete. In this matter, as Leibniz often puts it, God is inclined, though not necessitated. Further, more follows from this than that the world that God elects to create is richer than any other. Even if that would be achieved by something less than the replete world we have (say, by that segment of the actual world that simply excludes the Pyramids or the Taj Mahal), in his pursuit of supreme excellence we can see that God is bound to ensure that as much additional value is included as is possible. When it comes to his final choice of world, it isn't just a matter of choosing one collection of things that is better than any other. The world that is chosen will inevitably be as much better than the others as it is possible for it to be.

One might wonder at this point how many different possible worlds there may be that really compete for God's attention. Leibniz held that they are infinite in number, but we should be aware that there are severe constraints on their range. These derive largely from the thought that the monadic substances that go to make up the various possibilities are essentially active in their desires and their perceptions, and that in their finite way they are bound to reflect God's own essentially perfect nature. In particular, in their perceptions monads will tend towards (but no more) God's own omniscience, and this suggests that their perceptions are very similar to those of one another. If they all perceive everything – though necessarily with various degrees of distinctness and confusion, so that they are all none the less distinguished from one another – and if their active desires must be of a kind to be satisfied, then they will need to have bodies which themselves obey natural (for Leibniz, mechanical) laws. That in turn implies that there are relatively narrow limits to the kinds of world there could be and that even if they must all run by somewhat different sets of laws the possible range of variation falls within fairly narrow bounds. Whatever other worlds God might have chosen would in fundamental respects have to be markedly like our own.

Whether or not the active nature of simple substances really does entail that monads have bodies, the character of our own world obliges Leibniz to explain how there can come to be matter in a world whose ultimate constituents are only minds. He never discusses the topic at length, and passes over it in silence in the *Monadology* itself. It is a crux of his philosophy, though, and we should not follow him in this silence. This topic is the subject of Chapter 7. Further, when Leibniz does give the issue his attention, he repeatedly calls bodies 'phenomena', and that can easily encourage a mistaken understanding of what he is inclined to think. We have already seen that on the English side of the Channel Berkeley and Hume were inclined to phenomenalism, the view that the truth of statements about the material world is fully explicable in terms of actual and possible perceptual experiences. Leibniz's talk of bodies as 'phenomena' might likewise encourage the thought that a body of matter exists just in case all monads agree in having the same 'material' perceptions. However, to embrace any such reading of him would be to see Leibniz as explaining away the material nature of things rather than explaining it, and I have already said he is anxious not to do that.

Whatever the attractions of the phenomenalistic reading of Leibniz's thought, it can hardly have been Leibniz's own on at least two further counts. First, it overstrains the claim that bodily aggregates are compounded of monads, and then it also unacceptably weakens his thought that in their perceptions monads have true knowledge of the world they inhabit (even if their perception of it is indistinct and imperfect). A view much more consonant with Leibniz's writing is that groups of monads are perceived confusedly in the large as material blocks and as such blocks they exert physical force on other such groups. To perceive something confusedly, we must insist, is not to misperceive it. It is to perceive it correctly enough, only from the peculiar perspective of our own perceiving position. So for there to be matter is for there to be groups of monads that are jointly disposed to affect perceivers in that familiar confused 'material' way, much as we account for a paint's colour or a perfume's scent in terms of the way in which the paint or the perfume is liable to affect perceivers like ourselves. Correct or not, this is certainly not a phenomenalistic view of the subject. What it is that for Leibniz makes material bodies 'phenomena', as he calls them, is that their unity is no more than a conventional matter, depending on our classificatory interests and concerns. They are, quite unlike monads, not absolute unities in their own right but confused ones, or unities in relation to us and our ways of thinking. That view of their phenomenal nature is entirely orthogonal to a phenomenalistic construction of their existence.

The main focus of Leibniz's interest in the material world is taken up with man himself, and it is entirely to his credit that his treatment of men is one that allies them with other natural organisms such as animals and plants – though naturally enough there are metaphysically important differences among them. What these things all have in common is that their unity is in each case precisely not a conventional one. It would therefore be wrong to think of them just as physical bodies. Rather they are all natural *living organisms*. Such things, Leibniz believes, are to be understood as a unity of a dominant mind or monad, together with a number of other monads that form the organism's body. It is these living organisms that are the subject of Chapter 8. Being active, their dominant monads need a body through which to express their desires and facilitate their perceptions of the surrounding world, and whichever totality of monads serves these functions will count as the organism's body as long as the organism persists through time. The matter of that body though, taken apart from its dominant monad, has no true unity, since it is no more than a shifting mass of monads whose constitution changes from time to time. The whole organism, though, does have a strict unity, consisting of the dominant monad and whatever physical whole it governs as it expresses the perceptions and desires that are its. If monads are simple substances, living organisms have every claim to be composite substances and not just haphazardly compounded aggregates.

Since the dominant monad (and every monad must be dominant over some others) is eternal, and since every monad needs always to have a body through which its desires and perceptions are expressed, it will follow that any world that God might reasonably have created will be populated by organic life. What is more, and to the reader's astonishment, it will also follow that living organisms themselves will be naturally immortal, since if any collection of monads that adequately serves the expression of a thinking subject's perceptions and desires is its body, and if no subject can exist without a body to express those desires and perceptions, all individual monads must have their place in a permanent living organism of one sort or another.

This result looks totally at odds with the world of our experience. Surely, men and animals are born and die, plants germinate and decay. How can Leibniz refuse to acknowledge such obvious truths? His response is that we too easily misdescribe what observation teaches us. The metaphysics that has taken us to the recognition of everlasting living organisms is, he thinks, unimpeachable. Its conclusions cannot but hold. In consequence, we should revise the way we think of the natural processes we encounter in our lives. We have already seen that mere physical bodies – those that are not identified as facilitating the perceptions and desires of some dominant monad – have no more than a conventional unity. So we should say that the carcass or corpse that we are left with when an animal or person dies is really more accurately thought of as akin to the skin that a snake sloughs off as it passes from one stage of its existence to another. That skin, and hence that carcass, does not really have anything other than a 'phenomenal' unity to it and, properly seen, such things are no more than large collections of monads that make up a pretty haphazardly organized quantity of matter. On what we call 'death', the person or subject, i.e. the dominant monad who has shed that quantity of matter, continues to exist and continues to exist *with its body*, as does the snake, although maybe its body endures in a very different form than the one we are accustomed to thinking of as its. But there is no inconsistency here. What we must avoid saying is that the corpse is the body that the person once had. It isn't. It just consists of monads which once entered into that person's body. Now that the person no longer requires them for the expression of the perceptions and desires it comes to have, those quondam body-constituting monads cease to make up the body that they previously did, and others have simply come to take their place. The corpse is not the body that the soul has cast adrift; and what we call 'death' is not the end of existence. Rather it is merely a change of state of a natural organism, and the corpse merely matter that the persisting organism has shed to make possible a new stage of its natural life. Here reconceptualization of our accustomed ways of thinking is forced upon us, and not arbitrarily so. For Leibniz, it is forced upon us as long as we care to think clearly about ourselves and our world and follow those inflexible iron tracks that metaphysical reflection lays down for us.

To have said that the monad or soul needs a body to be properly active (and indeed to acquire perceptual knowledge of its world) implies that there is causality running between the two. Yet has not Leibniz already rejected any such thing? Certainly he has rejected one model of causality, that which conceives of it as the transmission of parts or properties from the causing agent to the receiving party, the effect. What he recommends instead, and thinks of as properly understood and intellectually respectable causality, is a version of a regular conjunction account of causation which is more familiar to us from Hume's rather later thoughts about the topic. Under this way of thinking, discussed in Chapter 9, one event causes another if there is a lawlike connection between events of the relevant kinds and where if the first (causing) event had not occurred the second (the effect) would not have done. Leibniz refers to such links in terms of a 'pre-established harmony' between the unfolding of monads' states over time, and sees it as applying ubiquitously wherever causal links are to be found. In particular, it applies without difficulty to causal relations between the distinct realms of mind and of matter. His proposal is quite general, though, and has no especially privileged bearing on the issue of interaction between mind and body or body and mind. Nevertheless, just because it turns its back on all need for the transmission of something mental to something physical (or vice versa), which had made Descartes' explanation of interaction in terms of the will's power to direct the waving of the pineal gland deep in the head so risible, Leibniz thinks he has answered one of the major metaphysical problems that his contemporaries and close predecessors had been unable to resolve. His conception of the unity of living organisms described above likewise seemed to him to have solved the other major difficulty in his period's philosophy of mind, namely how to account for the intimate unity that there is between mind and body, which had also baffled Descartes. Since it handles the issue in a way that allows our experience of the closeness of connection between soul and body to be smoothly integrated within the metaphysics, Leibniz was understandably proud of the intellectual reach of the system which made this possible.

I said that the overall aim of Leibniz's philosophy was to provide us with understanding of our world and our place in it. What we have somewhat laboriously gained so far is insight that by the objective standards of divine wisdom the world we are endowed with is the best there could be and that it shares very many features with any other world that could have seriously engaged God's creative attention. What is left open – and this is discussed in the final chapter – is the moral dimension of this metaphysical vision. Seeing the world as it teaches us we must, how should we conduct ourselves? While we are shown that God fashions his creatures in full knowledge of their natures and therefore with a full knowledge of what they will come to do once they are brought into existence, Leibniz is insistent that they act freely in the light of their own perception of the best. We, like God, are moved to act for the best as we judge it, although clearly in our case, unlike his, the lights by which we judge that best are fallible enough. Then, we have to allow that the good and bad that we recognize and the good and bad that we reap are necessarily this-worldly ones, since we cannot make sense of ourselves as ceasing to exist or as having a future in any other-worldly heaven or hell. Although Leibniz speaks of punishment and reward for our deeds on earth in an entirely conventional way for the period, in a way that is entirely unconventional his metaphysic obliges us to take these notions as immanent ones, whose full content is given in an entirely natural setting. Our good deeds will be rewarded in that they will conduce to good consequences, and our bad ones make the world worse for us. This may sound vacuously pious, but it is not. The reason is that the notion of the good itself must be closely tied to the sorts of natural creatures we are. There is no mystery about our choosing what course to pursue in the light of the understanding we have of that, and no mystery about such choices leading to consequences that are broadly liable to promote our good. Equally, if we get things wrong, then our errors will tend to make things worse for us. This may sound too impersonal and seem likely to make Leibniz's idea of moral reward and punishment inapplicable to the individual agent whose deeds he wants to say will be rewarded or punished. But Leibniz can plausibly argue that it need not do so, since for the most part we are not ignorant of the good or bad that we do, and our state of knowledge itself rewards or punishes us by generating a self-image that we are liable to find more or less tolerable accordingly. The hardened criminal or the wilful psychopath of course is not troubled by conscience or an intolerable self-image, but then he has the burden to bear of living in ignorance of himself, and thus standing at a further distance from God than those who are not similarly afflicted. That, for Leibniz, is his dire hardship.

These remarks about the strongly naturalistic strain in Leibniz's moral theory will seem quite empty if they are detached from his vision of what the human good itself consists in. That is ultimately provided by his theology. The world we have, the best world that there could be, is itself a reflection of the absolute good that God is taken to personify. Being an expression of God's own goodness man mirrors him in a finite way and therefore cannot but rationally pursue as best he can the goods that God himself is moved by. These are knowledge, and in particular knowledge of necessities, creative activity, concern for the world that comes over time to be the world of man's own making and care for the needs of those on whom our activities impinge, our contemporaries and those who succeed us in their passage to the state of reason. Reflectively driven, we are bound to temper our activity to the furtherance of such ends as these and in doing that find true fulfilment in what Leibniz calls 'genuine *pure love*'. Stated in such bald terms, this view may appear too unworldly or maybe just emptily conventional. Yet once we see these moral abstractions growing naturally from the metaphysical system that the *Monadology* erects their appeal will be felt to be more urgent and anything but arbitrary. Philosophy has often been charged with the duty of discerning the meaning of life, and often accused of failing in its task. Sympathetic readers of Leibniz's work who take the trouble to think through the system link by link may find at the end of their labours that they have met a philosopher who has taken that task to heart and found one who has not fallen badly short in its execution.

Further reading

Works referred to by author or editor alone under 'further reading' are listed in the select bibliography at the end. Leibniz's life and character are well portrayed in G. MacDonald Ross, 3–27; see also R. Ariew, 'Leibniz: Life and Works', in Jolley (ed.); the details of Leibniz's unsatisfactory relations with Newton are detailed in Richard Westfall, *The Life of Isaac Newton* (Cambridge, 1993), 98–101; his place in contemporary analytic philosophy is described more fully in Ishiguro, 8–13. The intellectual climate of Leibniz's day is discussed by S. Brown in 'The Seventeenth-Century Intellectual Background', in Jolley (ed.); see also Catherine Wilson, 'The Reception of Leibniz in the Eighteenth Century', in Jolley (ed.). For Kant's reading of Leibniz, see Wilson, 314–29.

Chapter I

Two Great Principles
(§§31–7)

> The foundations are everywhere the
> same; this is a fundamental maxim for me,
> which governs my whole philosophy.
>
> (*NE*, 490)[1]

Leibniz composed the *Monadology* in 1714, two years before his death, as a compact statement of his mature philosophical views. Within its narrow compass he sets out an elaborate account of the world presented though the lens of pure reason. It is an account that appears quite out of touch with the world as we know it. We are to understand God's creation as a collection of simple mental substances, a world of monads, and

---

1   Citations in the form '(*NE*, 000)' refer to P. Remnant and J. Bennett's 1981 translation of Leibniz's *New Essays on Human Understanding* (I am grateful to Cambridge University Press for permission to cite passages from this translation of Leibniz's work). The original texts of Leibniz's writings are to be found in *Die Philosophiscen Schriften von G. W. Leibniz*, ed. C.I. Gerhardt (Hildesheim, 1996), vols I-VII, hereafter referred to as *GP*.

to see ourselves as one particular kind of such thing, namely as minds having the power to reflect on ourselves and to understand the structure that the world necessarily has and to appreciate our privileged place in God's plan for the universe. We are to see ourselves and monads of other sorts as developing according to pre-ordained patterns, harmoniously attuned to one another and striving to achieve the good in emulation of God's own nature. The physical world is understood as consisting of compounds of these simple things and their perceptions, apart from which nothing else exists. For all its apparent defects we are brought to appreciate that of all the worlds that God might have created the actual world is the best, the one that mirrors his power, his knowledge and his goodness as perfectly as may be.

A common reaction to this metaphysic is to dismiss it as an extravagant fairytale, one that is not seriously concerned with the reality around us at all. The highly compact and apparently dogmatic nature of Leibniz's writing in the *Monadology* serves only to reinforce that impression. Nonetheless such a view is quite mistaken. As soon as we look beneath the surface we see that all the major claims that Leibniz advances are backed by reasoning that owes little or nothing to fancy, and it quickly becomes evident that the intricate story he tells is comprehensive, highly systematic and can lay claim to great explanatory power. It exemplifies to the fullest degree the rationalist conviction that the human intellect has the capacity to achieve adequate understanding of itself and of the world it inhabits, and it displays the philosophical virtue of subjecting the putative facts of experience to rigorous and taxing theoretical scrutiny.

With the *Monadology* Leibniz has bequeathed us a highly compressed file. The task of the commentator and guide must be to decompress it, and that is what I seek to do in this book. There exist fine books treating of Leibniz's philosophy as a whole and others on specialized aspects of it. Here I pursue neither course but, instead, restrict my attention to the *Monadology* alone and limit myself to asking how Leibniz may have expected his reader to understand that work on the assumption that he or she does not have access to the full body of his philosophical writings. It was, after all, written to gain a wider audience for his views than his more specialized writings reached, and it is reasonable enough to suppose that it contains within itself many of the keys to its own understanding. However, I some-times draw on Leibniz's other writings to support suggestions I make about the *Monadology*'s darker elements or to provide evidence about views germane to matters that this work discusses but which it passes over in silence.

For the most part I follow the text through in the order in which Leibniz presented it. The major exception to this strategy concerns the fundamental logical and methodological suppositions that underlie his general procedure. These make no explicit appearance before §§31–2, and they concern what Leibniz calls the two 'Great Principles' on which all his reasonings are founded.[2] It is with these principles, and with the existence of God to which they directly lead (§§38–45), that my first two chapters are concerned. Only after treating these topics will it make sense to turn attention to the exis-tence of the simple substances that make up the world, and whose introduction occupies the *Monadology*'s own opening sections.

The Principle of Contradiction

The first of Leibniz's two avowed principles is the Principle of Contradiction, whereby 'we judge to be false what contains a contra-diction and to be true what is opposed to or contradicts the false' (§31). In fact Leibniz is quite clear that there are two distinct ideas at work here, both of which operate throughout the *Monadology*. The first is the Principle of Contradiction proper, which he here phrases as a rule for recognizing a judgement to be false. When we find someone asserting both that something is the case and that it is not the case then we judge their composite assertion to be false. While it does indeed happen that people sometimes explicitly contradict them-selves, what more often occurs is that something someone says implies a contradiction that he does not notice, as might be the case were I seriously to say that the vixen lodged in my garden had just fathered cubs. In that case, too, Leibniz tells that we judge what is said to be

---

2 Citations in the bare form '§00' refer to the numbered sections of the *Monadology*. References to other of Leibniz's works indicate the titles of the writings concerned.

false because I have implicitly committed myself to the fox in question both being female and not being female.

Putting it in terms of what 'we judge', Leibniz makes it sound as if he is recording our behavioural response to contradictions. That would be to misunderstand him. As far as actual behaviour goes, as long as we do not notice a contradiction in what someone says then we are quite likely to accept it and judge it true on the assumption that our informant is trustworthy. This behavioural fact does not count against what Leibniz has in mind, though, for his 'Great Principle' is a normative matter, not a descriptive one. His thought is that we are rationally bound to judge contradictions to be false (assuming we notice them): we ought to reject them. The reason for this is that it is simply not possible for contradictions to be true, and we are rationally bound to judge false what cannot possibly be the case.

Someone whom Leibniz (mistakenly) thought would have disagreed about this was Descartes. At §46 he reports Descartes as holding that eternal truths are arbitrary and dependent on God's will. On such a view, it is only because God does not want the vixen to father cubs that my illustrative statement is false: there is no absolute impossibility about it. The suggestion behind this supposedly 'Cartesian' idea must be that there would be blasphemy in supposing God's power might be limited in any such way. If this were right, whether or not Descartes himself held the view, then Leibniz's principle would have to be rejected as long as it is seen as more than a rough-and-ready empirical generalization about our actual behaviour.

Leibniz is certainly not open to the charge of blasphemy. Also, he is well placed to say just what it is that makes contradictions impossible. As for the first, to say that God is omnipotent can only mean that God is able to do whatever can be done. To hold this is not to hold that there are limits to God's power. In particular, that something is impossible imposes no limitation on God's capacities, for what is impossible cannot be the case and so cannot constitute a limitation on the power of anyone, let alone God. What is it, then, that permits us to say that it is not possible both that p and that not-p – that a state of affairs and its opposite cannot both obtain? Leibniz himself does not tell us, certainly not in the *Monadology*, but that need not stop us answering the question on his behalf.

The 'Cartesian' supposition is that God could permit a determinate state of affairs and its opposite to coexist.[3] Now for a state to be a determinate one it has to be clear what condition must be satisfied if it is to obtain. For that to be clear it must also be clear what conditions are ruled out by its obtaining. So, for example, for it to be clear what it is for snow to be determinately white it must be ruled out that snow be black or green or any colour other than white. Were we to suppose that snow should be at once white and also some other colour, that would involve not just our supposing snow to be both, but in effect our not really supposing it to be white at all. So if it is determinately white it must be impossible that it should also be other than white. That impossibility is written into the supposition that white is the colour that it is. Likewise the impossibility of my vixen fathering cubs is written into the content of the thought that identifies the animal in question as a vixen. Her being male is something ruled out in the very supposition that that is what she is. However, since a condition of the animal's fathering cubs is precisely that it be male, the situation I have supposed myself to be envisaging could not obtain.

I have said that the first of Leibniz's two principles involves two ideas. This is essential for him to its having any positive utility. If we had only the Principle of Contradiction proper, as I called it, it would enable us to identify certain falsehoods, but not to assert any truths. The second limb of §31 enables us to do that by telling us that the opposite of a falsehood is a truth. Using this additional thought, we shall be able to assert as true whatever it is that is excluded by the falsehoods we have already identified, and Leibniz presumes that these will necessarily be the negations of the contradictions that have been identified as false, or of whatever propositions there may be that imply a contradiction.

In fact the ancillary principle that Leibniz is appealing to at this point must be the Law of Excluded Middle, the principle that for any

---

3   Historical accuracy will distinguish the 'Cartesian' position and Descartes' own. Descartes' view was not that there are no necessary truths, but that if *p* is a necessity, it is not a necessary truth that *p* is necessary.

proposition one might envisage either it is true or its negation is true. We could only use the second limb of §31 to identify 'not-*p*' as true if we are assured that that really is the opposite of the one that Contradiction proper has identified as false. Without reliance on Excluded Middle we should not be able to say what proposition was true when *p* itself was false. Just to be told, as Leibniz tells us, that we can assert as true what is the opposite of the false, whatever proposition it is that must hold if *p* itself does not, does not itself give us any clue what that proposition might be. For that we need to know that if '*p*' itself is not true then 'not-*p*' is true.

That Leibniz was aware of this is clear from the statement of the Principle of Contradiction he had earlier given in the *New Essays*, saying:

> Stated generally the principle of contradiction is: a proposition is either true or false. This contains two assertions: first that truth and falsity are incompatible in a single proposition, i.e. that *a proposition cannot be true and false at once*; and second, that the contradictories or negations of the true and the false are not compatible, i.e. that there is nothing intermediate between the true and the false, or better that *it cannot happen that a proposition is neither true nor false*.
>
> (*NE*, 362)

My own remark about the second limb of *Monadology* §31 does no more than bring out explicitly what Leibniz chose there to leave unstated. Although he always assumed Excluded Middle holds, he nowhere offers any defence of it. It is what he would call a primary truth which is known by 'intuition'. We can, as it were, see straight off that it expresses what he would loosely call an 'identity', and he thinks that it must be true because it scarcely does anything 'but repeat the same thing without telling us anything' (cf. *NE*, 361).

With the backing of Excluded Middle, then, the Principle of Contradiction proper can be put to work in the metaphysics. Contradictions are false because it is impossible that they should be true. Their falsity is *necessary* falsity. One way of reading the second limb of Leibniz's principle is to take the falsity whose opposite he says is a truth to be precisely the falsity of some contradiction or other – any contradiction you like – already identified as false by the principle's first limb. Then it will be the case that its opposite is true. What is more, since the falsehood in question is a *necessary* falsehood, we can conclude that its opposite is not barely true, but *necessarily* so. So, on occasion we shall see Leibniz arriving at metaphysical conclusions to the effect that this or that must be the case by showing that a proposition which is the negation of the thought expressing that state of affairs is itself a contradiction or that it entails a proposition which is a contradiction. In this way his first 'Great Principle' is not merely a trifling proposition that 'repeats the same thing without telling us anything', but is intellectually productive.[4] How productive it is we shall come to appreciate.

At §33 Leibniz introduces a division of truths into truths of reasoning and truths of fact. The former are necessary truths, truths whose 'opposites are impossible', the latter contingent truths, those whose 'opposites are possible'. While the Principle of Contradiction functions in its narrow form to identify certain necessary falsehoods and in its broader form productively to identify certain truths as necessary, that is not the sole way he thinks about the use to which it can be put. For Leibniz, occupied as he was with the need for philosophy to provide understanding, it also supplies answers to 'why'-questions as they are asked of truths belonging to the former of the two broad classes. So someone might wonder why π has no terminating decimal expansion and be shown by rigorous demonstration that it must be so, and that the alternative is impossible. It is so because it must be so, and that it must be so is either something that

---

4   In the *New Essays*, Theophilus, Leibniz's spokesman in discussion with Locke's representative Philalethes, says:

> Do you not recognize that to reduce a proposition to absurdity is to demonstrate its contradictory. I quite agree that no one will teach a man anything by telling him that he ought not to deny and affirm the same thing at the same time; but one does teach him something when one shows him, by force of inference, that he is doing so without thinking about it.
>
> (*NE*, 428)

The demonstration of the contradictory of an absurdity is often for Leibniz the demonstration of a metaphysical truth of the first rank.

can be demonstrated, or else is so primitive that it is discernible by intuition and 'cannot be proved and [stands] in no need of it either' (§35). To show that something is necessarily the case in this fashion is to explain it, to display why it is the case, and to do so by rigorous proof that is completely adequate to the demands of understanding. To the extent that we can do this, the rationalist aspiration to complete explanation and full understanding is satisfied without residue.

The Principle of Sufficient Reason

The second of Leibniz's 'Great Principles' is the Principle of Sufficient Reason, articulated at §32 as that principle 'whereby we consider that no fact can hold or be real, and no proposition can true but there be a sufficient reason why it is so and not otherwise, even though for the most part these reasons cannot be known by us'. The content of this claim is obscure and emerges gradually from the amplifications that §§36 and 37 add to it. However it is to be taken, Leibniz makes plain (§36) that it serves to assure us of the answerability of contingent truths of fact to 'why'-questions no less fully than its companion does for necessary truths of reasoning. That is, the Principle of Sufficient Reason assures us that all contingent truths must have their explanations, even though for the most part those explanations 'cannot be known by us'.

A first attempt to understand this second principle can be put in terms of facts or states of affairs. It appears to say that a condition of a fact or state of affairs obtaining is that there should be something or other – no matter what – that determines that that fact should obtain rather than any alternative. No fact or state of affairs can hold which is not completely accounted for and made fully explicable by reference to something else. No fact or state of affairs is accounted for by reference to anything which would equally well explain the occurrence of a different fact or state of affairs. Ruled out, then, are situations of which one might want to say: '*This* happened, but there is in principle no explanation why it happened'; equally ruled out are situations of which one might say: '*This* happened because of *that*, but *that* could equally well have brought about some other state of affairs than *this*.'

So, for example, it would be ruled out that there should be random events, or that at the end of the day all there is to say about some event of radio-active decay should be expressed in terms of the decaying element's half-life. Likewise it is ruled out that a doctor should truly say that his patient's asphyxia was provoked by the poison she ingested, but that that particular ingested dose could just as well have produced heart failure as asphyxia, where nothing else about the situation accounts for the occurrence of asphyxia rather than infarction.

If one reads it in this way, Leibniz's Principle of Sufficient Reason is of universal applicability. It admits of no exceptions,[5] and it cries out for some support. Indeed, so striking is it as an axiom for him to start out from that one might consider looking for an alternative and less daunting way of taking it. The text itself tells us that '[*we consider* that] no fact can be real ... but there be a sufficient reason', etc., and my italicized phrase might suggest not so much that there must always *be* a determining reason for what occurs as that it would be irrational for us to accept a proposition asserting something without being prepared to search for a reason that would explain it. This would be to recommend a readiness to look for reasons that account for things even if in the end there should be none, or that beyond a certain limit there are merely probabilistic reasons for things. Such a modest inter-pretation would not be excluded by Leibniz's open acknowledgement (§32) that most of the time we are unable to find the reasons why things occur, since that would still not make it unreasonable for us to hunt for reasons. We may strike lucky on occasion and come upon explanations which we should not do unless we were to look for them. Most of the time, though, we should expect to fail in our search.

Despite the attractions of caution, the use to which Leibniz actu-ally puts his principle obliges us to take the expression 'we consider' as having much the same force here as did the locution 'we judge' in the statement of the Principle of Contradiction, namely as expressing a norm that we are rationally obliged to respect, possibly because of the very nature of things, though that is something to be decided later. In that other case I said that we are rationally bound to judge contradic-tions false because it is impossible that they should be true. Equally

---

5   A point Leibniz emphasizes in section 44 of *Theodicy*.

Leibniz's view about sufficient reason seems to be not just that it provides a good maxim for the conduct of intellectual enquiry, but that were it not to hold in some domain there could be no truth there at all.[6] Confirmation of this may be found in the 1712 paper 'Metaphysical Consequences of the Principle of Reason', which at its outset asserts: 'The fundamental principle of reasoning is that *there is nothing without a reason*; or to explain the matter more distinctly that there is no truth for which a reason does not subsist.'[7] A more categorical commitment to there being answers to contingent 'why'-questions it would be difficult to imagine.

Why should Leibniz have thought any such thing? What support can he offer for it? Reflecting on these questions sixty years after Leibniz's death, Kant observed that before his own consideration of the matter it was just an assumption of common sense.[8] To deny it would be to accept the seeming absurdity that something can come from nothing: *ex nihilo aliquod* ! Yet, even though we may suppose that to be a brute impossibility, reason requires that we should be able to say something to show why it is, just as we did in the case of the Principle of Contradiction.

Reflecting on Leibniz's division of truths into necessary truths of reasoning and contingent truths of fact (cf. §33), one may well suppose that he can not have held his principle to express a very general but merely contingent truth of fact. For him it is an axiom that we start out from, not something that we come to by the patient amassing of data. So we might conclude that it must express a necessary truth, a truth of reasoning, 'explicable' by the Principle of Contradiction. Its assertion will then either explicitly express an

---

6 Although Leibniz never expresses himself so strongly, the following inference might appeal to him. Let *p* be true and suppose there to be no sufficient reason for *p*. Then *p* is not true. By Excluded Middle, which we saw Leibniz to have endorsed, if *p* is not true, not-*p* is true. So *p* is true and not-*p* is true. Then, either we argue by reductio that there is a sufficient reason for *p*, or we conclude from the contradiction that just any proposition is true. Faced with the choice between sufficient reason and ultimate intellectual catastrophe, Leibniz would not hesitate.

7 *Gottfried Wilhelm Leibniz: Philosophical Writings*, ed. G.H.R Parkinson (London, 1973), 172, hereafter referred to as Parkinson (ed.).

8 For Kant's discussion, see *Critique of Pure Reason,* A 200f./B 246 and A 783/B 811.

identity or else be reducible to one with the help of definitions, axioms and postulates (cf. §§34, 35). The trouble is that even if we phrase the principle in terms as clear as the familiar 'Nothing comes from nothing' – which, incidentally, Leibniz himself rejected[9] – it is just not right to say that its denial would be a downright contradiction. Nor does it seem at all promising to attempt to reduce it or analyse it in other terms than this, terms more acceptable to Leibniz, which then reveal its denial to be a contradiction. We seem just to be at the point at which Leibniz says (§35) we are concerned with 'primitive principles', principles which 'cannot be proved and stand in no need of it either'. This is unsatisfactory, because Leibniz believes that those primitive principles are, loosely speaking, identities, and this principle does not appear to be one.

Here one might proceed in either of two ways. One is to abandon Leibniz's thought that all necessities are ultimately reducible to identities or transparent conceptual truths. For us, plausible counter-examples might be that *Water is* H_2O, or that *Heat is mean molecular kinetic energy.* However, even if we think this is the right step to take – which Leibniz himself would surely have denied[10] – of itself that will provide no reason for holding the Principle of Sufficient Reason to express another 'non-identical', i.e. non-trivial, necessity. The only thing to add before moving on is that if it is a necessary but 'non-identical' truth of reasoning that there should be a full explanation for every truth, that will still leave ample room for Leibniz to maintain the

9 In his comments on Spinoza's philosophy, Leibniz observes that Spinoza overlooked the coming into being of modes (qualities) *ex nihilo*. 'Modes which arise really come from nothing' (Ariew and Garber (eds), 273). So certainly he would not have accepted Kant's diagnosis of the situation, nor his assimilation of Sufficient Reason to the familiar *ex nihilo* principle.

10 Only he never claims that it is given to us to perform the reductions in question. So he would say in these sorts of case that if we could make our ideas of water or heat 'distinct' we would then offer ourselves definitions in terms of their causes or causal powers, and then the identities will ultimately emerge. The identities in question do not give us the meaning of 'heat' or 'water' but provide an adequate account of the concepts under which we are bringing our samples, whether we know it or not. The Principle of Sufficient Reason hardly lends itself to this kind of treatment.

states of affairs that are explained by Sufficient Reason should be contingent ones. The necessity of the principle itself would be one thing, the contingency of what it accounts for another.

Let us suppose that we cannot regard the principle as stating a truth of fact, perhaps in part because we can not envisage anything that would show it to be false. Suppose, too, that we despair of offering any demonstration of it as a truth of reasoning. Without taking the matter further it is open to Leibniz to say we are bound to treat it as a methodological postulate. What I mean by this is that we are obliged take the principle to hold as a condition of the world being genuinely comprehensible to us. Just as the Principle of Contradiction answers 'why'-questions when they are asked of truths of reasoning, so as we ponder matters of fact it is only if Sufficient Reason reigns that we can be sure there are responses to 'why'-questions in their regard. Otherwise adequate understanding of the contingent will be beyond us. Refusing to pronounce on its modal status in this way, Leibniz could still say that this indeterminate way of putting it gives clear expression to his fundamental rationalist tenet, namely that the world we live in is a world that is penetrable to human understanding. It is even penetrable to an understanding of how penetrable to understanding it is, as we shall see. What is more, such a procedure does not even leave Sufficient Reason without the prospect of intellectual support. Leibniz may well say that its proof, like that of the proverbial pudding, lies in pursuing matters to the end of the course – in the case of the pudding to the end of dessert, in intellectual and philosophical cases to the end of the *Monadology*. If at the end of the day we find reliance on the second Great Principle leads to notable explanatory success and if that success could not have been achieved without making that assumption in the first place, then what the rationalist never doubts is systematically confirmed. Proof is supplied without it having to be decided whether what has found support is finally a very general matter of fact or a non-perspicuous truth of reason itself.[11]

---

11 It is always salutary to remind onself that the verb 'to prove' means little more than *to test* and that different matters are tested in different ways. It would be as absurd to insist one must provide a geometrical demonstration of a pudding to prove it as it would be to set about proving a theorem of geometry by eating it.

To the best of my knowledge Leibniz never explicitly chooses between these two alternatives – Sufficient Reason as a necessary truth or as a necessary methodological postulate – and commentary can do little more than point out the attractions of each. The first I set aside until the next chapter because it will involve consideration of Leibniz's theology. The second, the methodological proposal, is rooted in the thought that unless Sufficient Reason holds in full generality the world of fact will scarcely be comprehensible at all. Just what this commits Leibniz to needs elaboration, but that he is strongly drawn to the methodological thought comes out plainly in a striking passage from his Preface to the *New Essays*. There he writes:

> This distinction between what is natural and explicable and what is inexplicable and miraculous solves all the difficulties. To reject it would be to embrace something worse than occult qualities. Thereby one would be renouncing philosophy and reason and giving shelter to ignorance and laziness by a blind system that admits not just that there are qualities that we do not understand – of which there are all too many – but also that there are qualities that the greatest mind, aided as much as lies within God's power, could not understand, that is to say, qualities that would either be miraculous or without rhyme or reason. It would also be without rhyme or reason that God should perform miracles in the ordinary course of events, with the effect that this idle hypothesis would both ruin our philosophy, which searches for reasons, and God's wisdom, which supplies them.

(*NE*, 49f.)

Take it which way we will, as a necessary truth or as a methodological postulate, it was Leibniz's view that only if Sufficient Reason runs in full generality will we have any respectably grounded understanding of the world of fact. But just what does the demand that the principle hold in full generality come to? We have already seen that it takes us beyond a recommendation to act on the heuristic maxim of being prepared to look for reasons for any matter of fact. That would say little more than that in the pursuit of understanding we shall not succeed unless we are prepared to try. It certainly does not claim either that we shall always succeed, which Leibniz did not think anyway (§32) or, what he did think, that there is always success to be had.

Monadology §§36 and 37 provide Leibniz's anwer to the question of 'full generality'. If we take a particular state of affairs, a host of factors physical and psychological may enter into a comprehensible account of why it holds. Without grasping them the initial state of affairs would be opaque to us. Then similarly each of those physical and psychological explanantia depends for its understanding on a host of other factors in the absence of which it would not be comprehensible and which would then transmit its incomprehensibility to the very state of affairs it looked set to explain. This is what Leibniz has in mind when he says (§37) that, since all this differentiation of contingent things needs yet more differentiation to explain them, 'one is no further forward'.

The message is clear. For Sufficient Reason to hold it is not enough that there be an explanation for any given matter of fact, but more than that there must be an explanation for it that does not peter out. If one were to come to a dead-end in the pursuit of backward ramifying explanations, then the apparently successful account given of our initial explanandum would be just that: *apparently successful*, but not genuinely so. The utter mystery about why something happens where we reach a dead-end will transmit itself forward along the branch of explanations up to the initial explanandum itself and render what seems like intermediary or provisional success nugatory. So, if an event or a state of affairs is to be genuinely understandable there must be an account of it in terms of its antecedents that does not run into the sand. For Leibniz, this emphatically does not mean that as far as the provision of understanding goes *we* have to be able to trace things back and back and back. Given the endlessly ramifying nature of things, that would be impossible. What it does mean is that the understanding we take ourselves to have will be only dummy understanding and not understanding proper if the states of affairs that provide illumination of our original explanandum fail to have their own fully sufficient reasons.

One might suppose that in the light of this concern with backward ramifying reasons, Leibniz should be content if there were an infinite chain of backwards-stretching considerations, as we might well suppose there to be. Then even though there would never be an end to any chain one might embark on, no chain would peter out and so the full generality requirement would appear to be met. However, §37 makes plain that this would not suffice. Even if the series of explanations stretched back to infinity we should still be no further forward. This alarming thought had been at the heart of Leibniz's major treatment of the subject fifteen years earlier in the essay 'On the Ultimate Origination of Things', where he likens an infinitely ramifying series of explanations to the regressive explanation of the existence of a copy of a geometry book in terms of its being copied from a previous copy. There he puts it by saying that

> it is evident that, even though a reason can be given for the present book out of a past one, nevertheless out of any number of books taken in order going backwards we shall never come upon a full reason; since we might always wonder why there should have been such books from all time – why there were books at all, and why they were written in this manner. What is true of the books is true also of the different states of the world; for what follows is in some cases copied from what precedes (although according to certain laws of change). And so, however far you go back to earlier states, you will never find in those states a full reason why there should be any world rather than none, and why it should be as it is.[12]

The conclusion that Leibniz wants us to draw is that full explanation of individual states of affairs can only be provided from outside the series of explanatory states that give rise to them. Sufficient Reason can never be satisfied unless within the series explanations never peter out, and, in addition, there should be from without the series an explanation for the series as a whole. Furthermore, we may assume that the explanation provided for the whole must not give rise to a regress of its own.

---

12 Parkinson (ed.), 136.

At this point, one might wonder whether Leibniz is not succumbing to a simple fallacy in moving from a weak form of Sufficient Reason to his own peculiarly strong one. Is he not simply inferring that if there must be an explanation for any event there must be some explanation for all events?[13] Any such an inference about causes or explanations would be no better than a like inference from the need for all races to be won by someone to the thought that there must be someone who wins all races. It would, I believe, be both unwarranted and ungenerous to accuse Leibniz of gross logical error here. It seems much more plausible to think that the ultimate motivation for the need he perceives to look for explanation outside the series of things derives from specific considerations about explanation itself and from his conviction that it is obvious enough how the demand can be met. Many of us are susceptible to the thought that a chain of backwards-stretching reasons could never be the whole story about an event that we seek to explain just because, as Leibniz himself says, the question is left entirely open why that chain of reasons should obtain in the first place. Refusing to say anything about this, or, more accurately, refusing to allow that there must be something to be said about it, even if when it comes to the precise detail we cannot hope to say it, appears to leave our understanding of things unanchored in a decidedly perilous way. Certainly Leibniz thought as much, and if, like him, we consider that the anchoring in question could be adequately supplied by God, we might indeed suppose that the strong methodological postulate is one we should adopt. How Leibniz shows that God exists and how God is envisaged as supplying the needed anchor are topics for the next chapter.

Before leaving the discussion of these two principles, we need to appreciate how they operate in the construction of Leibniz's system. Put in the broadest terms, it is Leibniz's philosophical aim to establish how things must be and to explain why they are so. However, that way of speaking can be taken in either of two ways. A claim that it must be the case that p can be an assertion of the metaphysical impossibility for anything other than p to be the case. That claim will be held in

---

13 To put it in the perspicuous notation of first-order logic, is he not illegitimately moving from $AxEy\,(Fyx)$ to $EyAx\,(Fyx)$?

place by the Principle of Contradiction, first, by the demonstration that not-p involves a contradiction and, second, by the ancillary principle that permits us to assert the truth of p. Yet there are also truths that must hold whose denial is not a contradiction, and in their case they must hold because there would be no sufficient reason for anything else holding in their place. Here, we shall see, Leibniz is led by his rationalist cast of mind to seek to establish of contingent matters of fact that they must hold. By this means he finds a route to philosophical conclusions that his immediate predecessors either could not secure or else struggled in vain to make out on the basis of the Principle of Contradiction *alone*. Two illustrations will bring out the novelty of Leibniz's procedure and make it evident why he thought his systematic achievement was so spectacular.

Descartes' epistemology is constructed around the idea that knowledge demands certainty of a kind that the hypothetical operation of an evil genius set to deceive us would cast in doubt. Even if the existence of such a figure were as much as possible, knowledge proper would lie beyond our reach. The Cartesian strategy to counter this threat is to show that the idea of such a malign figure embodies a contradiction and that in the satisfaction of our quest for knowledge we can provide a logical guarantee that our best-evidenced beliefs are true. The philosophical approach to knowledge is thus conducted solely under the aegis of the Principle of Contradiction.

Leibniz, by contrast, finds no contradiction in the idea of our beliefs being systematically false, or our being deceived by an evil genius or otherwise being systematically misled. These are undeniable metaphysical possibilities (cf. *NE*, 375). Even so, our best-evidenced beliefs must be true and must furnish us with knowledge, because a world that could be fully explained would not display that delusive feature. In particular, it would be unreasonable for God to create a dream-world given the better alternative that stands open to him. Thus, with the aid of Sufficient Reason Leibniz arrives at the knowledge Descartes strove for without having to embrace the implausibilities that Descartes relied on to do so.

Or, consider the question raised by Locke whether matter might not think (cf. *Essay Concerning Human Understanding,* IV. iii. 6). To him, this appears an open question since no consideration of incoherence or contradiction can be drawn on to close off the possibility. For Descartes, by contrast, the question can be settled negatively just because, to his mind, the idea of thinking matter is self-contradictory. Leibniz finds neither approach satisfying. To his way of thinking, it is clear that God could have made matter think had he wanted to, by miracle as it were, and that the Principle of Contradiction is powerless to settle the issue one way or the other. Nevertheless, as we shall see in Chapter 9, there could be no comprehensible world that contains thinking matter, since its doing so would be utterly inexplicable. The first of these illustrations finds Leibniz using Sufficient Reason to establish a positive conclusion to the effect that something must be the case. Here he does the same to establish negatively that something cannot be the case. The details need not concern us. What we shall appreciate is that with a more generous methodology at his disposal Leibniz takes himself to be able to make real philosophical progress at points at which, in his eyes, his predecessors had been bound to fail.

Further reading

For the historical Descartes, see Hidé Ishiguro, 'The Status of Necessity and Impossibility in Descartes', in Amélie Rorty (ed.) *Essays on Descartes's* Meditations (California, 1986), 459–72; R. C. Sleigh, Jr, 'Truth and Sufficient Reason in the Philosophy of Leibniz', in Hooker (ed.), and 'Leibniz on the Two Great Principles of All Our Reasonings', *Midwest Studies in Philosophy VIII* (Minneapolis, 1983), 193–216; Rutherford, Chapter 4: 'Metaphysics and its Method'; David Wiggins, 'Sufficient Reason: A Principle in Diverse Guises, both Ancient and Modern', in S. Knuuttila and I. Niiniluoto (eds) *Methods of Philosophy and the History of Philosophy: Acta Philosophica Fennica* (Helsinki, 1996), 117–32.

Chapter 2

God (§§38–46)

The main themes of Leibniz's metaphysics depend on his theology. God exists of necessity, is the creator, fashioning the world he creates in line with his nature and in accordance with a highly specialized version of the Principle of Sufficient Reason. This is the Principle of the Best (§46). We are quickly led to understand that whatever world it is that God created – ours, to be precise – will have been the best of the alternatives open to him. The central lines of this theology are laid down in the sections immediately following the introduction of the methodological principles just discussed, and are presented as following directly from them. In particular, God's existence is derived from each of Leibniz's two great principles in apparent independence of one another. It is with this derivation that I shall initially be concerned. With that in place I will be able to turn to God's nature and the way his creative choice inevitably, but in Leibniz's view freely, comes to be made.

The first of the existence proofs is offered as a

simple consequence of Sufficient Reason itself. Once we accept the ambitious demand of reason for an anchoring of the whole series of contingencies, we see that it cannot possibly be provided from within the series itself. Whether chains of explanations peter out abruptly or whether they continue indefinitely, they could not suffice. A satisfactory resolution to a series of 'why'-questions that leaves no loose ends could only be supplied from outside. It is in that sense *extramundane*. So much is asserted at §37. Furthermore, the existence of what (in §38) Leibniz calls 'the ultimate reason for things' could not itself be a mere contingency, because if it were the Principle of Sufficient Reason would once again apply to it and the regressive argument that has driven us to look away from the series of contingencies within the world would come into play once more, only this time outside it. Hence Leibniz claims the successful quest for reasons must come to a halt with 'a necessary substance', by which he means a substance that exists necessarily.[1] The necessity of this substance's existence stops any further regressive 'why'-question arising. It exists because anything else would be impossible.

Bringing Sufficient Reason to bear in the way it has been understood since its introduction (§32), Leibniz claims that this necessarily existing substance must account for the series of worldly contingencies – the differentiation of contingent things, as he puts it – productively, as their source. Otherwise the demands of the principle will not be met. Nothing less than a necessarily existing creative source of all contingent truths bringing them about by an act of will could explain why the world exists and explain why it exists in the way it does. Anything less, such as a godly recognition that it would be good that the world should exist, and even that it should exist just as it does, would not do, for that recognition would not automatically carry with it any implications for the will. At best it would raise a presumption about what might be created, but that would not by itself explain the existence of what does exist. What is of the essence is that the very existence of the actual contingent series be accounted for, and the accounting in question can be supplied by nothing other than the

---

1   'A Résumé of Metaphysics' offers this argument for the necessity of God's existence at §3 (Parkinson (ed.), 145).

very creator of the series. Using the terminology of his day Leibniz says (§38) that the actual differentiation of things, the contingent series making up the world, exists only 'eminently' in this necessary substance as their source, meaning thereby that the substance we are led to posit, God, must have the power and the will needed to produce the series. It does not already exist, ready-made as it were *in* him, nor is it in any way identical with him, as it was for Leibniz's close contemporary Spinoza. Having arrived so far, Leibniz has completed his first proof, for as he says a necessarily existing substance that creates the world is just what we call 'God'. Setting out from the Principle of Sufficient Reason, the journey has been short and swift. There are a number of things to say about it.

First, although Leibniz's argument is a version of a 'first cause' or 'prime mover' argument I have avoided presenting it straightforwardly in that light. For one thing, it is important for Leibniz that God's activity – whatever it is that is done by God to create the world – should lie outside space and time. So it would be misleading to say that God's decision or decree that the world exist which produces the world is the First Cause. If there is a First Cause, the first in the temporal series, it will be the coming into existence of the world itself, the result of God's creative act – the Big Bang, perhaps, as we might like to think. The coming into existence of the world cannot be the act of creation itself. Usually we do something by doing something else, and one supposes that to create the world God, too, must do something, something like thinking imperatively: 'Let there be light!' Commanding this, with the appropriate outcome, is creating the world. It is as a result of this act that light and the world came to be. Thought of in this way, the creation of the world is not the first event, and God's creative act not the first cause.

A different reason for avoiding this way of talking is that Leibniz envisages the possibility of there being no first cause in his talk of the infinite series of differentiations. In such a series, whichever event one took would be preceded by some earlier event. To think in those terms, with there being no start of time, would not nullify the argument from Sufficient Reason, since as we have seen Leibniz insists that we must still ask for an account of the whole series without supposing that there has to be a beginning to it. Standard arguments for a first cause assume that something has to get in at the start, but Leibniz can distance himself from any such suggestion and simply say, as he does say, that God created the whole series (as unfolding according to certain determinate laws of change).

A second point is this. Leibniz moves from the requirement of a reason for the series to the necessary existence of a *substance*, and given that my exposition of the system starts here it might be thought that he is smuggling in material under that term without justification. Now it is certainly true that Leibniz is here drawing on presumptions that the *Monadology* does not discuss, but it is far from clear that making them imports any particular weakness to his reflections. The leading assumption, which will receive fuller treatment in the next chapter, is that substances are the sole things that are truly real. Such things must be true indivisible unities. Leibniz can say that as far as Sufficient Reason goes, the only thing that could possibly satisfy its demands would be the existence of something that is itself fully real. Anything less could not account for the existence of the series of real things. Only one thing more is immediately imported into the arena by the term *substance* – though the *Monadology* nowhere explicitly tells us so – which is that it must be active. The other popular piece of writing from 1714, the *Principles of Nature and Grace*, begins definitionally – 'Substance is a being capable of action' – and the same thought is offered in other places too. To insist on this from the start in talking about the *Monadology* is not to import anything illicit from elsewhere. Once we accept that Sufficient Reason requires there to be some real producer of the world, it *ipso facto* requires activity on the part of that producer in some way or other. That this activity should be activity of the will adds a little specificity to the idea. God cannot be other than a substance, and as the originator of all other substances he must be the Supreme Substance exercizing his will.

The appeal to the will, to God's choice in effect, is not merely theologically grounded. It is not simply a reflection of the traditional conception of the world being created by some intelligent agency in pursuit of some grand goal. No doubt it is that, but for Leibniz this picture is forced on us because the alternative could be nothing else than mindless, mechanical, causal agency which would just add to the series of things that appeal to God is supposed to explain from outside that series. Once that option is excluded, all that is left over which could possibly provide an explanation why this or that is the case is that it should result from some desire for the series as a whole and from a decision to fashion the series accordingly. In our case, the desires we pursue and the decisions we take must have their explanations, so they do not put an end to the quest for explanations, but in the present case the goals which Leibniz's God is envisaged as pursuing are the goals of a necessary substance acting from its nature. That is supposed to make further enquiry otiose. It can be admitted, though, that until more is said about God's nature all we have is a thought about what would be needed to close the chain of explanatory reasoning that would account for any series of contingent things that might obtain. We do not yet have theological information rich enough to reveal why it should be *this* universe that came to be rather than any one of a large number of possible alternatives.

Having arrived (§38) at the existence of a necessary substance creating the world through its activity, Leibniz quickly assures himself that there is only one God, and that that one God is, as he says, enough. If we are moved by Sufficient Reason alone, these assertions are mere ancillaries to the existence claim and cannot be said to have been secured in any convincing way. The most that the reasoning used to date will tell us is that there must be at least one God and that there must be enough Gods to provide a total explanation of the series of contingent things. Monotheism would be one way in which these demands could be met, but perhaps polytheism could work as well, though unlike the Greek gods each member of any polytheistic group recruited for the purpose would have to be as necessary a substance as the one that Leibniz envisages and also have its productive role assigned to it of necessity. However, so far as Sufficient Reason goes, all we can say is that a monotheistic regime would be good enough and that, respecting the demands of an austere methodology, entities should not be multiplied beyond necessity. Whether Leibniz does not have a surer path to the uniqueness of any Supreme Substance is something to which I shall briefly return shortly.

Setting aside the form in which explanation is to be provided from outside the series, let us ask precisely what Leibniz would now be committed to. That will depend entirely on how the leading demand for Sufficient Reason is taken. I have rejected reading it as a modest heuristic maxim, since that would not encourage dissatisfaction with merely *intramundane* explanations, whether or not they be terminating explanations. Neither has any reason been produced thus far to treat it as a necessary truth. So for the time being we should view it as a methodological postulate to the effect that if the actual differentiation of the world is to be comprehensible, there must exist a necessary substance that is creatively responsible for its being as it is.

There are two claims of necessity here, but neither of them amounts to the categorical affirmation that God exists. The first of these is just the necessity of the conditional: if the world is comprehensible, then it will have a necessarily existing creative source. With that, the creative source of the world is not asserted to exist, for we are not yet in any position to say that the understanding we seem to have of the world is genuine understanding and not simply understanding of a spurious kind. Then the second necessity is internal to what it is that must be true if the world is indeed genuinely comprehensible and not just apparently so, to wit: the necessary existence of what explains it. In our present position, even if we have accepted everything that happens up to §39, we shall still not have committed ourselves to God's necessary existence. We can say that his necessary existence is something we should only be justified in accepting if we accept that the world is explicable, but that still awaits its proof. Maybe God exists, maybe not. If he exists, then maybe he exists necessarily, maybe not. Of course, if God does exist necessarily he will do so whether or not we recognize it, so we must not say that whether he exists or not depends on whether our methodological postulate holds. All we are concerned with for the present is whether Leibniz has yet provided a categorical reason to suppose that God does necessarily exist. To that question the answer is unequivocally 'No'.

Things would be different if the Principle of Sufficient Reason itself expressed a truth of reason. Then it would indeed be necessary that there exists an adequate reason for the contingent series of things, and from accepting that we would be rationally bound to accept that God exists of necessity. Otherwise we might just provisionally postulate the holding of Sufficient Reason yet find that even given the conditional acceptance of the necessary substance that that brings with it we still did not have an adequate account of the contingent series. In that case, provisionally accepting the principle would lead us to reject that very principle and, in consequence, to suspend judgement about God's existence and its modal character as necessary or contingent.

If we look at texts other than the *Monadology* it is hard to resist the thought that what Leibniz in fact believed was that the Sufficient Reason holds as a truth of reason. Evidence of this is supplied in the unqualified assertions that nothing happens without a reason made in the 1697 paper 'A Résumé of Metaphysics' and in slightly different terms in 'On the Ultimate Origination of Things' of that same year, from which I quoted towards the end of the last chapter. Additionally, in the *Monadology* Leibniz makes parenthetical reference to other available writings of his that direct the reader to fuller treatment of the topics that the *Monadology* so concisely summarizes. Thus, at the end of §§32 and 38 he directs us to sections 7 and 44 of *Theodicy*, both of which use Sufficient Reason to derive God's existence categorically. Admittedly, §44 of the latter work does speak of the principle as a generally exceptionless rule, one 'which would be seriously weakened if there were exceptions to it', and that might suggest that exceptions are possible though unwelcome and hence that the principle will therefore hold as a matter of contingent fact. However, it seems to me more in keeping with his metaphysical ambitions to hear Leibniz's way of speaking there as recognition that unless Sufficient Reason held of necessity much of his system would be pure speculation and not underwritten by reason, as he takes it to be. This impression would be immeasurably strengthened if we could see a way for Leibniz to derive that principle from the Principle of Contradiction itself. The direct proofs of God's existence offered between §§43 and 45 suggest a way in which he might envisage this being done.

While the proof of God's existence in §38 is in its way *a posteriori*, as Leibniz observes at §45, setting out as it does from the contingent nature of the world we know and from reflection on what is needed for that to be comprehensible, Leibniz now passes to *a priori* proof independent of the obtaining of any contingencies whatever. Although the line of argument is obscure, at least two different considerations are offered in taking us to the desired conclusion. The first of these concerns things which are not actual but merely possible. As I understand it, these are what Leibniz calls 'essences' (§43), in contrast with actualities, which he calls 'existing things'. It is, he says, only because God exists that there is any reality in possibilities, an idea that one might rephrase by saying the truth of any statement to the effect that something is possible presupposes God's existence. Why should that be? The reason must be that what is possible could be actual, and a condition of that is that God should choose to make it so. In the absence of God there is no way in which a state of affairs might pass from being unrealized (being merely possible) to being realized (to its being actual), and then it would effectively reside in the same dark limbo as contradictions, which is to say not be possible at all. If the argument is taken in this way, it must clearly rely on considerations closely akin to those introduced by Sufficient Reason. Otherwise one could find oneself saying it is possible that this or that will happen tomorrow, but for no reason at all, completely unforeseeably, or else for some reason confined entirely to the intramundane series of contingent things. Other than by appeal to considerations already canvassed and found wanting, there is nothing here that obliges us to rule that out.

It seems that §44 deploys another version of the same argument. There Leibniz considers eternal or necessary truths themselves, not just true statements of possibility, and he suggests that their reality – or truth, as we may prefer to put it – likewise depends on something actual and existing. So, once again, the existence of the Necessary Being, or God, is supposedly derivable. Quite why Leibniz thinks that eternal truths are existence-involving is obscure. Certainly some necessities are, namely those asserting essential truths about individuals or species that we pick out by indirect or direct reference. 'Leibniz was a man' is one example; 'gold resists cupellation' another perhaps. But neither of them directly involves the existence of God, and neither is a necessity in the sense that it would be true no matter what the world was like. If Leibniz had never existed, 'Leibniz is a man' would never have been true.[2] In a world containing no gold, it is

---

2 They express *de re* necessities, truths that must hold of Leibniz or of gold, wherever they exist.

arguable that the thought that gold resists cupellation would lack a determinate sense, and so would not express a truth either. However, I doubt whether Leibniz had such examples as these in mind when talking of eternal truths. It is far more likely he was thinking of claims like 2 + 2 = 4, or propositions of Euclidean geometry, or relational claims such as 'if A is sharper than B and B sharper than C, A is sharper than C', and these would not be false in any world at all, even (for the first claim) in worlds containing no countable objects and (for the second or the third) no spatially extended things. Perhaps the idea is that the necessity of such truths has to be explained in terms of their holding no matter what world should have come to exist, and that would be so only if there could have been worlds other than our own. That then would be thought to presuppose God's existence in the way just discussed, for his existence would need to be presupposed if it made sense to talk of such worlds as possibilities again. However, if this is Leibniz's idea it once again depends on his reflections about Sufficient Reason and has no plausibility apart from them. Let us therefore move on.

Happily, §45 offers a very different consideration, and one which Leibniz says is sufficient by itself to afford knowledge of the existence of God *a priori*. It is stated with extreme brevity and is presented as if it were a special case of the argument I have just rejected. 'God alone, or the Necessary Being, has this privilege, that He must exist if He is possible.' However, we need not see it in that light. Instead we can take Leibniz to be offering the thought that if it is so much as possible that God exists, then it is necessary that he exists. For if God exists he exists necessarily, and if it is so much as possible that p is necessarily true, then p itself must be true, i.e. p is necessarily true.

The main premiss of this little argument, that if it is possible that p is necessary, then p is necessary, is a widely accepted principle of modal logic, in particular of that version of modal logic (C. I. Lewis' S5) which has been perceived by many as being best able to furnish a correct account of the logic of necessity and possibility. We can make Leibniz's acceptance of it intuitive for ourselves by some such reflection as the following. If some arbitrarily chosen proposition, p, say, is possible, then it is hard to resist the thought that it could not but be possible, that is, if it is possible that p, it is necessary that it is possible that *p*. By contraposition, it follows immediately from this that if it is not necessary that *p* is possible, it is not possible that *p*. Given that possibility and necessity, as those ideas are used here, are interdefinable (i.e. it is necessary that *p* if and only if it is not possible that not-*p*), we can further conclude that if it is not necessary that *p* is possible, it is necessary that not-*p*. Again drawing on the interdefinability of the two notions we can rephrase this first as saying if it's possible that *p* is not possible, it's necessary that not-*p*, and then as saying that if it's possible that it's necessary that not-*p*, it is necessary that not-*p*. Noticing that the proposition *p* that we started with was arbitrarily chosen, it is evident that at this last step any proposition other than not-*p* could legitimately be substituted for it, *q*, say, or even *p* itself. Doing that, we arrive at the thought we wanted to make intuitive, namely, if it's possible that *p* is necessary, it is necessary that *p*. Applied to Leibniz's case, this yields the premiss that if it is so much as possible that God exists necessarily, God does exist necessarily.[3]

Is it possible that God necessarily exists though? Not if the concept *God* contains an incoherence, and not if he does not actually exist. I shall not argue the first issue. Leibniz was always clearly aware that he needed to show the concept was consistent, and it is true that he thought it demonstrable that it was so. We ourselves may not be so sure that the idea of the possession of all perfections, around which the concept *God* revolves, is indeed a coherent notion. Certainly Leibniz's observation (§45) that nothing can prevent the possibility of that which has no limits, no negation *and consequently no contradiction* (my emphasis) will not pass unchallenged. Be that as it may, and supposing that the concept *God* is as unimpugnable as Leibniz believed it to be, the proof cannot usefully be carried through without our already being able to affirm that God exists. Failing his existence,

---

3 Using 'L' for 'necessary' and 'M' for 'possible' the steps above are just these:

(1) M*p* $\Rightarrow$ LM*p* (Axiom)

(2) $-$LM*p* $\Rightarrow$ $-$M*p* (by contraposition)

(3) M$-$M*p* $\Rightarrow$ L$-p$ (by definition)

(4) ML$-p$ $\Rightarrow$ L$-p$ (by definition)

(5) ML*p* $\Rightarrow$ L*p* (substituting '*p*' for '$-p$')

it would not be possible that he exists necessarily. Here, surely, is a crucial weakness of the proof, namely that if we are to use it persuasively we already have to know whether it is true or false that God exists, and to secure that knowledge we must use some other route than this one. It is notable that in section 44 of *Theodicy* Leibniz tells his readers that without the Principle of Sufficient Reason one could not prove that God exists. In the light of the observation just made this thought takes on a significance it might otherwise lack, since here we are trying to derive God's existence from the Principle of Contradiction alone in order to provide the Principle of Sufficient Reason with metaphysical credentials that make it more than a methodological postulate. It seems we have failed.

Whatever we may think of it, Leibniz himself is convinced by the proof of §45. Once God's necessary existence is in place, it may look as if Sufficient Reason will recommend itself as a simple consequence of that. To Leibniz's way of thinking, what guarantees the necessity of God's existence is that God is a being who is incapable of limitation, and he must therefore contain just as much reality as is possible (§40). What this comes to specifically is the subject of §48, but at the point at which it is introduced the characterization of God offered is rather more formal: God is incapable of being limited and contains just as much reality as is possible. If Leibniz is to be able to derive Sufficient Reason from the Principle of Contradiction everything will hinge on this formal characterization of God generating what is needed for this. In the first place, it will have to be here that we find the root of the idea that God is the creator of the world, an idea that would otherwise find its place only if Sufficient Reason was already secured. Perhaps there is something here with which we can sympathize.

Suppose that God does exist and is unlimited. Then he is, among other things, unlimited in his power. So he must have the power to create the world. This cannot mean that he has the power to create the world as long as it does not exist already, for that is already to conditionalize and so limit that power. The world's existence must be seen not as a limitation on his power but as a manifestation of it, not something that sets limits to his power but something that involves the exercise of his unlimited capacity. If this is so, Leibniz could conclude that the ultimate explanation for the contingent series of things that actually exists, no matter what that should be, must be attributable to God. And it looks as though it is none other than the thought that God must provide a sufficient explanation or reason for the whole 'succession of things or the series of detailed contingencies, however infinite it may be' (§37). So, from the Principle of Contradiction alone God's necessary existence is supposedly derived. His necessary existence guarantees his maximal reality. That in turn ensures that he is necessarily creator, and hence that he must supply the effective reason for contingent truths. Thus there must be such a sufficient reason for them, and categorically so. That was what was thus far no more than an undemonstrated postulate.

Let us now turn to the way in which Leibniz uses the idea of God to generate information about the sort of creation to which God himself can give rise. In doing so we must not forget that whether we view Sufficient Reason as a consequence of the Principle of Contradiction or as holding independently of it, the way the former operates is liable to narrow down the range of things which might be explained by an appeal to God the creator as their ultimate reason. Whether this is so, and the extent to which it is, will depend on the specific information Leibniz thinks we are in a position to deploy about the way in which God's creative choices are made. This information is set out at §48 and is derived from the formal characterization of God as absolutely perfect offered at §41, a section which itself is seen as a direct consequence of God's infinite (that is, unlimited) nature as presented in §40.

Using the idea of God's unlimited capacity as a lever, Leibniz moves quickly to the point of claiming God to be absolutely perfect (§41), though as yet we know nothing about the specific ways in which he is so. What we can say is that to be perfect in a particular respect is to be maximally endowed or all-embracing in that respect, and that is a simple consequence of being absolutely unlimited. Bearing in mind the etymology of the word we can say that God's perfection is *infinite*. (*Finis* means 'end' or 'limit'; cf. *Finisterre*, meaning 'land's end'.) Whatever essential character God has, then, he has to an infinite maximum. We have to wait until §48 before we are told what that character is, character in the sense of the essential qualities, possessed to an infinite degree, in the absence of which nothing could be God.

These endowments are there revealed as power, knowledge and will, and they constitute a well-established orthodox conception of God's attributes or essential nature. In §48 Leibniz does little more than announce what God's attributes are but, theological orthodoxy apart, it is not difficult to see why the choice seems to him such an obvious one.

We know that whatever exists has depended on God's choice to create it. His choice was a choice among an unbounded range of alternative possibilities – the range of logical possibilities. It cannot have been an arbitrary choice, but was one made for a sufficient reason. If God's choice were arbitrary there might be some explanation of why the world came to be (God created it), but no explanation why *it* came to be rather than any other possibility that God could have chosen. So, if Sufficient Reason is to explain the world by reference to God's creative choice, his choice must itself have been made for a sufficient reason. In consequence, it must have been guided by the perception that some possibilities are better than others, and that one is best of all. Thus it is that Leibniz says (§46) that when it comes to contingent things God's will is guided by 'their *fittingness* or God's choice of *the best*' (emphasis added). It is only if that were a truth about God's psychology that the Principle of Sufficient Reason, as I have discussed it thus far, could be satisfied.[4]

To be able to choose to create a series of contingent things according to the Principle of the Best, God must obviously know just what range of possibilities lies before him and know also which among them are better than others. So *knowledge* is indispensable to the Supreme Substance that supplies the reason for what exists. Likewise *power* is indispensable, since, as Leibniz sets it out (§44), the range of possibilities is the range of possibilities that can be made real, and what can be real is so only because it can be produced by God. Without the ultimate reason for things essentially possessing creative power, nothing could come to be. Finally, we are to ascribe

---

4   If Sufficient Reason is thought of as holding of necessity, then the Principle of the Best becomes a necessary feature of God's psychology. If its modal status is left indeterminate, then maybe, as far as God's nature is answerable only to the demands of Sufficient Reason, there is room for Leibniz to say that God's choice of the best is a free choice, one to which by his nature he is inclined, though not necessitated.

will to God since without that, even if he had knowledge of the whole range of alternative possibilities and of their ranking by merit, and even if he had the power to realize any alternative in the range, no decision to exercize that power and to exercize it in the light of the known ranking of alternatives could be taken and hence no creative act accomplished. So, at the very least, power, knowledge and will are essential to God's fulfilling the role of Sufficient Reason through decisions about what to create arrived at in accordance with the Principle of the Best.

The three attributes discussed in §48 make no explicit allusion to two features of God that are important to Leibniz and which he distinguishes from one another much later on (cf. §86), namely God's *wisdom* and his *goodness*. It may be that wisdom is a facet of God's knowledge, namely the ability to discern which of the known possible alternative series of contingent things is better than another, whereas goodness is a particular determination of will, namely, the will to choose the best. Then God's wisdom will be nothing other than his perfect knowledge and therefore need not appear later on as a novel and disconcertingly unattached attribute. Equally God's goodness may be nothing other than the perfection of his will. Assuming it to be just that, some speculation about why this should be so is in order.

One might suppose that instead of a perfect God having the role of being the ultimate reason for things a malevolent deity might do just as well. Being a deity, such a being would, of course, have unlimited power and unlimited knowledge for the same reason that God himself has them. Equally this being would need will to put his choices into effect. The difference between God and such a figure would be that while God creates according to the Principle of the Best, the imagined malevolent deity is pleased to leave the best uncreated and selects a world that is systematically subject to Murphy's Law or Sod's Law, or worse. For Leibniz, such a supposition must be incoherent. Just like God, the malevolent deity must have a reason to choose what he does. His reason can only be that what he chooses seems best to him. The curiosity is that what seems best to him must also be what he knows to be less than the best, for his unlimited knowledge will prevent him from being mistaken in this regard. Yet if his perfect knowledge prevents him from misidentifying the best, it can hardly be the case that something other than the best seems best to him. It sits at odds with his perfect knowledge. Hence, Leibniz will think, for a God, though not for limited and finite creatures such as ourselves or Ovid's Medea, it would be impossible to say *video meliora proboque, Deteriora sequor* ('I see and approve the better, I choose the worse').[5] So he could hardly entertain the idea that an unlimited or perfect will could be other than a good one.

Following Leibniz's usage at §48, I have called God's power, knowledge and will his 'attributes'. In the language of the day, those were the necessary – essential – properties of substances in contrast with their accidents, those features or properties which they possess as a matter of contingency. Since Leibniz is using the term 'God' to designate the necessarily existing Supreme Substance, its possession of omnipotence, omniscience and perfect will (benevolence or goodness) will be a matter of necessity. It should be clear that that is inevitable once God's choices are assumed to be motivated by Sufficient Reason. Not only is it necessary that any divinity sensitive to that principle must possess these features, but if those features are not to inject something that fails to be self-explanatory into the picture each one must of necessity be possessed by such a deity. This will inevitably raise the question whether this conception of God's nature is compatible with the freedom of choice which Leibniz thinks it proper to ascribe to him.

That question is, I think, still an open one, for it might be said that the reasoning which has led to my saying that God must be the creator did *not* say that God is logically obliged to create a contingent series of things, but took the form rather of saying that if any such series exists, then, by Sufficient Reason, God must be creatively responsible for it. So, it might appear that, consistently with his being omniscient, omnipotent and benevolent, God might not have created anything. In that case, the fact that he did create something – our world – would have been a pure act of grace, something to which he was inclined by his goodness but not necessitated by his nature. However, traditional theological discussion of God's perfections – his perfect knowledge, perfect power and perfect goodness – assigns them to God's essential

---

5   Ovid, *Metamorphoses* VII, 20, 21.

nature, so that God necessarily chooses for the better. In this envisaged case, then, he would necessarily have chosen to create some world rather than not create a world at all. Not to create anything would itself have been one of the logical possibilities that confronted God, but it could not have been endorsed because, by both Leibnizian and orthodox standards, the existence of something is necessarily better than the existence of nothing. So orthodox 'perfection theology', which envisages God as having a perfect nature that is through and through essential and resolutely non-accidental, can hardly grant God freedom at this point.

Leibniz certainly disagreed. God is *inclined*, not necessitated. To secure this disposition, he is obliged to envisage some feature of God's nature being contingent. If God necessarily exists and is necessarily omnipotent, omniscient and benevolent, then he will necessarily choose what he does in accordance with the Principle of the Best. The world that God chooses will necessarily be the best one. Of course, if some other world than ours had been the best, then God would have had to select it, so we have room to say that the necessity of choosing by the Principle of the Best leaves it open whether he had to create this world. However, it seems to me that the ordering of worlds as they present themselves to God for selection is conceived of as a rigidly fixed one (otherwise what would his knowledge that one was better than all the others answer to?). I doubt, therefore, whether this apparent loophole is something that Leibniz might happily exploit.

Occasionally it seems that Leibniz is inclined to regard God's benevolence or moral perfection as something that does indeed belong to his nature, only *contingently* so.[6] That would make room for freedom in God's choice, both in the choice to create some world rather than none and in his choice as to which world that should be. But it is entirely questionable whether Leibniz can consistently allow that and still maintain adherence to Sufficient Reason. If it is a

---

6 For example, at §13 of the *Discourse on Metaphysics* Leibniz tells us: 'It is reasonable and certain that God will always do the best, though the less perfect does not imply a contradiction' (Parkinson (ed.), 25). The problem, though, is how this can be justified on the premises from which he sets out. That he believes it to be true is not in question.

contingent matter that it is God's nature to be benevolent, then by application of Sufficient Reason itself there must be some reason why it is so, and to say merely that God is by his very nature so inclined is in effect to be content with the assertion of a brute, if benign, inexplicable fact. If that is what we are ultimately forced to in the extramundane domain, there will be little compelling reason not to be prepared to do so equally in the world itself. At that point, the rationalistic quest for the world's total intellectual transparency to our understanding will have broken down irremediably.

I shall not pursue this issue further. Before ending this chapter by tidying up a couple of loose ends, I shall draw attention to one more leading feature of God's choices that finds expression in these sections of the *Monadology*, a feature that will be important in what follows. To say that God's creative choice is (whether necessarily or not) guided by his concern for the best leaves it entirely unspecified what the best is. What, one might wonder, are the values that impress themselves on God in his exercise of his power, his knowledge and his will? The most explicit answer the *Monadology* provides is given at §58: God aims at producing as much perfection as possible, identified there in terms of his producing as much *order* and *variety* as is possible. Later on, this will be seen to have determinate consequences for how we come to understand the world that is ours. But apart from this rather bland conception of the good, God's essential concerns are given rather more content in §48, although rather *en sourdine*, where Leibniz sees the creator as moved by the desire for perfection by way of the replication of his own infinite perfections on a finite scale. That is, God cannot simply reproduce his own perfections to infinity since that would make us into gods ourselves, which we most certainly are not. But at least he can create the world in his own likeness, embodying within it *finite* degrees of activity, knowledge, power and benevolence. If these are features of the Supreme and Perfect Substance, then it cannot be a fortuitous matter that in his desire for perfection the world he chooses exemplifies them as far as is possible. To emphasize this aspect of God's concern for the best early on is to focus on something that reference to variety and order passes over in silence. We do well to keep it in mind as the analysis progresses.

I have said that it is certain we are not gods. But why should God not be able to produce gods? Or, to pick up a line of thought I left open before, why is Leibniz's theology not as welcoming to polytheism as it is to monotheism? Two considerations based on the Principle of Contradiction lead to a monotheistic stance, whereas reflection on Sufficient Reason does not. The first is that any god would have to have infinite power, knowledge and benevolence. If to be omnipotent is to be able to do anything that is logically possible, then it would seem that distinct gods engaged in creating the one Universe that comes to be might disagree about its contents. One of them might seek to exercize its power to make snow white, and the other to make it black. Suppose that either option is coherent. Still the Principle of Contradiction will ensure that one or other of the gods cannot have its way among the open atomic logical possibilities. But then he would not be omnipotent. The inference is that a plurality of gods is not a possibility, and this would supply the best of reasons why in his creation God does not create other gods. It does not lie within his power to do so. He is the only God there could be.

A more characteristically Leibnizian argument to the same conclusion is also available. As will be seen when the discussion focuses on the nature of worldly substances, one of Leibniz's logical principles is that distinct things have to have distinct qualities. If there were more gods than one, they would have to be differentiated from one another. Our methodological principles forbid our supposing figures of the extramundane realm to be exempt from this requirement, and we have seen that they must possess the qualities they do as a matter of necessity. However, the features that God possesses of necessity are features he has in virtue of his divinity, and hence features that would be shared with any other god sharing the same nature, which is to say with all of them. So no gods could be distinguished from one another by the possession of different properties. Hence, if any gods exist at all, there is only one, and polytheism is excluded by Contradiction if not by Sufficient Reason.

The second loose end I have in mind also has to do with uniqueness, not with the uniqueness of God himself, though, but with the uniqueness of the best that he chooses. As applied to God's motivational psychology Sufficient Reason tells us that in choosing what to create God acts according to the Principle of the Best. Additionally, if there is to be a choice between alternatives it must be that the preferred candidate has something to recommend it to the chooser that other candidates lack, the possession of which is not nullified by some countervailing defect. If there were a precise and exact balance between two candidates for God's choice, he could have no reason for preferring one to the other. The upshot is that in saying God acts according to the Principle of the Best Leibniz is bound to view the best world not just as an optimal world but as the uniquely best world that outstrips all other possible alternatives in value and worth. Only if it is that could God come to choose it. The thought that the best has to be the uniquely best is nowhere argued for.[7] It must just be another of those 'axioms and postulates, in a word primitive principles, which cannot be proved and stand in no need of it either'.

With so much said about God and God's nature, we can turn next to the nature of his creation, that is to the simple monads that necessarily make up the world. It is with discussion of this topic that the *Monadology* itself sets out, and from here on, with the fundamental principles of the system as firmly in place as they are, it will be convenient and helpful to follow Leibniz's own order of exposition.

Further reading

Russell, Chapter 15, 'Proofs of the Existence of God'; Adams, Chapter 5, 'The Ontological Argument' and Chapter 7, 'The Root of Possibility'; David Blumenfeld, 'Leibniz's Ontological and Cosmological Arguments', in Jolley (ed.); G. Oppy, *Ontological Arguments and Belief in God* (Cambridge, 1995); A. Kenny, *The God of the Philosophers* (Oxford, 1979); Edward Craig, *The Mind of God and the Works of Man* (Oxford, 1987).

---

7 Though, at the very end of the *Theodicy* (section 446), we find Theodorus dreaming of Pallas Athene explaining to him that '[a]mong an infinity of possible worlds, one is the best of all, because otherwise God would not be minded (*déterminé*) to create any at all ...'.

Chapter 3

Simple substances (§§1–3)

This chapter discusses the *Monadology*'s first three
sections. The first of them says what monads are; the
second gives us reason to believe such things exist; and
the third infers from the first two that monads are the
true, non-physical, atoms of nature. To be clear in
one's mind how to understand these initial sections is
already to be on the way to possessing a good understanding of the whole work.

In Leibniz's late philosophy, monads are simple
substances. Both elements of the description –
substantiality and simplicity – require elucidation,
something that Leibniz supplies in the shortest of
measures. To make good that omission I start with the
idea of *substance* itself. Modern speech has come to
confine the term pretty much to stuffs of various
kinds. A list of prohibited substances – substances
which may not be legally produced, imported or sold –
might under some easily imaginable regime include
things like uranium, heroin, dynamite and tobacco. We
would not find on that list sparrow-hawks or orchids,

although their sale, breeding and importation might equally well be prohibited. Colloquial usage, however, is distinct from that current in eighteenth century (and modern) philosophy. Its practitioners inherited the word *substance* as a technical term from their Aristotelian forebears and its prime philosophical use then, as now, applied to those individual things whose existence and character make true or false the thoughts and utterances that we aim at the world. In this sense, the individual sparrow-hawk that makes true the reflection that some predator is terrifying my pigeons is a substance, as is each of the orchids in the meadow that account for the correctness of my assertion that the field harbours a few exotic flowers.

Of particular importance for Leibniz is that substances, be they simple or compound, are what is properly speaking *real*. That, after all, is why they can make what we think or say true. Further, he assumes that such things can only be individuals. Each must be a unit, a singleton, a one. Such are the sparrow-hawk that preys on the pigeons and the individual orchids that populate the meadow. By contrast, the things we are more likely to call 'substances' today, such as whiskey or tobacco, are not individuals, but stuffs of one sort or another. Leibniz does not judge them to be genuinely real, and calls them instead 'phenomena'. Equally, he would discount as genuine substances individual samples of such stuffs which we single out in speech with the help of an individuating term, like a *glass* of whiskey or a *plug* of tobacco. For Leibniz the unity or oneness of these things is too arbitrary and depends too much on our conventions and interests for them to count as fully and genuinely real; so, too, with those particular kinds of stuff we call a whiskey or a tobacco, a Highland Malt or Caporal, say, for what encourages us to account them individuals is only their possession of some common property that invites us to talk of them as specific abstract individuals. They are not what Leibniz would call unities on their own account, unities *per se*.

In later chapters I have something to say about what it means for Leibniz to represent something as a phenomenon. For now, though, I leave that topic to one side and ask why the idea of substance, that which has a unity *per se*, forced itself upon him as the central notion of his metaphysic. Ultimately its position derives from the presumption, noted in Chapter 1, that through the exercise of reason we may aspire to understanding of ourselves and of the world that is ours. If reason is to enlighten us at all, it must articulate truths. The truths that most happily fit into the pattern of the (Aristotelian) logic that Leibniz inherited will standardly fit one of the four forms

- All *S* is *P*
- Some *S* is *P*
- Some *S* is not *P*, and
- No *S* is *P*

the paradigmatic subject–predicate forms of the day, and what will make assertions in one or other of these forms true (or false) can only be how things stand with individual instances of the subject terms. These, Leibniz takes it, can only be units or singletons or things that are one. If there are thoughts that do not lend themselves to expression in forms such as these, their truth (or falsity) will derive from the truth (or falsity) of thoughts that do exemplify these patterns, and hence their truth or falsity ultimately depends on how things stand with individuals enjoying a *per se* unity.

Setting off, then, from the axiom that what is real lends itself to investigation by reason, we quickly get to the conclusion that what is real and what is a unit are one and the same thing. Leibniz expressed this thought succinctly in a letter of 1687 to Arnauld saying, 'ce qui n'est pas veritablement *un* estre, n'est pas veritablement un *estre*' ('what is not truly *one* being is not truly a *being* at all'), and again a few years later, in correspondence with Des Bosses, by saying '*ens* et *unum* convertuntur' ('*being* and *one* are interchangeable ideas').[1] This thought, equating the *real* with *being* and *being* with *what is one*, is fundamental for him, and it is in tracing out its consequences that many of those details of the *Monadology* which we initially find so fanciful are forced upon him. It is in his quest for the truly one, for the real *par excellence*, that we find him at the start of the *Monadology* defining monads (a formation from the Greek *hē monás* for a unity or single thing; cf. Plato, *Phaedo*,105 C) not merely as substances in

---

1 Parkinson (ed.), 67 (*GP* II, 97 and *GP* II, 304, respectively).

general but as substances which are simple, and as such have no parts. These alone, he says elsewhere, 'have unity and absolute reality'.[2] We need to know just what this refinement brings with it and what leads Leibniz to it.

A common use of the term 'part' is to pick out a separable element of a thing, one which has a particular function. When the army recruit is first given a rifle, he is taught to disassemble it into its functional elements, the stock, the barrel, the bolt, the firing pin, the magazine and so on, and he learns to name those parts for future reference. However, it is not in this sense that Leibniz denies a simple substance has parts. If it were, that would allow us to class as monads or simple substances a dinosaur's thigh-bone or a plastic ping-pong ball, each of which is an individual capable of rendering thoughts true, but neither of which has clearly distinguishable elements serving a specific function in the economy of the whole. In such cases we also speak of parts when we have in mind sections or segments of the things that amount to less than the whole. So, as I unearth the dinosaur little by little on site I may uncover its thigh-bone gradually and see a greater and greater part of it emerging from the surrounding soil. Equally I may pick up from the floor a fragment of a ping-pong ball that one of the children has crushed beneath a clumsily misplaced foot. Talking of parts in this second way we are not concerned with the functional elements of a thing but with any segment of it that amounts to less than the whole. According to this second usage, a part may be a functional element of the whole, but it need not be. It is in this latter way that Leibniz is thinking when he defines monads as simple substances having no parts. In no way at all is it possible for less than a whole one to exist. Consequently, when we speak of monads we only do so correctly so long as we talk of things for which it would be impossible to identify anything less than the whole. This is not just the (true) thought that there cannot be a part of a ping-pong ball unless there is or was a whole one from which it originated; rather it is the thought that where we have to do with monads nothing whatsoever could

---

2 To de Volder (1704?) 'I show a corporeal mass not to be a substace, but a phenomenon that results from simple substances, which alone have unity and absolute reality' (*GP* II, 275).

count as the existence or the manifestation of less than a complete one. Not even God could conceive of the existence of less than a monadic whole. The manifestation of a simple substance is the manifestation of something that cannot exist except in its entirety. Thus it is that monads are essentially simple.

So why does Leibniz think it is simple unities that must lie at the centre of our attention and deserve introduction in the very first paragraph of the *Monadology*? Why, as metaphysicians, need we bother with simples at all? To engage with this question is already to approach the topic of §2, concerned as it is with our reasons for thinking that monads exist. It seemed perfectly adequate before to say that what made my thoughts about the fauna of the forest and the flora of the meadow true were sparrow-hawks and orchids, and those things are not simple substances by any stretch of Leibniz's imagination. Why are we to look away from them in our quest for the absolutely real to something else that is quite unfamiliar? Leibniz's answer is that unless monads exist such familiar things could not exist, but the most obvious and frequently given reading of §2 that might tell us why this is so fails to get to the heart of the matter.

In the case of the sparrow-hawk and the ping-pong ball it might be supposed that Leibniz is relying on some version of the reflection that here we have to do with composite material things, and what accounts for the truth of sentences about them will inevitably depend in the end on the existence and configuration of their smaller parts. Now these smaller parts must themselves be either simple or composite. If those parts are themselves composite the same reflection will apply, and reapply repeatedly until finally we arrive at ... simples. So it might be supposed that at the end of this imagined procedure it must be the existence of truly non-composed simple things that ultimately accounts for the truth of my thoughts about the bird of prey taking my pigeons or the ping-pong ball that has been crushed beneath my child's misplaced foot. Such is the most natural and the most common way of reading §2, where Leibniz moves from the seemingly innocuous fact that aggregates or compounds exist to the existence of monadic simples. At the very start of *Principles of Nature and Grace* he says that 'there must certainly be simple substances everywhere, for without simples there would be no compounds', and my examples of the hawk, the flower and the plastic ball all seem to be illustrations of that very point.

It is certainly true that Leibniz does think that the material mass that constitutes the ball and the body of the hawk must ultimately consist of simple elements, and he does also think that these will be simple substances, but it is also certain that the argument I have used to introduce them is one he would firmly reject. In the letters of 1715 to Samuel Clarke, for example, he declares that 'the least corpuscle is actually divided *ad infinitum* and contains a world of new created things, which the universe would lack if this corpuscle were an atom, that is a body all of a piece and not subdivided'. Just because there is an infinity of smaller material parts in the material atom, no matter how often we envisage dividing up the material thing we start with we shall never arrive at an unextended whole. Indeed, the very idea of completing an infinite series of operations to arrive at ultimate simples is a nonsense for Leibniz, as it is for us. The most we can say is that no matter how often we divide some material thing we shall always find ourselves with something else material which is not a simple whole. So the route to monadic simples by the imagined division of material objects cannot succeed. The unwillingness of Leibniz, remarked on earlier, to use a simple First Cause argument to underpin his introduction of the Principle of Sufficient Reason adds support to the thought that he was unmoved by analogous considerations in motivating his concentration on substances that are simple. Some different explanation is called for.

If we think back to the introduction of Sufficient Reason, it will strike us that while Leibniz did not pretend we can provide answers to an infinite series of 'why'-questions, he was happy to say that the regress of explanation-seeking queries has to be stopped and happy also to use this thought as one of the main proofs of God's existence. So here, too, while he does not think we can divide up complex individuals or quantities of stuff until we come to their simple elements, he is inclined to think that the only way we have of stopping the regress of divisions is to recognize that at the end of series there must be individual simples, even if we can never actually reach them.

Thus he wrote to Arnauld (*GP* II, 96) in 1687:

I believe that where there are only beings by aggregation, there are not even real beings, because every being by aggregation presupposes beings endowed with true unity, because it obtains its reality only from the reality of those of which it is composed, so that it will have no reality at all if every being of which it is composed is again a being by aggregation, or else we must seek some other foundation for its reality, seeing that by this means it can never be reached, even by searching forever.

The desire to stop a regress is admirable, of course, but only if there is a regress to stop. Someone who was not already convinced of the need for simples may wonder, though, why God might not create a world that consisted just of quantities of water and ice and snow or else a world that consisted of complex individuals like the sparrow-hawk and the ping-pong ball and the dinosaur's thigh-bone. In the one case he would have dispensed with unities altogether; in the other he would have created unities, but not simple ones. To such a person it would seem as if God's massy or complex creation would have its reality, only without there being simple unities in either case. So for him there is no regress in the offing. Maybe the world of water, snow and ice can be set aside as not lending itself to treatment within the framework of Leibniz's subject–predicate logic, but that would still leave Leibniz needing an argument to persuade the unconvinced reader that there is some other and better reason for the introduction of simples than any consideration stemming from the divisibility of matter. Before anything else happens we need to be persuaded that a divisible aggregate is not a unity, and the regress argument can only get started if one is already convinced of that. It cannot be used to introduce the need for simples in the first place.

The course of Leibniz's reflection on simplicity was a developing one. The term 'monad' first appears in a letter of 20–30 September 1690 to a scientific correspondent, Johann Bernouilli, and there as here, in what we can call Leibniz's late philosophy, it is used to designate real existences.[3] Only at this earlier date real existences are not

---

3   *Leibnizen's Mathematische Schriften* ed. C.I. Gerhardt, III, 542.

the monads of the later work. To Bernouilli he wrote: 'What I call a complete monad or individual substance is not so much the soul as the animal itself, or something analogous to it, endowed with a soul or a form and an organic body.' Quite what *soul*, *form* and *organic body* are need not detain us now, but what is notable is that the things which are real are indeed units, are one, just as they are later on, only the prime examples of such things are naturally existing objects in the world, such as men, or animals like the sparrow-hawk and individual plants like the orchids of my example. In 1690, however, there is no suggestion whatever that such things must be simple in the sense of having no parts. The fact that I can remove a pouch from the orchid or see the wing or the rump of the hawk (i.e. less than the whole) did not then impugn the claim of those whole things to be truly real. Now, however, by 1714, things have changed. The animal or the organic body are no longer monads but are understood in a different way – as aggregates or compound substances. Monads have to be simple, and the explanation for this refinement must be that Leibniz has come to hold that only simples enjoy a true unity, a unity *per se*, and in accordance with the *ens et unum* doctrine they alone have an unassailable claim to reality, and the composite that is the hawk or the orchid 'borrow' their reality from them in a way he will need to explain.

What would have made such a thought compelling? The answer lies, I believe, in the way Leibniz understood the ultimately Aristotelian account of natural substances to which he had firmly subscribed since the mid-1680s. (See, at this point, the *Discourse on Metaphysics* and the ensuing correspondence with Arnauld.) The individual man consists of a certain kind of matter, its changing corporeal mass, and a form which lends that changing mass the peculiar organization that men have. In our own day we are inclined to hear such suggestions, and indeed to read Aristotle's own texts, as saying that a man is a bodily being that enjoys a certain kind of organization or one that functions in a number of specific ways, just as the eye (Aristotle's favoured example in *De Anima*) is a bodily organ unified by the function it has of enabling its possessor to see. But to Leibniz this conception of the individual form or soul as the function of the whole would have been quite alien. For him, the form is conceived of as a distinct and theoretically autonomous element of the composite whole which binds together the animal (or the organ) as a unity. So, in the letter to Bernouilli the man or the ox is a unit in virtue of its bodily mass being held together and is given its particular human or bovine organization by its own dominating and unitary 'substantial form'. The move to simple substances is the consequence of that view. (How near Leibniz comes to abandoning that view will be discussed in Chapter 9.)

Consider the matter that at any moment makes up a man's body, apart from the form or soul that organizes it as the sort of body it is. There there is nothing other than a swirling mass of corpuscles, any one of which we now know contains an infinity of smaller parts. In that swirling mass there is nothing that makes that bodily item truly one thing. Equally there is nothing that makes the individual corpuscle one thing if we imagine that small chunk of matter apart from the form organizing its various minute elements as one mass of sub-corpuscles. So, in any case in which we consider that we have to do with a composite whole, a substantial aggregate, that which makes it an individual or a unit, that which accounts for its *bona fide* reality, must be a form, something which itself is distinct from the bodily matter of the larger whole, and something which has no parts, which is a unity in its own right and which by its very nature endows the animal or the corpuscle with its unity by organizing the matter that goes to make it up.

Implicit in the Bernouilli letter, so understood, is the recognition that the human beings and the animals which Leibniz was then calling 'monads' get their identity from an individualizing element of their constitution, from their form or, in the human case, their mind or soul. This element is, I repeat, not just seen as the way in which their bodily matter is organized, but is itself a distinct and partless individual unit in their constitution. In the absence of such individual forms or souls, the whole being, the hawk or the man, the very smallest atom there might be, would simply have no unity, and then by the *ens et unum* doctrine would have no genuine being at all. The *Monadolology*'s doctrine that monads or true unities must be simples articulates the idea, present but unremarked upon in the Bernouilli letter, that material things which we take to be true unities acquire their unity from something else, their forms, and it is for this reason that such things, partless as they are, must lie at the centre of the meta-physician's attention.

We can see now why Leibniz's own introduction of monads at §2 is so puzzling: 'There must be simple substances because there are compounds and a compound is nothing other than a mass or aggre-gate of simples.' As a persuasive proof that there are simple substances, this is unsatisfactory for at least two reasons. The first is that it misleads us about the breadth of the claim that Leibniz is advancing, and the second is that it is blatantly circular. As for the first point, it is made to appear that we can appeal to our experience of compounds or aggregates in order to warrant the inference that there are simples. Now, it is evident that in speaking of compounds Leibniz has in mind just the sorts of substance which in the 1690 letter to Bernouilli he was happy to call 'monads', first and foremost men but also animals and plants. Other things we encounter, such as celestial bodies or microscopic viruses, will also qualify as aggregates, though even in this earlier period Leibniz was hesitant whether they would be sufficiently animal-like to count as true compound substances rather than mere phenomena. But this path to the existence of monads by way of such gross observable things suggests that if the part of the world that falls within our purview had been very different, or if God had elected to create an altogether different kind of world from ours, there might have been no aggregates and no compound substances, and so maybe no simples either. Since the *Monadology* suggests no other reason for thinking that there are monads than the one given here, it would be tempting to infer that the only monads we have reason to believe in (setting aside God himself) are those that enter into the constitution of such compounds as our world contains. So the existence of monads might be restricted to this world and those other worlds that are closely similar to it and not feature in a large number of further worlds that God might have decided to create. Even in our own world it seems a possibility that such things should be denser on the ground in London than in the Orkneys. Thoughts like these quite misrepresent Leibniz's intentions.

Second, if a compound or an aggregate is definitionally a compound of simples, it is analytically true that there are simples if there are aggregates, but it must be an open question whether the fishes and trees and other natural creatures we encounter are compounds at all in this sense. Admittedly they are material things, being divisible and having various functional parts; but we are as yet in no position to say that this is the same as being composed of Leibnizian simples of the kind adduced in §1. To appeal to aggregates as a way of introducing simples misfires as long as the idea of an aggregate is itself explained via the notion of simplicity. Experience can give us no way of deciding whether the things we bump into in the course of our everyday experience are aggregates of that kind or not. So, on the face of it, §2 fails to make clear why the metaphysician should concern himself with simple monads at all.

We should perhaps not be too worried by such points as these. Leibniz's way of writing may do little more than reflect his desire to convey his thinking easily to a philosophically naive audience. What is important is that he should have something else at his disposal to justify the introduction of his simple monadic unities, and we now have enough in hand to see what it might be. Presuming that the reality that there is is what reason can explore, and noticing that what reason's exploration of the world needs if it is to yield truths is the existence of individuals, Leibniz simply draws on the assumption remarked upon above that any individual we come across, or indeed any individual that could possibly exist, must either have a unity *per se* and be something that is one on its own account or else be explainable in terms of things that are unities *per se*. The unity possessed by anything else will be a merely accidental unity, a unity *per accidens*.

Some hint of this thought is found even before the letter to Bernouilli of 1690. Four years previously Leibniz was writing to Arnauld:

> There is as much difference between a substance and such a being [a unity *per accidens*, such as a block of marble] as there is between a man and a community – say a people, an army, a society or committee, which are moral beings, yet they have an imaginary something and depend on the fiction of our minds. Substantial unity calls for a thoroughly indivisible being. This characteristic can not be found either in shapes or motions, both of which involve something imaginary.... It can however be

found in a soul or substantial form, such as is the one called *me*. These latter are the only thoroughly real beings (*les seuls estres accomplis véritables*).[4]

Eight years later, in 1704, he is reiterating the connection he sees between what is real and what enjoys a true (non-fortuitous) unity when he writes to de Volder:

A thing which can be divided into several is an aggregate of several, and ... is not one except mentally, and has no reality but what is borrowed from its constituents. Hence I inferred that there must be in things indivisible unities, because otherwise there will be in things no true unity, and no reality not borrowed. Which is absurd. And where there is no reality not borrowed, there will never be any reality, since this must in the end belong to some subject.[5]

Whatever we think of the correctness of this train of thought, it does avoid the objections I raised before. It makes it plain that when we consider the options available to God at the moment of creation the choice that confronts him is not between some world of monads and some other sort of world. As long as creation is undertaken at all it will necessarily be of a world of monads. Just as with the Principles of Contradiction and Sufficient Reason, this is no external constraint on God, preventing him from doing something he might otherwise have done. It delimits the very possibilities among which he might choose. Here there is no external constraint, only metaphysical necessity.

Then there is no circularity in this way of understanding the introduction of simple monadic substances. We set out from what I call the *ens et unum* axiom and acknowledge that the only true unities are simple unities. If God creates anything, he creates something that is through and through real. Consequently, either he creates things that have a unity *per se*, simple substances, monads as they are understood

---

4   To Arnauld, 28 November–8 December 1686 (*GP* II, 76).
5   *GP* II, 267.

in the later phase of Leibniz's thinking, or, alternatively, he creates things which do not have a unity *per se*, such as a sea of plasma or complex individuals like the sparrow-hawk and the orchid of the earlier examples. In these cases the reality of what God creates, the plasma or the flower, is 'borrowed' from the unities *per se* that enter into their constitution. Either way, Leibniz will say, wherever anything real is found there will be monads, and since reality is equally distributed between London and the Orkneys there is no question that the distribution of these simple beings might be scarcer in one place than in another, and no question but that other worlds God might have made real would have been as replete with monads as we are obliged to take our own world to be.

The reasoning that moves Leibniz sets out from a quest for the real unity that underlies that which we accord to individual animals or men. Only, as I have just written, it seems as if he must also be prepared to argue to the existence of monads from the existence of quantities of stuff or matter, like the sea of plasma, that have no unity of their own. This is what we find in another late work, the *New System* of 1695, where he says:

> Furthermore, by means of the soul or form there is a true unity corresponding to what is called 'I' in us. Such a unity could not occur in artificial machines or in a simple mass of matter, however organized it may be. For such a mass can be compared only to an army or a herd, or to a pond full of fish, or a watch made of springs and wheels. If there were no true substantial unities, however, there would be nothing substantial or real in the collection.[6]

The assumption here, I think, is that there is indeed something real in a mass of plasma or a tot of whiskey, and that reality has to be accounted for by reference to some unbreakable unities or other. That is how they can be real things, even if not real *individuals* like the bird or the flower. So the *ens et unum* doctrine can be applied

---

6   Parkinson (ed.), 120.

here too, and we can say that even if God had not created individual composite substances such as the hawk and the orchid, but had restricted himself instead to making a world of pretty uniform magma, he could only have done so by creating monads that combined themselves together in that massy way.

Of necessity, then, if anything exists, monads exist. We know that some physical things exist, and whether we think of them as unities or not – as individual birds or flowers, say, or mere quantities of matter of óne kind or another – a condition of their claim to reality is that they be constituted of simple substances. It is a further question whether we can say that monads themselves exist of necessity. By this I do not mean whether any particular monad that exists exists necessarily – that is the privilege of God alone – but whether it is necessary that some created monads or other exist. This is not a question that the *Monadology* raises, but it is one that it already allows us to ask, and it is also clear how Leibniz would want to answer it. Time and again in his mature period he adverts to a distinction between *absolute* and *hypothetical* necessity. A proposition is said to be *absolutely* necessary if its denial expresses a contradiction. A proposition is *hypothetically* necessary when its truth is grounded in Sufficient Reason, when it must hold if God sees that it is for the best. Now, while it is an absolute necessity that there could never have been a time when no created monads existed, it is no more than a hypothetical necessity that there must exist created monads. The existence of time itself depends, for Leibniz, on the existence of monads that change their states, so naturally he thinks there would be a straightforward contradiction in the idea that there might be a time when there were none. But this leaves open the possibilities that God should have created no monads and that there should have been no time either. It is therefore not an absolute necessity that there be monads. It is, however, a hypothetical necessity that there be such things. Whether or not anything exists must have an explanation. That is guaranteed by the Principle of Sufficient Reason. In either case the reason will be because God in his wisdom chose it to be so. God's choice is governed by the Principle of the Best, and, that being so, he will prefer to create something rather than create nothing, because of necessity something is better than nothing. Since to create anything God has to create monads, monads must exist given that God chooses and acts for the best. For Leibniz this necessity is no more than hypothetical since, in his view, there is no necessity that God act in accordance with the Principle of the Best. His nature merely *inclines* him to do that; it does not oblige him to do so.

Setting out from the initial ontological commitment to substances and the late-come realization that, properly speaking, substances must be simple wholes, in §3 Leibniz proceeds to draw what is for him the immediate inference that they cannot be physical things: 'where there are no parts, neither extension nor shape nor division is possible'. We need to appreciate, though, that there is a significant inference being made here, since the only uniform content that my exposition has given to the idea of the simple is that it is what is a *per se* unity, something which is a fundamental unit of existence. Whereas considerations of the infinite divisibility of material things must not be used to justify the existence of simples, once their existence is secured in some other way they do have their utility in telling us what monads cannot be.

It is obvious enough that what can be divided can be divided into separate elements, each of which is less than the whole. Since simples cannot exist other than as wholes, nothing that is divisible could be simple. That is so whether the things we think of as divisible are physical or not. If we concentrate on the physical and corporeal, and remember the Cartesian background against which Leibniz was writing, his observation that nothing that is extended can be simple entails that no bodies can be monads and hence that bodies are not true unities *per se*. The argument is the same as before. Take anything that is extended. Let it stretch from point A to point C in one dimension, and from point A to point E in another direction. On the line AC there must be an intermediate point B, and similarly some point D on the line AE at right-angles to AD. In that case we can construct a triangle ABD whose extension is smaller than that of the whole from which we started. The operation can be iterated as often as we like and applied to any extended figure whatsoever. So no extended figure can be simple. Any extended whole, any Cartesianly conceived body, must possess parts smaller than the whole. No body is simple, so no body is itself a monad, a true element of God's creation or, as Leibniz puts it, 'a true atom of nature'. Of course, we must take care not to think that Leibniz's argument rests on the assumption that when it comes to bodies we can always actually divide them up into smaller and smaller pieces, which are their parts, or that we can identify the parts by sight or touch down to even infinitesimally small ones. That is not what he is counting on to make his point. Rather it is that for any body, no matter how small, given that it has particular boundaries, there will always be narrower boundaries, falling within the original ones, that define something less than the initial whole. That we may not be able to specify where these boundaries lie is neither here nor there. Their existence is guaranteed by the idea of continuous dimension which is internal to our notion of extension. That is what lies at the root of Leibniz's thought that of necessity anything extended has extended parts.

Bodies are not monads, then, for bodies are not true unities. However, that is not to say that such things do not exist. Indeed, we have seen (§2) that Leibniz explicitly acknowledges that there are compounds and infers the existence of monads from them. Clearly, he here has in mind material things. The issue is going to be how it can be intellectually satisfying to see these as aggregates of simples, for if simples have no parts, and hence no extension, an aggregate of simples can hardly possess any extension either, or so it would seem. How Leibniz can handle this topic is material for Chapter 7. Let me say here just that he is careful not to conceive of monads as extension-less mathematical points out of which somehow lines and dimensions may be constructed. Leibniz is quite clear that points are not parts of lines, but the limits of lines, and so can be introduced only in terms of the lines that they delimit.[7] They are not, therefore, independently existing items as monads must be; hence they cannot be the elements from which things possessed of physical dimension might be built up.

Even to mention mathematical points encourages an image of monads which is quite misleading and which it is as well to dissipate as early as possible. That is the image of Leibniz's monads being

---

7 In 'Primary Truths' (*c.* 1686) he writes: 'However, the continuum is not divided into points, nor is it divided in all possible ways. Not into points, because points are not parts, but limits' (Parkinson (ed.), 91).

essentially very, very small, so small indeed as to take up no space, not even a point of space. This is utter nonsense. Even to talk of something being small is to think of it in spatial terms, and the expression 'smaller even than a point' has no sense whatever. All that Leibniz is committed to is that monads are not things with parts, hence not with extended parts. They have no size, therefore ('no shape' is what he says in §3, and this implies no shape of any size), and are radically misdescribed if said to be small or minute, and so on. Perhaps it helps one to resist that temptation to recall that the one monad we have already met – God, the Supreme Simple Substance – is never thought of in dimensional terms, and certainly never as 'small'. It is no more proper to think of any other monad in such terms.

Having remarked that monads cannot be extended, Leibniz adds in §3 that they are the 'true atoms of nature', and the 'elements of things'. This takes us further than anything we have yet seen, since it enables us to say that monads are ubiquitously present in the matter of the world. Wherever we find that there is something real there must be monads, since even that which is not a true substance borrows what reality it has from the true unities that enter into its composition. Leibniz put the idea in a letter of 1687 to Arnauld in these terms: 'I do not say that there is nothing substantial or nothing but what is apparent in those things that have no true unity, since I allow that they always have as much reality or substantiality as there is true unity in what enters into their composition.'[8] So while we might initially suppose that what gives unity to the sparrow-hawk or the orchid is its own peculiar (indivisible) form, and that its body is some ultimately irreducible mass of smaller parts, now we know that even its body consists of simple unextended elements because, while the sparrow-hawk's form or soul makes the whole a unified compound, unless its bodily parts inherited their reality from other true unities the soul or the substantial form (or, as Leibniz will later say, the dominant monad) would not find anything else that is even derivatively real to which it might supply a unity.

These further unities, together with the monads that are the substantial forms of men and animals and the like, are the atoms of

---

8   Ibid., 67 (GP II, 97).

nature. These are not physical atoms as Lucretius conceived of them or as latter-day physical science does. They are *metaphysical* atoms, the non-physical units which have to exist if anything else is to do so. It will be one of the major tasks of commentary to explain just how Leibniz does think that a congeries of monads can constitute a material thing, and why it is, as he puts it in §2, that 'a compound is nothing other than a mass or aggregate of simples'. It will also fall to later to say why even where we are inclined to say that nothing extended is to be found somewhere in the universe but empty space, there too there must exist these monadic metaphysical atoms.

To close this chapter I want to stress that however much it may seem as if Leibniz is focussing his attention on the world that is so familiar to us and offering an account of how we need to think if we are to understand it, in truth his concern here as elsewhere is quite universal and applies to any world whatever that God could have created. Just as the Principle of Contradiction and the Principle of Sufficient Reason would have their application to any world that God might have chosen, so too we can say that the true atoms of any world that might have come to be would have to be monads and that no matter what external forms such worlds might display their elements could not be anything other than simple immaterial and unextended things. As the epigraph to Chapter 1 I took Leibniz's observation: 'The foundations are everywhere the same. This is a fundamental principle of my philosophy' (*NE*, 64). Here, at the very start of the *Monadology*, is one place at which these universal foundations are shown to be in place. As we progress, we shall repeatedly see that same thing recurring, even in the area of moral reflection where perhaps we might least expect it. It is notably at work in the next topic I address – Leibniz's discussion of what we can say negatively and positively about the character and nature of any possible world's true monadic elements.

Further reading

Russell, Chapter 4, 'The Conception of Substance', and Chapter 8, 'The Philosophy of Matter'; R. C. Sleigh, 'Leibniz on the Simplicity of Substance', in Kuhlstad (ed.).

Monadic nature (§§4–13)

There must be simple substances if there is to be anything at all. About such things we know no more than that they have neither extension nor size and are in consequence non-physical. Between §§4 and 13 Leibniz supplements this meagre characterization, first, in §§4–7, with a number of negative claims and then more positively in §§8–13. The negative doctrines are consequences of monads' essential simplicity; the positive and highly abstract claims I shall be concerned with are consequences of that simplicity together with another Great Principle that has not yet appeared. In both cases, the doctrines Leibniz endorses are meant to be universal and necessary. Nothing in these sections applies to some monads rather than others, and nothing is specific to one possible collection of monads rather than another. While the first three sections have told us what monads *are*, now we are to learn what they *are like*.

I begin with the *negative* claims. §§4–6 affirm that in the natural course of events monads can neither cease to exist nor come to be. They come to be 'all at once', by creation; they cease to be 'all at once', by annihilation – and neither creation nor annihilation are events that take place in the natural course of things. To that extent they are genuinely miraculous occurrences. In the world as we know it we have to do mainly with composite things, and composites come to be by being formed quite unmiraculously out of existing material through the gradual assimilation of matter and the conjunction of parts. The tree grows from the seed by absorbing nutriment through its roots; each year new leaves come to be through the organization of matter taken up from the soil. Things are entirely comparable in the case of artefacts. The joiner makes a door from planks of wood he has cut from his tree, and he furnishes it with handles and locks taken from other sources. By parity of reasoning, when the tree or the leaf ceases to exist, it slowly decays or is cut up and burned until the matter of which it is composed is dispersed into the air or the earth whence it came. The door ceases to be when its constituent elements come apart and can no longer be reassembled. With monads, however, things must be different, for being essentially simple they have no parts and so can neither perish nor be assembled. They are immune to corruption and generation.

Are we then to say that monads endure eternally? Is it that once a monad exists it must exist forever? Here there are two questions. One is whether even if some monads have a limited span of life there are others that are everlasting. The other is whether it is even metaphysically possible for any monad to have less than an unlimited span of existence. §6 suggests no clear answer to either question, but what Leibniz's response to both must be is not hard to discern. It cannot be a strict metaphysical truth that monads are eternal, for God has the power to create and the power to destroy. So divine decree could bring about the existence of new monads at any moment. Equally, divine decree might annihilate any monad that actually exists. That much is conveyed by the text itself. Similarly, against the background of the creation myth, it is natural to suppose that God's existence in the absence of any created monads whatever has to be possible. How else might he come to create them? If that is so, then God's existence too, when monads have ceased to be, must be possible. How might he, the necessarily existing being, otherwise annihilate them?

Nevertheless, we need to take care. While *space* for Leibniz is nothing other than the order of coexisting things and their states, *time* is the order of non-coexisting (i.e. successive) things and their states.[1] Given that if anything exists monads do, as long as there is time monads will have to exist, for otherwise there will be no things possessing states at all, whether coexisting or not. Consequently, there was no time before monads existed, and time will cease should they cease. In one way, then, it is indeed a metaphysical truth that monads are everlasting. Such things must persist from the very beginning of time until its very end. Admittedly, this carries absolutely no implication for the individual monad. As long as time flows, any particular monad may in logic cease to be, and new monads may in logic be created (by decree, of course, though not by composition).

This last is an *a priori* truth. Using an idea we met in the last chapter, it enjoys *absolute* necessity and depends on nothing other than the Principle of Contradiction. Surprisingly, perhaps, if we now bring to bear the Principle of Sufficient Reason as well, we can see that Leibniz has every reason to think that while it is not of the essence of the individual monad to endure forever, it is a *hypothetical* necessity that each one should do so. Consider how it might be otherwise. If a monad were to last less than eternally there would have to be some reason for it to cease to exist before the end of time or for it to have come into existence after time has begun, or both. Reflect on the latter part of such a monad's existence. Were God to annihilate it at a given moment, he must have sufficient reason to do so. A sufficient reason could only be that a better state of affairs should result from the absence of this particular than would obtain were it to continue in existence. 'Better' here will be understood in the light of §58, which tells us that the good that God effects is to be calculated in terms of considerations of variety and order. Acting according to the Principle of the Best (§46), and thereby expressing his nature, God generates as much perfection as possible – that is, 'as much variety as possible is achieved, though with the greatest possible order' (§58). So the

---

1   Cf. letters to de Volder of 20 June 1703 and 30 June 1704 (*GP* II, 253, 269).

annihilation of a given monad will need to make way for a greater perfection than its continued existence would allow for. We can also say that before the imagined act of annihilation God must have had sufficient reason to create our chosen monad along with all the rest. His omnipotence and omniscience exclude his having created it as a result of a mistaken calculation or of carelessness in the execution of his original design, errors that he might rectify *post factum* by some corrective annihilative act. As Leibniz wrote to Samuel Clarke in 1715: 'I do maintain that [the corporeal world] is a watch which goes without needing [God's] *correction*: otherwise we should have to admit that God keeps improving upon his own work.'[2] The issue, then, will be whether God could have reason both to create our sample monad and later on to destroy it without his doing so being thought of as a correction of his initial calculation of the best.

The only possibility must be that our hapless substance is obliged to give way to the creation of others, to yield its place in the grand whole for the sake of a greater perfection brought about by later comers on the scene *with whose existence its own is incompatible*. Just such a thought might be encouraged by the reflection that we ourselves are late-comers on the earth's stage and that our presence here had to be prepared for by the existence of other species now extinct. So, it might be supposed that, by Leibniz's lights, the total goodness of the world is properly measured in diachronic terms and that that may involve the creation of new monads during its course and the destruction of others to make way for them.[3]

Such a quasi-evolutionary model happily applies only to composite things, though, not to simples. As far as composites go, Leibniz will say that new sorts of things come into being by the rearrangement of already existing simples. So, at the level of simples it provides no

---

2 Leibniz–Clarke correspondence, Leibniz's Letter 2 paragraph 6 (Parkinson (ed.), 209).

3 Tenuous evidence that Leibniz could have had some such thought in mind is offered by §47, which says that monads 'originate so to speak through continual fulgurations of the divinity'. The passage conjures up an image of God's creative activity as being somehow akin to that of a spider spinning her web out of herself, but whatever we are to make of it, it hardly consists with Leibniz's considered metaphysic to think of the world's simple elements gradually emanating from God over time.

support at all for any continuous creation hypothesis. In the present context that image can be no more than suggestive, permitting application to simples only if the value that supposedly accrues to the world from the addition of new members to its original number could not have coexisted with the earlier 'preparatory' states that preceded their advent. However, if the existence of some monads should be incompatible with the existence of others, as Chapter 6 will show, that can only be because their doing so would be at odds with the operation of general laws governing the action and behaviour of the individuals falling under them. Yet we shall also see that conflicting laws cannot obtain at different times in one and the same world. Consequently, it is ruled out that there should be situations in which some monads are obliged to make way for others whose existence under a novel set of general laws increases the total value of God's creation. If the new-come monads increase the perfection of the already established collection, then God would have no reason not to have included them in that collection in the first place. We may conclude that in all consistency Leibniz must permit that even a diachronic measure of the world's perfection does not allow there to be sufficient reason for God to engineer the destruction or creation of monads in time. The only other thought that might encourage one to suppose that he could not have allowed the old and the new to coexist would be that he needs the material of the old to constitute the new, but the very simplicity of monads excludes that as a possibility.

If, then, God has reason to create a given monad, he has reason to create it at the outset. Since the perfection of the world containing it can scarcely be increased by that monad's subsequent annihilation, there can be no natural reason for a monad that earns its place in the original dispensation to cease to be later on. *En passant*, we may think that analogous reflections would furnish Leibniz with grounds for holding that it is a further hypothetical necessity that once time has begun it should never end, and in consequence not merely that the world of created monads will last forever but also that no single monad, once created, should ever cease to be.

A protest that Leibniz evidently encountered at this point, one which enjoys perennial charm for the piously inclined, is that it is sacrilegious to suppose our finite reason could so much as begin to comprehend God's infinite powers. Must not what satisfies His reason be entirely different from what we are inclined to judge reasonable? If so, may God not well abide by Sufficient Reason in His own reflection, his calculation and his decision making, yet still find reason enough to create worlds which we cannot fathom? In that case, it would be arrogant of us to deny it to be a real possibility that short-lived monads should exist in full conformity with Sufficient Reason and that the somewhat surprising hypothetical necessities I have outlined would be no more than deluded philosophical fantasies.

The right response to this must be to say that by 'reason' is meant *reason*, viz. what *our* use of that term picks out. God's reason cannot be different from ours in a way that is not captured by our own developed usage of the language. What is proposed here as a possibility is not in fact one. This is not to deny that God could, by miracle, cut short the existence of monads where there is scarce reason for him to do so. Only that is to say no more than that God's omnipotence extends to the boundaries of what is logically possible, the boundaries of what is not forbidden by the Principle of Contradiction itself. On this subject Leibniz himself observes quite sharply:

> I should not wish us to be obliged to have recourse to miracles in the ordinary course of nature, and to allow the existence of powers and operations which are absolutely inexplicable – otherwise we should be granting too much licence to bad philosophers on the strength of what God can do.[4]

While we must not expect to find in the world around us empirical confirmation of the monads' claim to everlasting or eternal existence, we can insist on the hypothetical necessity of individual monads persisting throughout all time. Later (§76), Leibniz will extend this claim to natural composites as well, in particular to humans and animals, which he thinks never suffer complete destruction, even at what we call 'death'. The grounds for that astonishing assertion will receive comment when we come to it. So far, our reasonings apply to simple substances alone, about which we can make only *a priori*

---

4   *NE*, 61 (*GP* V, 54).

claims. For what it is worth, though, we know from the 1686 letter to Arnauld, quoted in the last chapter, that Leibniz identifies the self with a simple monad, you with one, me with another, and readers who have been carried along with the flow of the argument mounted here will already be able to draw the consequence that, for Leibniz, they are not merely protected against decay and dissolution, but as simple substances have no beginning and no end in time. If there is immortality to be had, then, as Leibniz sees it, you and I have it already, not in some distant celestial sphere, but in the very world in which we live.

I have pursued the discussion of the duration of monads at some length – and rather beyond Leibniz's own text – because it illustrates so well and so early in the work the evident rationalistic ambition of his thought. As the story develops we shall see that the metaphysic we are offered is rarely governed by the Principle of Contradiction alone, but by that principle in comfortable harness with the Principle of Sufficient Reason, just as §32 leads us to expect. In consequence, we would be making an error if we were to think that the central claims of the *Monadology's* ninety sections express absolute, metaphysical, necessities. Not even the claim that monads exist does that. Instead, we have an intricate set of interrelated hypothetical necessities, truths which must hold as long as God's choices are rationally governed by the Principle of the Best. The result is that we should not read the *Monadology* as telling us that every world that is possible must be structured in this way or in that. Instead, we are asked to accept that any *intelligible* world must be so structured, or that any world that presents itself to God's mind as a serious candidate for his creative decisions should be so. Only a rationalist vision of things more extreme than any endorsed by Leibniz would suppose that what was logically possible and what was rationally intelligible must coincide. No such vision was his, though it may well have been the vision of Spinoza, who was already dead when Leibniz came to elaborate his own mature thought.

Putting it a little more accurately, we see absolute and hypothetical necessities elegantly nested within each other in Leibniz's monadological vision of things. It is an absolute necessity that God exists. It is a hypothetical necessity that he creates a universe. Given that he does create a universe, it is again an absolute necessity that any universe he creates should consist of monadic atoms. That the monadic atoms which actually exist compound to form men is a hypothetical necessity, relative to which it is absolutely necessary that men should be rational intelligences. At any point at which we discover Leibniz committed to some necessity, it is interesting to ask just where in the nested system it is right to see him locating it. In what follows I try to keep track of the status of each of the main claims that Leibniz makes.

A second important negative claim about the essential nature of monads is introduced at §7, where we come upon the famous assertion that monads have no windows. With this Leibniz maintains that monads are not amenable to external influence. No change in them can be brought about from outside by any created thing. This thought is often understood as denying that there can be causal relations between things, as if Leibniz thought that the incidence of light on plants is causally unconnected with their growth. In fact he holds nothing of the kind, but merely wants to warn us against a particular conception of causality, one according to which changes take place in things by their acquisition of the properties of other things. To illustrate the idea to be rejected, we may imagine a boy playing a game of rugger. In the scrum someone's elbow bangs the boy's nose, which bleeds over his white shirt. His shirt becomes red in places by absorbing the blood that he has shed. When his mother washes the shirt after the game, the water turns red and the shirt returns to its original colour. Washing it has caused the shirt to become white by removing the red that was there and absorbing it into the water. In Leibniz's view, it is all too easy to misunderstand what has really happened.

The way Leibniz articulates the prevalent understanding of causation is initially, and somewhat mischievously, to construe it in terms of a thesis concerning the transfer of *parts* from what is involved in the cause to what is involved in the effect, as if when the water absorbs blood from the shirt a part of the shirt has entered into the water and become part of it. In relation to monads, such a conception could have no application, since simples can have no parts and therefore could not possibly change by acquiring parts from others. This is the point of the observation that monads have no windows by which anything could come in or go out. However, that does nothing to discountenance the popular account of causality in general, but only (and at best) its application to simple substances. Later in the same section, however, we are offered a more general and more pertinent reflection which extends Leibniz's criticism of this 'transitive' conception of causation to aggregates. This turns not on the simple nature of monads, but on the general nature of accidents or properties: they 'cannot detach themselves from substances and wander about outside them' (§7).

What Leibniz has in mind is to remind us that while I may perhaps lose and gain qualities as I change over time, I cannot acquire particular instances of qualities that once belonged to something else in the way that I can inherit a piece of property. In my example, when the water turned red and the rugger shirt white again, the water did not come to possess the quality of redness that was a passing feature of the shirt. The redness in the water is not the particular redness that was once in the shirt (that trope), even if the washing has made the shirt white again by absorbing and removing the blood that had stained it. Once the point is made in this way it is not the windowlessness of monads that stands in the way of 'transitive' causation so much as the logical tie of qualities to their subjects. Leibniz sees that we must resist the temptation to reify them and then to think they might be detached, as self-standing individuals, from the subjects to which they originally belonged. Having said that, though, there is no reason why one monad should not bring about or cause changes in another as long as there is available an account of causation that involves neither an exchange of parts nor the transference of qualities. That Leibniz does indeed have something positive to put in its place will emerge when later I come to discuss his understanding of the relation between mind and body.

So much for the negative claims of §§4–7. In the sections immediately following Leibniz embarks on what can be said *more positively* about monads. §§8–10 may be read as counterparts to the passages just discussed. Thus §8 argues that while monads cannot have parts, they must have properties; §10 shows that while they do not come into existence or go out of existence, monads must continuously change through time; and §11 explains that though they do not affect one another 'transitively' from without, their changes take place in accordance with an internal principle. §§12 and 13 extend and refine the thought offered in §11. These are dense paragraphs, and they deserve to be taken one by one.

'However, monads must have some qualities ... otherwise they would not be anything at all.' Leibniz's quite general point at the start of §8 is surely correct. Whatever exists must have some feature or other. If we were to try to imagine something without any properties at all we should be at a loss to know how we had supposed it to exist in the first place. How, for all properties F, could anything be neither F nor not-F? Since we know already from §3 that the properties of monads cannot be corporeal ones, it will be left for later (in fact for §14) to identify exactly what sorts of features monads necessarily possess. §8, however, does more than affirm that monads have to possess some properties: it proclaims their need to possess properties that differ from one another. If they did not, we should be unable to account for one of the most salient features of the observed world, the fact that it harbours change.

This may well strike one as an odd way for Leibniz to proceed. For one thing, the impossibility of monads being undifferentiated in their qualities is not advanced in the text categorically but rather hypothetically, on the basis of actual detectable gross variation in composite things. As a quite general thesis, or even as a thesis tailored to capture the nature of simples, it appears unsupported at the point of introduction. This omission is quickly repaired in the next sentence, where Leibniz commits himself to the fundamental dependence of the character of the composite on that of its underlying simples. 'For what is found in compounds', he says, 'can only come from their simple ingredients' (§8). In the present case he thinks that observed change in something, say, from hot to cold, could not be accounted for if the simple monads composing the object or the liquid in question were all uniform in character. There would be nothing in the uniform base which could possibly account for the higher-level observed variety.

The argument from gross change would in fact be happier had Leibniz used it to underpin the necessity of monadic change over time rather than of fundamental synchronic monadic diversity, for the change in a liquid from hot to cold might (just) be thought of in terms of a uniformly constituted set of monads changing uniformly from being hot at one time to being cold at a later one. What Leibniz would want the example to show, though, is that the monads involved could not themselves be uniformly constituted, and that the example does not do. Nevertheless, a slight adjustment to the text will make the point well enough. If the compound world is dependent on the world of simples, observed synchronic variety in the world of aggregates will require at least some synchronic variety among the simples that make it up. Hence a world containing both synchronic and diachronic variety at the level of compounds cannot dispense with variety at the monadic level in either way.

Even incorporating this adjustment, we are still only able to argue to monadic diversity if there is diversity at the level of compounds. That, however, seems to be a contingent and empirical matter. To get from the restricted nature of the claim to a fully general one, one that gives us information about any possible world that God might have created, Leibniz's next section (§9) introduces the thought that no two beings ever have all their properties in common. The language he uses is lax. First he speaks as though this is just an observed fact about the world, and that could not possibly underpin the claim that all monads must differ from each other even in this world, let alone in other ones. There could be no empirical basis for asserting any such thing. Then, although Leibniz is here speaking of monads, he talks in far too epistemic a vein, speaking of our '[finding] some ... difference' between things. Except for a few possible exceptions (the selves we encounter, perhaps), *finding* any such thing must lie well beyond the reach of our earth-bound investigative powers.

It is plain from other texts, as well as from the use which Leibniz makes of it in the *Monadology*, that he views this principle not as an empirical matter but as a logical truth which applies to all possible subjects of thought. So we need to add it, the so-called Identity of Indiscernibles, to the growing list of axioms we see shaping the Leibnizian metaphysic – to the Principle of Contradiction, the Principle of Excluded Middle, the Principle of Sufficient Reason, the Principle of the Best, the *ens et unum* doctrine and to the latest arrival, the Dependence of the Compound on the Simple. Taking §9 as endorsing a principle of logic, then, Leibniz envisages the Identity of Indiscernibles holding in a notably strong form. That is, he is saying more than that the requirement that monads have different properties from one another can be satisfied by their differing in respect of their relational properties, so that simples which were in themselves alike might differ in their age, say, or their relationships to God or to each other; rather, he is claiming, the principle ensures that they differ from one another in their *internal – non-relational –* features, and that in consequence each monad taken in itself must differ qualitatively from every other monad taken in itself. It is not difficult to see why Leibniz should think this principle must hold and hold in this strong fashion.

First, it is entirely reasonable to think that if things must be distinguished by some property or other, relational properties cannot do the trick. For two things to stand in distinct relation to each other they must already be two, and hence already be distinct from one another. So, if the Identity of Indiscernibles holds at all it must hold of them already, and they must therefore differ from one another internally. Furthermore, when we think of God deciding to creating a world, he needs to be able to specify the particular items he envisages the world containing. To identify them, he has nothing available to himself other than a full description of the candidates for existence given in terms of the properties they are to have. He can do nothing else to single them out, such as laying a hand on them or strictly referring to them, since they do not yet exist to be taken hold of or otherwise be demonstrated. The only thing that will serve to distinguish one prospective individual from another will be a uniquely identifying description of it that God can bear in mind and with which those individuals will comply when he comes to issue his creative edict. In the absence of such a unique description there will be nothing to distinguish one putative candidate for creation from another. In consequence, when the moment of creation comes, the things that come to be will be bound to differ from each other in the properties they possess, and specifically in their non-relational properties. Since this reflection is entirely general, it will hold in any possible world, not just in the world in which we find qualitative difference between the things we come across. This new logical principle will have rich and unexpected consequences for the kind of world Leibniz can suppose it is open to God to create.

§10 addresses the theme of *change*, an idea which figured only marginally in §8. All created things are subject to change; so too are monads. Furthermore, Leibniz asserts that the change is continuous in each case. We are urged to take these claims for granted, and no support is offered for them. Nevertheless we do have in hand what we need to supply one argument for adopting them that Leibniz would be happy to endorse. It has wider application than merely to the actual world and to other possible worlds that closely resemble it.

Suppose there was no change in any monad. Then there would be nothing to distinguish the several times at which each displayed the same constant features. We could not then speak of constancy at all, since, as we know, for Leibniz time is not properly conceived of other than as the order of successive states of things. It is nothing like an absolute container into which monads are inserted at different temporal points. It must be a mistake to imagine time on that model, Leibniz thinks, since under the Identity of Indiscernibles empty parts of time would simply collapse into a single moment. In addition, we would be trying illegitimately to think of something as a basic existent that was other than a simple individual substance. (What properties would the container, empty time, have? Would it have a direction? Or an extent?)

With no change in the world of monads, there would be no change in the world of aggregates, since from §8 we know that the properties of aggregates depend on those of simples. However, the most that this reflection can show is that there must be some change in the monadic structure of things if there is to be any temporal flow, not that every monad must itself change over time. Yet if one accepts Leibniz's version of the Indiscernibility Principle, any such limited conception of monadic change will have to be abandoned. To appreciate this, consider a single monad apart from its relations to others. We may like to think of it persisting unchanged whatever other monads around it might do. Our sample individual is to be supposed to endure stably alongside them. To do this, though, there must be something about it which will distinguish its later stages from its earlier ones, something non-relational apart from their being contemporaneous with successive states of other changing monads. That requirement is forced on us by the strong version of Indiscernibility. Yet if our sample monad displayed no change, there would be nothing to permit us to say that it had endured at all. Consequently, our supposition is incoherent. For a monad to endure it must not just be subject to change ('subject to change', as Leibniz rather mildly expresses himself), it has actually to undergo change, and indeed undergo change from moment to moment throughout the whole course of its existence.

This still does not entitle us to the general thesis I have attributed to Leibniz, the thesis that in all possible worlds monads must undergo continuous change, because it leaves open the possibility that there are worlds which are themselves timeless and embrace no change. I do not see that it is a possibility that can be closed off by inference from anything Leibniz has yet told us. However, it will be ruled out as soon as we draw on one further crucial feature of 'substance' that is introduced later on, and which Leibniz used definitionally at the start of the companion treatise to the *Monadology*. At the very beginning of *Principles of Nature and Grace*, he says: 'Substance is a being capable of action' (*PNG* §1). To be capable of *action* is to be capable of changing in the pursuit of the satisfaction of appetite or desire. If we consider changeless and hence instantaneous monads, it would make no sense to attribute desire to them, nor to think of them as active. Once the capacity for action is introduced, change becomes inevitable. With that on board, timeless worlds can be seen to be an outright impossibility.

Of course, the question arises how this idea can consist with the belief that God is the Supreme, yet changeless, Substance. Is it not of God's essence, as it is of ours, to be active? Certainly Leibniz wants to say so. But unlike us, God does not have to satisfy his desires by means that involve change in him. We may suppose his desire for the good is satisfied outside time by creating a world of changing things. In doing that God mirrors himself within the limits of the possible, and that is done not by the sort of physical or mental labour that would involve change in him but by simple decree. Our position, though, and that of any other finite substance, however unlike us it may be, is quite different. We cannot achieve our ends by fiat but only by means that bring about changes in the surrounding world. As a consequence of the view that there can be no 'transitive' causation, we shall see that this inevitably means for Leibniz that as we do that, unlike God, we ourselves also have to change.

The final claim advanced by §10 is that change in each monad is *continuous*. If this means that at no two immediately successive moments can any monad be in the same state, then we already have seen one way in which Leibniz might do other than 'take it for granted', as he puts it in the opening words of the section. The strongly interpreted Identity of Indiscernibles proscribes the existence of such states. However, it may well be that Leibniz has an even stronger claim in mind. The French word *continuel* that he uses here could be taken to mean not so much *continuous* as *gradual*, and the Law of Continuity according to which 'nature never makes leaps' is something Leibniz thinks of as being 'one of [his] great and best confirmed maxims'.[5] If this is indeed what he has in mind here, his claim would be that changes in monads do not take place digitally, in discrete steps, but do so by gradual analog variation of the kind displayed by the ageing process or by the dimming of lights controlled by a domestic rheostat. One may wonder whether there is reason for him to think that.

While he does not insist on the view in the *Monadology*, apart perhaps from the allusion he makes (§13) to changes taking place by degrees, there is at least one passage, in a letter written to de Volder in 1699 (*GP* II, 168), which suggests he sees it as an *a priori* truth. He says there that 'not only does experience confute all sudden change, but also I do not think that any *a priori* reason can be given against a leap from place to place which would not militate also against a leap from state to state'. The underlying thought is that if we trace a substance through space, continuity of its pathway will be a condition of its identity. If there is a gap in its spatial track there is better reason to say that on the two sides of the break there are distinct substances than that one substance has moved from one path to the other without crossing the intervening space. Spatio-temporal continuity is thus a condition of substance identity. In the de Volder letter Leibniz suggests that the same consideration will force one to say that if there is substantial identity through change in a single monad's properties then there can no more be a discontinuous change in it there than there can be a breach in the track it traces through space and time.

---

5   *NE*, 56 (*GP* V, 49).

Why Leibniz should have thought that emerges from another letter written to de Volder five years later. If we try to think of a substance changing radically and discontinuously over time, there will be nothing about it that enables us to say that it is genuinely the same substance at different times, even if we think of our subject as occupying a stable place in space. For example, if at one moment I were confronted by an elephantine thing, and the next by something fully muscarine, then it would be natural for me to say that the elephant had been replaced by a mouse. I could only be tempted to say that the beast had changed into something mouselike if it had gone through a rapid shrinking and transforming process. However, while that might seem reasonable enough when we consider a sufficiently large proportion of an object's qualities, or a set of qualities that is sufficiently salient, it seems far less reasonable to say the same when we consider stepwise reductions in the intensity of one property among many, say in an object's brilliance or its hue. But Leibniz's thesis is quite general, and should be understood to outlaw all non-continuous change. Thus he writes:

> The succeeding substance is held to be the same when the same law of the series, or of continuous simple transition, persists; which is what produces our belief that the subject of change, or the monad, is the same. That there should be such a persistent law, which involves the future states of that which we conceive to be the same is exactly what I say constitutes it as the same substance.[6]

There is perhaps one line of enquiry that might have moved him more surely in the direction he wants to go, and one which exploits a difficulty with temporal discontinuity of the same sort he clearly finds with that of space. Just as no substance can persist over spatial gaps, neither can it survive temporal discontinuity. So the way the individual persisting monad has to behave must allow the construction of temporal continuity for it, and it will only do that, he might think, provided its successive states can be coherently arranged in a

---

6   Letter to de Volder of 21 January 1704 (*GP* II, 24).

smoothly continuous series. What permits this can be nothing other than that the states which we identify as successive states of one and the same substance should be no more than minimally different from those which we assign to it at the next earlier moment, and while there cannot be temporal *minima* we can at least require *a priori* that there should be minimally differentiable temporal segments. This is only possible in the construction of time if there are no sharp discontinuities in the variation of the features that the monads possess. The very continuous nature of the ordering of the series requires proximal moments to be minimally different from their neighbours. Failing that, temporal continuity will break down. It is the *a priori* continuity of time that presupposes a smoothness in the continuity of change.

There remain three claims in §§11–13 that I propose to say something about before moving on. We may assume that we already know that simple substances must have some non-relational properties that change gradually as long as they exist. In logic this condition could be met in the simplest of ways. One might think of a disc that did nothing else than continually expand. There is nothing to it except that it gets larger and larger. A non-corporeal version of such a disc (whatever that might be, and setting aside the question whether its expansion is a genuinely non-relational matter) might fit this very thin description of monadic substance. §12 claims that monads must have a wide range of properties and that any such exiguous picture as I have just drawn will miss the point §13 insists that in the gradual changes that monads undergo there must be some stability as well as some alteration, and §11 requires that whatever sorts of change monads undergo, including of course that envisaged by §13, take place according to an *inner principle*. How these assertions are to be read is anything but clear, for once again we seem to be pulled between two extremes, neither of which is satisfying.

Pursuing one line of thought, we might wonder whether these refinements of the highly abstract characterization of monads we are offered do not simply fill out the sketch of features that monads possess essentially, of absolute necessity. Then Leibniz would be telling us not only that monads must have changing properties, but that they must have many properties of which at any time some must be changing and others remaining stable. But that claim does not seem to be motivated. If one recalls that we ourselves are monads, then a possible analogue of the expanding disc of the previous paragraph might be a conscious mind whose experience consisted of nothing other than an ever-louder and louder bell-like ringing, a sort of continuous tinnitus *sempre crescendo*. That sort of substance seems not to infringe the Principle of Contradiction. Then the requirements that the monad should enjoy myriad properties and that there be 'a unity in the plurality' (something stable amid the change) and that the change be governed by an internal principle appear arbitrary.

On the other hand, if we look at our own world we are presented with many-featured things which undergo some change all the time and which remain in some respects unchanged from moment to moment. Furthermore, we do think that the changes that come about are in large part principled and law-governed changes. Given the doctrine of the dependence of the aggregate on the simple (§8), it makes good sense to say that in our world the simple constituents of the aggregates we observe should have multiple features undergoing regular and lawlike changes. Yet that way of looking at §§11–13 is also unsatisfactory. It might indeed correctly capture the nature of some of the monads that go to make up our world, but it provides very little ground for saying that all the monads of our world behave like this. Anyway, it is not until much later in the work, until §63 that is, that Leibniz begins to marry the general theory of monadology elaborated in the early sections to the world in which we live. Somehow or other we need to assimilate these recalcitrant paragraphs to the general theory and not to allow them to flow from the local particularities of our own situation.

The solution I propose is that we should for the time being view the refinements Leibniz is offering us in §§11–13 of his general characterization of the monad as pretty obvious consequences of God's creative choices being dominated by the Principle of the Best. The sorts of world that God might be drawn to create must all reflect his power and his wisdom. A world containing no more than a single monad suffering from continuous tinnitus may not be a logical impossibility, but it is certainly far too impoverished a world to be a serious candidate for God's creative attention. Given that God has the capacity to create many monads, infinitely many even, a minimally fulfilling world can be reasonably expected to be a richly populated one. The Identity of Indiscernibles suggests that each member of the rich population would be qualitatively differentiated from every other, so each monad will be bound to be complex in the features it possesses. This is a kind of formal truth, if one is willing to assign negative properties to monads as well as positive ones, but even if one supposes that Leibniz would regard it as a cheap way of introducing individual complexity to the equation, the reflection on God's power and wisdom that motivated the introduction of some density of population into the monadic world would also motivate the introduction of positive qualitative complexity into the nature of the individual. So one might say that, for Leibniz, any *intelligible* world must be richly populated by qualitatively complex simple individuals.

It is a further step to insist on stability in the character of the monad's properties as well as change, as Leibniz does at §13. There is of course no incoherence in the idea. We could think of the monad as being at any time in a complex state which we could write schematically as *a is F and G and H* ... Then we can say that over time it is bound develop in such a way that at minimally distinct moments one or more, but not all, of the elements entering into its momentary states must be minimally different from how it was immediately previously. Thus at one moment it may be that *a is F' and G' and H'* ... and the next moment it will be true that *a is F' and G' and H"* ... where *F*, *G* and *H* in each case is a positive property enjoying intensive magnitude and changing by degrees.

Why might Leibniz suppose that an intelligible world must contain monads that enjoy a measure of stability? Why shouldn't each element itself of the complex monadic state be constantly changing? That at least may not be ruled out by Leibniz's requirement that there be a plurality in the unity, that something must remain while something changes, for it would be natural enough to hear him saying no more than that in each individual monad which persists over time there must be change, and not that it must possess unchanging features as well as changing ones. What remains the same, one thinks, need only be this individual monad, and perhaps its persistence is possible while all its properties undergo change. When Leibniz goes on to say 'All natural change being gradual, something always changes and something always remains', he could be doing no more than repeating this point, stressing that, given the enduring nature of monads, even to think of their qualities as continuously changing requires that they themselves remain the same individuals throughout.

It is probably true that we are not yet in a position to say much more than this. But one thing we certainly can say: as long as we are concerned with enduring monads, they carry their past with them, and while their past becomes more and more complex as they age, nonetheless everything that was true of them at earlier moments continues to be true of them – in the past tense – at every future moment. So, even if through successive moments of time a monad changes from being F' and G' and H' ... to being F'' and G'' and H'' ..., at the later moments it will be true of that monad that previously it had been F' and G' and H', and that at every moment of its existence thereafter it will earlier have been F' and G' and H'. That is a truth about it that will never change. So, at least, while monads may be constantly changing, as they do so something about them remains the same, namely their past. In some such way as this we could even argue that it is an absolute necessity and not just a hypothetical one for active simple substances to display some constancy in the features that are theirs.[7]

Section §11, which I have left until last, is the pendant of the reflection that changes in a monad's states cannot come about by 'transitive' causation. They have to be accounted for from the nature

---

7 At *NE*, 239 Theophilus says:

> An immaterial substance can not be 'stripped of all' perception of its past existence. It retains impressions of everything which has previously happened to it; but those states of mind are mostly too minute to be distinguishable and for one to be aware of them, although they may perhaps grow some day. It is this continuity and interconnection of perceptions which make someone really the same individual;....

Since monads' states are indeed perceptions (§14), it would seem that Leibniz really did want to advance some such argument as this and not just rely on the persistence of the same individual through time to account for the something that remains the same.

of the monad itself and arise from an internal principle. That is the only acceptable alternative. What we cannot allow is that God simply decides at every moment what changes should come about and that he, so to speak, imposes his decisions upon the individuals he has created by decree that they change accordingly. That picture cannot be correct, since it would suppose that God has already had reason to create monads which would not change but for his later decision that they should. But then he would have chosen them on the basis of their being disposed not to change, for had he not come to impose his decree upon them they would not have changed in the way that is being supposed. Yet if he did choose to create a monad which was disposed not to change, he would have had sufficient reason for doing so, and hence sufficient reason not to decree that it should change. So, if monads change they must do so from their nature, not by reason of any decision of God's imposed on them by fiat. We know that they are bound to endure and that, enduring, they must undergo change. Consequently their changes have to come about from some internal principle. Graphically put, Adam does not sin because God decreed that he should; he sinned by reason of his own nature. God just permitted that a man of such a nature should exist.[8]

It is a question whether talk of an internal principle means anything more than that monads are naturally disposed to change in the ways they do, or would do if God were to create them. Metaphysically speaking it may not do. However, we have had occasion to notice that when God chooses what to create according to the Principle of the Best he does so in the light of considerations of variety and order. Ordered worlds are worlds whose workings are regular and lawlike. So it may well be that when Leibniz speaks of changes occurring from internal principles he has in mind that any intelligible world, any world that God could plausibly have a sufficient reason to create, must be a world of monads whose dispositions to change are governed by general principles. If this is so, we can see the claim of §11 preparing the way for the much later discussion of the pre-established harmony between substances and

---

8   Cf. *Theodicy*, section 369.

between souls and bodies that occupies §§78–9 and which is discussed below in Chapter 9.

Having outlined in the most abstract way possible the general nature of monads, Leibniz is now ready to speak of the ways in which these truths can be realized. The claims he advances on this score are set out in §§14–19. They merit a chapter to themselves.

Further reading

Russell, Chapter 5, 'The Identity of Indiscernibles and the Law of Continuity'; Rutherford, Chapter 6, 'Substance'.

Perception and appetition (§§14–19)

Monads' states are necessarily non-physical states. So monads cannot possess any of the traditional primary qualities of objects such as shape, size, bulk or texture. Nor do they have any secondary qualities either, since to possess those they would have to possess primary qualities too. Yet whatever qualities they do have must be of a kind that give rise to truths about physical objects and to their possession of primary and secondary qualities, since the dependence thesis of §8 insists that 'what is found in compounds can only come from their simple ingredients', and at the very least our own world contains physical compounds aplenty, fully supplied with qualities of both sorts.

§14 identifies the fundamental states of monads as *perceptions*, and with this identification we are immediately confronted with one of the most notable features of Leibniz's late metaphysics. This is that his ontology of simples, on which everything else depends, is an ontology of incorporeal mental sub-stances, or minds (though we may note that at §29 Leibniz expressly reserves this last term – *esprits* – for those highly developed simples which, like ourselves, engage in reflection and have knowledge of necessary truths).[1] Just how the physical is dependent on the mental is something that we shall have occasion to explore in due course. What is noteworthy for the time being is that with this first positive identification of monads' states as perceptions Leibniz is firmly committed to the claim that the basic elements of any world (not just ours, but any other possible world too) can only be mental things. Indeed, if we take strictly the *ens et unum* doctrine that we met in Chapter 3 and accord genuine reality only to unities *per se*, while discounting the claims of entities *per accidens* and other aggregates, then it would appear at first sight that the only genuine realities there are must be purely mental ones.

At the very outset it may well seem questionable for Leibniz to say that monads' passing states are perceptions, since as we use the term we think that for someone to enjoy perceptual states they need themselves to be materially embodied. This will be either because perception involves the causal impact of the perceived objects upon the perceiving system or else because we cannot envisage ourselves or anything else enjoying perceptual experience unless the subject of such experience is a physical subject. Leibniz is confident that neither consideration poses a serious threat.

As for the first, it might be said that a perceptual state is not of itself essentially a state in which a subject is aware of something distinct from itself. The hallucinatory states in which it appeared to the poet Gérard de Nerval that he was accompanied on his forays into the world by a pink lobster would certainly have counted for Leibniz as perceptual states, even though no actual lobster was ever present to make its impact on the poet's mind. Even though this is true, because Leibniz holds it to be the special nature of minds to represent bodies (cf. *Theodicy*, section 130), meaning thereby that they represent accurately bodies that do in fact exist, appeal to the intentional nature of perceptual states does not answer the question.

---

1   Leibniz's most general description of monads is as *entelechies* (§14) or *incorporeal automata* (§18).

Rather Leibniz will meet the first challenge by saying that whatever interchange of parts may take place between bodily aggregates in cases of veridical perception, the perceiving subject's experience in the total situation does not and cannot involve it acquiring parts or properties from outside. Instead, it will be because its perceptual states occur as they do in harmony with the flow of other monads' perceptual states that one monad perceives bodies that are constituted by other monads. As he puts it at §51:

> In the case of simple substances, one monad has no more than an ideal influence on another;.... Since created monads cannot exercise any physical influence on the inner nature of others this is the only way that one of them can be dependent on another.

Obviously enough, the resulting account of veridical perception will need to be worked out in detail, but at this early stage it should suffice to note that Leibniz is ready to accept any challenge the reader may want to throw down to account for it in terms that do not require physical interaction and exchange between perceiving subject and perceived object.

That the perceiving subject is not and could not be a purely physical subject is assumed rather than argued for in the *Monadology*. Section 17 comes as close to doing that as Leibniz gets, for there he says that 'we must admit that perception and everything that depends on perception is inexplicable on mechanical principles, that is, in terms of shapes and movements'. We are invited to imagine ourselves wandering round a machine (such as an enlarged version of the physical brain) and observing its wheels and levers at work. Were we to do so, it seems evident to Leibniz that nothing we might come upon of a physical and mechanical kind would *explain* the occurrence of perceptual experience. Since he thinks that matter is governed by mechanical laws and only by mechanical laws, the utter inexplicability of matter coming to have perceptual awareness in mechanically describable situations ensures that it cannot happen. The unresolvable mystery of any such thing occurring would force us to regard it as a miracle, and we have already seen that miracles infringe the Principle of Sufficient Reason. That was the thought that Leibniz relied on in the Preface to the *New Essays* to dismiss Locke's speculation whether matter might not think.

This topic will occupy us further in Chapter 9, but it is worth noting now that Leibniz's intransigence on this score draws not only on this use of Sufficient Reason, but also on the general, though tempered, sympathy he has for Descartes' ontological dualism. Even if bodies are aggregates of monads, the metaphysical atoms of which they are constituted and whose fundamental states are perceptual and representational states could not be material atoms, since the mental character of these states requires that they be attached to mental, hence non-physical, subjects. The hold that this Cartesian commitment has over him makes it difficult for Leibniz to envisage that any reconceptualization of the physical might make it explicable how physical systems should naturally enjoy perceptual experience. Consequently he finds the selection of perceptual states as the fundamental determinations of monads to be utterly natural. As far as he can see, they alone generate the right consequences, and no place can be found for them in our thought except as properties of incorporeal substances.

Even at this early stage of the *Monadology* Leibniz is in a position to supply refinement to the Cartesian stance to which he was sympathetically drawn. For one thing, he has immediately available a proof that the self must be constantly engaged in thought, something that Descartes had previously asserted (cf. *Meditation* II) on decidedly shaky grounds.[2] First, we have seen already that Leibniz will reject any suggestion that perception depends on the body in the sense that the

---

2 After discounting perception as his fundamental nature (because it is impossible without the body, of whose existence he is uncertain), Descartes goes on:

> Thinking is another attribute of the soul; and here I discover what properly belongs to myself. This alone is inseparable from me. I am – I exist: this is certain; but how often? As often as I think; for perhaps it would even happen, if I should wholly cease to think, that I should at the same time altogether cease to be.

If there is an argument here, it appears to derive a metaphysical conclusion from an epistemological premise. At all events improvement is called for, and Leibniz is happy to oblige.

subject of perceptual experience must be a physical thing. So if he thinks of perceptions as perceptual experiences he may happily take their occurrence as instances of thought. As §8 has argued, monads have to have some properties, and since physical properties are ruled out, all that is left are mental ones (*scilicet*, perceptions). So, as long as the individual monad exists it must have some perception or other. Quite unlike Descartes, Leibniz arrives at this conclusion through a purely metaphysical route, uncontaminated by epistemological considerations. This fact forces onto him a sharp revision of the Cartesian picture at the very outset.

For Descartes, we can only say we think as long as we are aware we are thinking. On this basis Descartes is inclined to think both that if at any moment we take ourselves to be thinking something we are indeed thinking that thing, and also that unless we are aware of thinking we cannot be engaged in thought. For him the mind is utterly transparent to itself. To Leibniz, however, it is apparent that at times we are not consciously aware of any thought going on at all. Not that we catch ourselves not thinking anything – for then some thought *would* be going on – but rather we want to say that we have persisted in existence without having enjoyed conscious awareness throughout the period. So when we come round from the anaesthetic, we remember going under but have no recall of anything after that and certainly were aware of nothing as the operation was being carried out (cf. §23). Nonetheless, just because we have persisted throughout the period we must have had some properties throughout the period. And since we are essentially immaterial things, we are bound to attribute perceptions to ourselves even without being aware of them. It is a condition of our persistence that perception flows on, even though conscious access to it is only intermittent.

The revision of the Cartesian position is subtle and striking. It enables Leibniz to envisage the existence of some monads, those he calls 'bare monads', as having perceptions without consciousness at all. Why they are required in his scheme of things is not all that obscure. Many things we encounter in the world around us display no signs of conscious experience. Within a Leibnizian understanding of them we are obliged to construct them from monadic elements. Since they display no signs of consciousness, it would be gratuitous to attribute consciousness to them. Yet we know we have to attribute perceptions to them as a condition of their existence. So it would seem that we have good reason to suppose that the world contains bare monads. Apart from them, the same kind of reasoning leads us to suppose that there are also monads whose perceptions make them conscious, without however their being self-conscious. We shall want to find a place for them on a Leibnizian interpretation of much of the animal life that we find around us. Explanatory caution will deter us from attributing self-consciousness to the monads that enter into their constitution. Finally, there are monads that are self-conscious, monads whose states are what Leibniz calls 'apperceptions' and which can think of themselves in the first person as perceiving this or that. Such are we and our kind. But it is only unreflective Cartesian prejudice that could encourage us to say that all incorporeal mental subjects are necessarily self-consciously aware of all their states.

Rejecting the doctrine of the transparency to their bearers of mental states not only prepares the way for a plausible adjustment of the known world to its monadic underlay, but promises to make room for some eschatological and theological presumptions that would otherwise appear questionable. §14 ends by criticizing Cartesians for confirming ordinary people's confusion of a prolonged stupor with death 'in the strict sense'. What Leibniz has in mind is that if the mind is necessarily transparent to itself, then when we are not aware of anything we are not thinking. Then, if no thought is going on, we must have ceased to exist. So setting out from the Cartesian presumption we conclude that when animals or people die, they cease to be. As Leibniz says, misguided minds are thus confirmed in a belief in the mortality of souls. We have already seen that monads do not naturally perish, so at what we call 'death' there may well really be no more than a prolonged stupor in which monads cease to be conscious or self-conscious about their mental activity but where nonetheless mental activity itself still persists (cf. §21). This topic is taken up again later on between §§73 and 77, and it will occupy us more fully when we come to those late sections of the work.

Although Leibniz does not explicitly assert the existence of the 'bare monads' whose possibility is affirmed at §19, they are not just needed for an explanatorily adequate account of the natural world.

Theology itself demands that such things should exist. The perfect God mirrors his nature in the world he creates. The omnipotence of his nature must be expressed, and in consequence he will have reason to create a world that contains as much reality as may be. If one of the fundamental possibilities is that there should be bare monads, then only a world which contained such things could appeal to God at the moment of creation. It is not that only such worlds are logically possible. There is no contradiction in the idea of worlds that contain no bare monads, only God could have no reason to create one of them rather than a world that realizes that possibility along with others. If this reflection is correct, any world satisfying the demands of Sufficient Reason will be replete with monads enjoying all the various possible grades of perceptual awareness.

This last thought should alert us to the wide range of states Leibniz takes to fall under the general term 'perception'. At the bottom end of the scale there are perceptual states of which the subject is neither conscious nor self-consciously (reflexively) aware. At this state there is not even sentience. Monads whose mental lives are no richer than this are *bare monads* or '*entelechies*'. *Souls* are monads which attain to sentience and memory. Their perceptions are generically no different from those of bare monads, but they are more distinct. Finally there are *spirits* or rational souls or *minds* which are reflexively aware of their perceptions and in addition attain by reason to systematic understanding of the world. Their perceptions are amplified by theory and insight into recognition of necessary truths (§§28–9). While souls are not reflexively aware of anything and are conscious of a good deal, they may of course be unconscious of some of their states. Equally, while minds are reflexively aware of some of their states, they may have states many of which they are merely conscious and of some of which they are not even that. The degree to which we are reflexively aware of our mental life, and the extent of the penetration of reason throughout it is something that differs from case to case and from person to person. The idea of a fully rational life, one permeated by reason through and through, is an ideal which, if it is realized in nature at all, is realized only by spirits belonging to a higher rank than we do. The theological reflection of the last paragraph may move us to the humbling thought that among God's creatures we are probably not the most nearly similar to him.

I have suggested that perceptions are generically of a kind, even though our access to them differs from case to case. So how should we characterize them? The *Monadology* is largely unrevealing, but not totally so. §14 introduces the idea of perception as a transitory state which 'contains and represents a multitude in the one, or in the simple substance', and in doing that it goes beyond the claim of §13, which represents the multiplicity in the monad as no more than a multiplicity of its various states. Now the states are made representational states, and the multiplicity in question is internal to what they represent as much as loosely indicative of their sheer number (cf. §16). So I take it that at different times our representations of how things are must be different (if they were not, then we would not be able to introduce differences of time anyway), and that at any one time what our perceptions represent must itself be internally complex. This is not simply a reflection of the world we are familiar with, one in which our perception of objects as tables and chairs and people cannot be detached from a highly complex set of beliefs about the world, but a quite general truth about any world of monads whose perceptual states could provide them with more than minimal knowledge of the world of which they were part.

Any world that is a serious candidate for God's creative attention will be a complex world. It will also be a world whose creatures mirror God's nature as far as is possible. So their perceptual states will be ones that reveal their world to them. As section 130 of *Theodicy* puts it, it is the nature of minds to represent bodies, assuming of course that the worlds they inhabit are (maybe even must be) populated with monads that enter into physical aggregates. Were they not to do so, they would be perfectly possible worlds, only from God's point of view worlds of little interest. So we can say that any world God might have seen fit to create would have contained monads whose perceptual states were highly complex in their representational content and which in their content answer to the nature of the world of which they are part. It remains to be proved that any such world must be a physical world, but the essentially complex nature of the content of monads' perceptions does not depend on that.

In entertaining perceptions we have knowledge of the surrounding world, more or less self-consciously as the case may be, and this despite the fact that strictly speaking the only states of which we can be aware are our own.[3] Leibniz's British contemporaries struggled in their various ways with the seeming impossibility of combining these two thoughts. Locke thought that our immediate perception of our own ideas made our speculations about the world beyond the mind highly precarious (cf. *Essay,* IV. xi); Berkeley and Hume in their different ways dispensed with that further world; Reid held we were immediately acquainted with things other than our perceptions. By contrast, Leibniz thinks that in awareness of our own perceptual states we must be aware how things stand in the rest of the world because as long as our perceptions are constantly and systematically related to our surroundings their occurrence will provide us with knowledge of our surroundings. We do not need to observe that they are constantly and systematically related to them, as the empiricists thought would be necessary, to know that they are so related. Relying on the Principle of Sufficient Reason we can see that God could have no reason to create a world in which his creatures did not possess knowledge of their situations, and arguing from the theological principles already discussed Leibniz can say on *a priori* grounds that our world must be one in which there is a constant and systematic correlation between monads' perceptions and such aggregates as make up their world. Knowledge is possible as long as there is such system and assured as long as God operates according to the Principle of the Best. Epistemological embarrassments that so exercized thinkers on the northern side of the Channel are confidently bypassed. Indeed we shall see later that the theologically driven need for perceptual knowledge supplies Leibniz with useful ancillary ammunition in the detailed construction of his general metaphysical picture of how worlds of monads must be structured if they are to exercize a serious claim on God's creative beneficence.

Leibniz has told us in §10 that monads are subject to change over time. We know that such change cannot be explained in mechanical

---

3   Cf. *NE,* 135.

terms since that would require them to be other than simple, so §11 hypothesizes an internal principle to account for it. Change, of course, will be change in the perceptual states that monads possess, and we can ask whether we can give any substance to the obscure internal principle to which Leibniz alludes and which he says we can call an active force.

A negative reading of the 'internal principle' would say that there is nothing to it except the denial that changes in our perceptions are the product of external forces impinging on us, either by way of transitive causation or by direct intervention from moment to moment in our lives on the part of God. I am the sole source of the changes that befall me. But this suggestion seems more modest than anything that Leibniz has in mind, since it would be entirely compatible with the occurrence of random changes in my perceptual life which lent it no internal order at all. In §15 Leibniz tells us that the source of change is appetition, and we may understand this reasonably enough as an expression of the thought that changes in my perceptual states come about because they are the consequences of actions I undertake to secure the goals I embrace. I find I am hungry. To satisfy my hunger I have to busy myself in the kitchen, and as I do that and move around it in search of provisions and cooking utensils my perceptual states change accordingly. So my perceptual states change as action is directed to the satisfaction of my desires. Having satisfied one desire and finding myself with a perceptual state appropriate to that, I am liable to find myself with a new desire – to occupy myself with a book, perhaps, now that I am no longer hungry – which gives rise to novel perceptual states in my pursuit of satisfaction of this new desire.

In this lightly sketched model of monadic psychology (not meant as a caricature of developed human psychology, rather a schema that applies equally to any active substances, be they actual or merely possible) there is still nothing that answers to an internal principle. It would be perfectly consistent with my being the subject of a sequence of disconnected desires, although as we consider progressively less integrated sequences of desires and satisfactions the less willing we shall be to think of their subjects as active and free (as Leibniz wants them to be) and the readier we shall be to describe ourselves as mere slaves of our passions. That won't do at all, though, if only for the reason that while infinities of worlds populated by such monadic slaves are logically possible, in none of them would God's perfect nature be adequately reflected.

At this point, we can begin to make something more positive of the internal principle of §11 that does not lead to its being treated as a mere encapsulation of the series of changes that in fact make up the perceptual course of the individual monad's existence. At section 369 of *Theodicy*, Leibniz suggests that Adam's sinning stemmed from a fixed internal disposition and was not responsive to a stray volition wished upon him by God. I do not think we should say about the particular example that Adam's fixed disposition was *to sin if tempted by Eve*, because any such reading would inevitably give rise to as many different fixed dispositions in a subject as there are discriminable actions that that subject performs, and then the appeal to an internal principle would serve no purpose at all. What makes far more sense is to suppose that Leibniz sees Adam's decision to eat of the forbidden fruit as a case of what seemed to him to be the way of acting for the best, very probably that it seemed to him at the time to be the action best calculated to serve his own interests. (Like so many eighteenth-century thinkers Leibniz was a rational egoist in ethical matters.) If that is so, we may suppose that there is just one fixed internal principle that governs the change of desires and perceptions to which monads are subject. This is that they form desires in particular situations in response to a generalized striving for their own good, and that their perceptions change as they attempt to satisfy their desires, and their desires change in the light of this principle and the perceptual situations to which response to unsatisfied desires gives rise. In this way their perceptual and appetitive states are systematically linked to one another and we have a means of understanding how Leibniz can appeal to the internal principle as a way of ensuring that the changes monadic states go through can be thought of as free actions, autonomous in a far stronger sense than is secured by the simple denial that they are brought about by external forces of one sort of another.

Why, if monads are essentially incorporeal, should the satisfaction of their appetitions have anything to do with changes in their perceptions? Is it that Leibniz simply thinks of perceptions changing in response to monads' wishes? Why should they connect their good with a situation in which their perceptions are in any way different from the perceptions that they find themselves with at a given time? It may seem that Leibniz introduces desire to account for change, and that he needs change to be able to say that monads endure over time. But the fundamental idea of desire as a perception of lack (i.e. desiring = *wanting*, as in 'to be in want of') looks as though it can have no place in the psychology of the monad, as it is first presented to us. It may seem also that even if my suggestion about the nature of the internal principle makes some sense of monads that are most nearly akin to creatures with psychologies like our own, as we go down the hierarchy of monadic types all sense of reality deserts us. If possible, something should be said to assuage both worries.

As for the first, we have seen that Leibniz's most general description of monads is as *entelechies* (§14) or incorporeal automata (§18). However, later on (§62) he tells us that 'although each created monad represents the whole universe, it represents most clearly *the body to which it is most particularly attached* and whose entelechy it is' (my emphasis). In the same section he also says that the soul 'represents the whole universe in representing that body which belongs to it in a special way'. So it seems that to fulfil their representational tasks monads must *have* bodies, without of course themselves *being* bodies, and it is through their bodies, which they perceive with especial clarity, that they act. We may also say, I think, that it is in relation to their bodies that the idea of their well-being is given content. Once this is allowed, and once we recognize that the well-being of the monad is intimately connected with the well-being of the body that is its, there is no particular difficulty in seeing why monads should have desires that relate to their perception of the physical world. For it is through changes in the physical world impinging on the monad's psychology through its perceptual states that its desires are satisfied, and it is in relation to the world as it is perceived by the monadic subject that it comes to recognize what it needs for its well-being.

The same thought bears on the second query. No matter how simple the monad – that is, whether we are talking of bare souls (mere entelechies) or more highly developed minds (*esprits*) – every monad has its body and a well-being related to that body's well-being.

Governed by the internal principle (of §11) that directs change of perception in response to sensed needs, even the simplest monads can be understood as undergoing changes in perception and appetition of a fairly systematic kind. What precisely the perceptions and desires are will naturally vary according to the particular sorts of monad that are in question and according to the situations in which those individuals find themselves, but the general mechanism that makes for change is one that applies throughout the created realm. If it is right to identify this as a striving for its well-being – the Leibnizian version of Spinoza's famous *conatus*[4] (cf. *Ethics* III, 6–9) – and right also to pinpoint this as what makes it possible for us to think of monads as active, then the internal principle of change which Leibniz calls on to account for the change in monads' states is not just common to those monads that God actually creates, but would govern the changes in the perceptions of monads in any other worlds that might have reflected his omniscience, his omnipotence and his goodness.

I shall be concerned with the topic of monads' bodies later on and do not develop that subject here. However, looking forward a little we can already see that some strain is emerging on the *ens et unum* doctrine. For if monads are essentially active and need bodies to be so, then they could hardly exist unless bodies existed. If bodies are aggregates of simples, and as such are accidental things, *entia per accidens* in the jargon, then by the *ens et unum* doctrine they are not truly real. But how can what is truly real, the monad, depend on something that is not truly real?

We should not be too anxious to accuse Leibniz of inconsistency here. For one thing, in his correspondence with Arnauld he denies that he accords only a diminished reality to things that have no true unity, writing that 'there is as much reality or substantiality in them as there is true unity in what enters into their composition' (*GP* II, 97). Along these lines, we might well hear him saying that monads alone are absolutely real, but that other things such as bodies have a solid

---

4   Not the same thing though, since Spinoza's *conatus* is seen by Leibniz as a mere striving of a thing to maintain itself in existence, whereas he lays stress on the pursuit of the good. See his remark that 'the will tends toward something more particular [than striving to persist], and towards a more perfect way of existing' ('Comments on Spinoza's Philosophy', in Ariew and Garber (eds), 279).

enough place in the world as – what he elsewhere[5] calls – 'well-founded phenomena' in so far as they are composed of things that are themselves absolutely real.

For another thing, and more intriguingly, it is open to us to ask whether the conjunction of a monad and its body really does make up an *ens per accidens*. As far as Leibniz is concerned, as we shall see, the body a monad has is one it never loses and from which it cannot be detached. If there is an unbreakable unity here, then the prospect opens up of there being an application of the *ens et unum* doctrine that extends beyond monads taken by themselves and embraces certain psycho-physical wholes.[6] For the moment, we may note this possibility and consequently refrain from concluding that we can only understand the flow of perception and appetition in terms of which Leibniz characterizes the fundamental states of monads if we abandon the underlying metaphysic that moves him to introduce them in the first place.

I end this chapter by commenting on Leibniz's description at §18 of all monads, no matter how little or how much developed they may be, as *entelechies*. The term, whose etymology suggests the possession of a goal or end, is taken from Aristotle (see *De Anima* I, 4, 408a28; *Metaphysics* θ 8, 1050a20, Γ 4, 1007b25–30), who uses it to designate the goal or end for which things of a particular kind strive and towards which they tend. So for Aristotle the entelechy of the eye would be seeing, and the soul (rational thought) would be the entelechy of the living human body. Leibniz's use of the term is rather different, being intimately related to the internal principle of which I have just been speaking. Monads themselves are said by him to be entelechies in that, being active, they have their perfection within them, meaning thereby that the changes they go through they go through for the sake of attaining that perfection or end. The end in question, I have suggested, is one or other specification of the individual monad's well-being, different in the case of a monad whose

---

5   See the letter to de Volder (*GP* II, 275) quoted in note 2 to Chapter 3 above.

6   As we pursue this line of thought we should bear in mind that room needs to be left for *entia per accidens*, and that in doing this take care not to abolish well-founded phenomena altogether.

body is that of a blade of grass than in the case of one whose body is that of a tadpole, but one which in either case operates in the formation of the (certainly unconscious) desires and the ensuing perceptions suitable for the blade of grass and the slightly more conscious appetitions and perceptions in the case of the monad which has its tadpole body. The etymology of 'entelechy' that Leibniz refers to at §18 (*echousi to enteles*, i.e. having their perfection within them) fits the term's applications to monads, since it is from their drive for their well-being that all changes of their states derive. Just because their changes cannot be explained in terms of external or mechanical influence – remember the etymology! – Leibniz can say (§18) that monads enjoy a certain autonomy and freedom.

This may be surprising, but it is important to appreciate that for Leibniz the need to account for the changes monads undergo in terms of this internal principle does not commit him to the predictability of the course of monadic histories or to any associated form of determinism. When God considers what world to create he does indeed take into account the complete history that individual monads would have were they to exist, and he is able to do this in virtue of his omniscience. But God is not omniscient in virtue of being a perfect predictor or on account of the substances he reviews having to fall under strict deterministic laws. So his knowledge extends smoothly to cover the precise moment of decay of radio-active particles which we know can be foreseen only probabilistically in terms of their half-life. Equally, when it comes to the desires and perceptions of monads such as ourselves, Leibniz can say that God selects a certain world for creation in the light of his possessing a complete specification of the states its elements will go through, but that this does not imply that our changing states follow one another as a matter of strict law. All we can say is that we and other monads strive to realize what we more or less consciously recognize to be our good, and that we adapt our behaviour to our present awareness of things in the light of that sensitivity. Thus it is that Leibniz can say that, just as with God himself, in any particular situation the inner principle moving us inclines us to do what we do, though it does not necessitate our doing it.[7]

---

7 Thus at section 369 of *Theodicy*, Leibniz expressly says: 'Adam sinned freely and

It is frequently said that in living out their lives Leibnizian monads fulfil a certain program inscribed, as it were, on their hearts at the very outset, and that in calling them 'entelechies' Leibniz gives expression to that idea. There is something highly misleading about this way of talking, since it suggests falsely that when the perceptual appetitive system gets into a certain state its 'program' determines what state it will move into, or that unless there is a uniquely determinate answer to the question 'What moves are open to it?' we shall not be concerned with a truly Leibnizian program. Now, it is certainly true that Leibniz holds that the monad will make no move, will not change its state in a particular way, unless it sees better reason for moving to a given new state rather than to any other, but all that commits him to is that what we undertake we undertake in reaction to our judgement about how best to achieve our well-being. There is no reason to think that when in a given situation S, say, I judge that the appropriate state for me to move to is S', were I again to be confronted with S I should *eo ipso* be bound to judge it appropriate for me to move to S' once more. Today's thirst on return from work may call for a whiskey, tomorrow's for a beer. Nor is there any reason for Leibniz to suppose that the same internal principle driving us all should lead to us desiring the same things in similar circumstances, however similar they might be. I may know that at the end of the opera my twin brother will want a drink as much as I shall, but it would be rash of me not to ask him what he wants and simply to order him champagne just because I know that that is what I shall want when I finally hear the Rhine engulfing Valhalla and its gods.

While the world of monads is a world of simple substances often changing in rational though unpredictable and undetermined ways, the world of aggregates that those simple substances conjointly makes up may well itself be subject to precise deterministic laws. Nothing said in the passages that deal with the nature of monads' changing states has any direct bearing on that issue. Whether in creating the

---

... God saw him sinning already in conceiving the very possibility of Adam which became actual.... It is true that Adam was determined to sin in consequence of certain prevailing inclinations [of his inner nature]: but this inner determination destroys neither contingency nor freedom.'

material world God is bound to create a strictly law-governed world is for the moment an entirely open matter. As it happens, Leibniz believes that the material world that is ours is subject to strict mechanical laws. It is entirely possible that any other world that might have engaged God's creative attention would have been similarly ordered.

Further reading

Russell, Chapter 11, 'The Nature of Monads in General'; M. D. Wilson, 'Confused vs. Distinct Perception in Leibniz; Consciousness, Representation and God's Mind' in *Ideas and Mechanism* (Princeton NJ, 1999); Robert McRae, *passim*.

Further reading

Chapter 6

Worlds (§§53–6)

Given that simple monadic substances are the sole self-standing realities, one might suppose that while God is bound to create a number of them if he creates anything at all, it is open to him to elect any possible constellation of monads that he pleases. Our world would then be nothing more than that constellation which pleased him best. That is not Leibniz's picture of the way God's choice operates. In his view, application of Sufficient Reason shows there to be severe constraints on any constellation that might be worthy of God's attention. The limitation that will principally occupy me is this: no collection of monads making up anything less than a complete world could merit God's attention. A second limitation that I touch on is that each monad must reflect every other. This is the famous mirror thesis of §56. What these two requirements amount to and why only such internally reflective complete worlds should be contenders for the original creative decree must initially seem quite obscure.

For Leibniz 'world' is something of a technical term, designating a maximal collection of monads whose existence is, or would be, compatible with one another's. Speaking of the actual world he expresses the idea in a letter written for Spinoza in 1676: 'My principle is that whatever can exist and is maximally compatible with other things does exist.'[1] Early on in *Theodicy*, at section 8, we find him saying:

> Even though one should fill all times and places, it still remains true that one might have filled them in innumerable ways, and that there is an infinitude of possible worlds among which God must needs have chosen the best, since he does nothing without acting in accordance with Supreme Reason.

Putting the two ideas together it becomes apparent that each member of that infinitude of possibilities will consist of a maximal set of compossibles. That notion does not itself single out our world of course, as the Spinoza letter might seem to suggest, but it does characterize any world that God might reasonably elect to create. We need to see why that should be.

Every simple substance is subject to the Law of Excluded Middle. As we saw in Chapter 1, Leibniz regards that logical commitment as integral to the Principle of Contradiction, and he expounds it as the claim that every proposition or its opposite is true. If we consider a proposition about a single monad, e.g. the proposition that Simon is proud, Excluded Middle will allow us to affirm the disjunction: either Simon is proud or Simon is not proud. Since this is an entirely general thought, we can say, for any individual substance at all, and for any properties it might have, either that that substance has the property affirmed of it or that it lacks it. It will follow from this that every substance has what Leibniz calls 'a complete concept', meaning thereby that every monad, be it actual or possible, is completely determinate in that one or other of '*F*' or 'not-*F*' holds true of it for all

---

1   From 'A Note on Spinoza's Philosophy' (2 December 1671), in Couturat (ed). *Opuscules et Fragments Inédits de Leibniz*, 530.

predicates that could possibly apply to it, or for all properties that it might possess.[2]

It is Leibniz's assumption that any complete substance concept could be actualized. That is what came to pass in an infinity of cases when God originally created the monads that he did. He chose to make real a large, in fact infinite, number of possible individuals by producing instances of their complete concepts. Because the concepts instantiated are complete ones, it cannot be that any of them should have had more instances than one, for the very completeness of their concepts ensures that there could be nothing that would distinguish between one instance of such a concept and another. The Identity of Indiscernibles implies directly that only one individual can answer to any monad's full concept. However, while any single such concept could be actualized, Leibniz holds that only some of them can be jointly actualized. God's decision to create one set of monads automatically excludes the creation of others. So, in creating one world, God is obliged to leave other worlds uncreated. That, however, does not tell us why, when he decides to create a number of individual substances, he is bound to create all those substances that are compatible with one another or why he could not be content with a subset of such compossibles.

Leibniz is clear in his mind that God could not create several worlds because the very idea is incoherent. For that to be the case the putatively plural worlds' members would have to be compatible with one another, and if they were that they would all belong to a maximal set of compossibles, and thus all belong to one and the same world.[3] Plurality here is a logical impossibility. By the same token, neither could God create several sub-worlds, those being less than maximal selections from distinct possible worlds. Evidently, no substances

---

2 The idea of the total set of properties can be indicated only by reference to the range of God's limitless conceptual repertoire. It clearly outstrips our own linguistic competence and the range of properties that are positively exemplified by items in the actual world.

3 'I call "world" the whole succession and the whole agglomeration of all existent things, lest it be said that several worlds could have existed in different times and places. For they must needs be reckoned all together as one world, or if you will, as one Universe' (*Theodicy*, section 8).

from distinct worlds could coexist with one another. So, the existence of proud Simon in our world must be incompatible with the existence of any monad that belongs to a possible world other than our own. Equally, if any of those other excluded monads had been selected by God for existence, then Simon would not have been. These truths are independent of God's will. They just set out the framework of possibilities within which his creative decisions come to be made.

Let us now turn to the question of how God's creative choice is made. About that there are a number of things to say. The first is that those sets of possibles that make up a world that God decides to create must be fully specified in his thought as he comes to make his choice among them, specified not only with regard to a world's individual members but with regard to the properties (the perceptions and appetitions) that characterize them. This requirement arises from the need for any set of simples that God considers for existence to be amenable to precise evaluation. Unless that were possible the psychological embodiment of Sufficient Reason, the Principle of the Best (cf. §§48, 54, 55), could not operate, and God would be envisaged as making his creative choice on the basis of a less than omniscient grasp of things. That we know to be impossible.

As things go with us humans, we can often come to an evaluation of something less than an exhaustively specified collection of things. For example, I can set a value on the stamps I have stuck in my album up to and no further than a certain page or a certain country. I can jot down their value provisionally at the bottom of the page, and then turn my attention to something else before going on. Equally, to calculate the value of my whole collection I do not need to bear in mind anything about the particular weight or provenance of the paper on which the stamps were printed. Those properties, we may suppose, are neither here nor there as far as the worth of the collection itself goes.

For God, however, things are unlike that (as they often are for us too). The Principle of the Best is sensitive to the overall value of a world judged in part by the advertized criteria of variety (of its contents) and order (of their behaviour). As §58 puts it, the way that the greatest amount of perfection is obtained is by combining as much variety as possible with the greatest possible order. Each element of this dual measure, variety and order, yields a value for a given set of items not by progressive summation, as did the stamps in my album, but as a totality. What value any particular item has will depend on what other things belong in the collection, so the variety and order that any individual imports to the whole cannot be accurately assessed independently of what other things go to make up that whole. For instance, the high degree of variety or order that God sees as characterizing a particular segment of a given totality may make the totality of which the segment is a part less varied and orderly than would some less varied and less integrated ordering of that initial segment.

It is a direct consequence of the holistic nature of the value of worlds and sub-worlds and their contents that God could not evaluate anything less than the totality of possibilities of which he entertains complete specifications. Even though it may be possible to say that with respect to the determinate elements of a set its value is provisionally N (for variety) and M (for order), the matter left unspecified or unconsidered may operate to increase N and to diminish M (or vice versa). So it is only in the light of his perception of the global value of the whole that God could decide if it is best to create a constellation of monads that contains elements which taken by themselves would be valued at N and M. Whereas we, on moving house, might reasonably decide to take with us a collection of things that contains some prized family heirlooms and a few pieces of furniture we are particularly fond of, and just go on from there, it would not be rational for God to act in any such way. Following the Principle of the Best as we know he must, he cannot say for instance that come what may he will create a world that contains men, or decide on principle not to create unicorns and take matters on from those fixed starting-points.[4] The value that

---

4 I mean 'men' here quite specifically. Because considerations of order and variety fall within the general conception of God as mirroring his own infinite perfections in the finite world that he creates, it may be that nothing could outweigh the presence there of *rational spirits*. If so, any possible world worthy of God's choice would have to leave room for them quite independently of whatever else they might contain. But men are only one sort of rational spirit among a host of others we may presume.

men have and the effect of the non-existence of unicorns depends entirely on the contribution they make to the value of the whole, and that cannot be determined except in the light of what other possibilties the worlds to which they belong contain. In this way Leibniz's God is anything but anthropocentrically oriented.

Just as it is only a full specification of the members of a world that enables God to assess the whole for its relative perfection in comparison with other worlds, so too it is only by bearing in mind the full specification of the properties that characterize each member of the total set that God can come to a proper assessment of it. What properties possible things would have, their perceptions and appetitions, fixes the order and variety they bring to the worlds that they belong to. As before, because the contribution that the individual makes to the whole depends on its complete concept, so the provisional value of a totality of members that is considered on the basis of anything less than full specification of their proporties is an inadequate guide to that totality's overall value, and hence is an unsatisfactory way of selecting one totality in preference to any other.

Now we can see why when God's creative choice of some whole is made it can only be a choice among worlds and nothing less, and why we may be confident that our world is indeed a maximal world despite that being at odds with the way we are naturally inclined to think about it. We think that, marvellous though they are, neither the Wallace Collection in London nor the Frick Collection in New York is as rich as is the British Museum or the Metropolitan, though both the Wallace and the Frick are closed – completed – collections and the other two are still making acquisitions. Our world is (still) rich in fish and trees, but, rich though it is, there might well have been more herring in the sea, and more mahogany in Cuba, than in fact there have ever been. How can Leibniz deny such things?

He can certainly agree with us that it seems as if there might have been more herring in the sea. That is not evidently excluded by the Principle of Contradiction. Nevertheless reflection that invokes Sufficient Reason will reveal that it is definitely ruled out. If there could have been more herring in the sea, the Identity of Indiscernibles would ensure that any additional fish would have been individually different in their qualities both from each other and from any actually existing herring. So they would have added variety to the world as we have it. On the assumption that to add herring to the world requires the relevant laws remaining the same as they actually are (otherwise the world would not be enlarged by *herring*), we can say that the order in the world would remain invariant under its imagined fishy augmentation. Since God's choice is guided by Sufficient Reason in the guise of choice for the sake of the greatest perfection possible, the augmented world is bound to be more highly evaluated – and, given God's omniscience, accurately so – than the unaugmented world just because it is no less fully ordered but is more varied. Now since our world has in fact been selected for creation it must have been the most highly valued of the various possibilities that God envisaged (viz. all of them). Hence our world could not have contained more herring than it does. More generally, a rationally eligible world, a possible world that will satisfy the demands of Sufficient Reason, will be bound to consist of a set of monads that is, contrary to appearances, *logically* incapable of augmentation in any particular direction *without incurring greater loss elsewhere*. In this way it will be a maximally valued set of compossibles. If there had been more herring, then something else would have had to make way for them, which would leave the world diminished and not augmented, and then its value would have suffered a diminution by overall loss of variety or of order, or of both.

Just as the world could not be augmented, neither could it be depleted. If we think of things from our own perspective, we have no difficulty in envisaging our world existing just as it is, but with the sole difference that it lacks some salient landmark, such as the Pyramids or the Taj Mahal. We can also think of progressively diminishing dispensations, each of them being possible ways our world might have been, and each one, we might suppose, a reasonable candidate for God's creative election and each one obviously augmentable. For Leibniz, this must be a mistaken idea, since any dispensation alternative to the maximal one which ours must be can be ruled out straight away as incompetent to satisfy the demands of rational choice.

This does not of itself mean that there is no competition among worlds for existence. There is, but the competition each time is between fully replete, maximal, collections of fully specified monads engaging God's attention on account of the distinct balance of order and variety that each such set would display if once made actual, not among variations that our own world (or any other maximal set) could tolerate. It is a curious consequence of this picture that in the comparison of the totalities of monads that offer God a significant choice about his creation there will be many that come to be disregarded in the upshot of God's calculations that are less worthy of his choice than are many incomplete worlds that are automatically eliminated from the start. Maybe this should not surprise us. Our world as it is, though without the Pyramids or the Taj Mahal, is doubtlessly a richer place than many worlds that are serious candidates for God's creative attention. Nevertheless, because the Pyramids could be effortlessly thrown in as it were (effortlessly, that is, as far as logic goes), the depleted version of the actual world that I have imagined hardly merits a second thought. It can be weeded out before any calculations about relative values come to be made.

There will be those who will protest that my exposition has neglected an important doctrine about substance which has the effect of preventing the hasty elimination of less than replete worlds and which extends the computational reach of Sufficient Reason quite ubiquitously, on the grounds that the very idea of a less than perfectly replete world is itself incoherent.[5] Such persons will be thinking here of Leibniz's own application, not yet mentioned, of the complete concept doctrine as supplying strict identity criteria for individual substances. Taking it in this way, and not just using it to secure them an exhaustive specification of substances and the worlds they inhabit, we forbid ourselves from thinking that any particular individual might have had properties other than it does have on the grounds that that would be to suppose something existing with a set of properties distinct from those that specify it, and hence to suppose some different thing to exist other than this particular one – not this very

---

5 It is not that Sufficient Reason isn't involved in discounting less than replete worlds. It is. Since there is no contradiction in supposing that God could have created the world without the Taj Mahal, its rejection must depend on Sufficient Reason. The thought is just that what makes such a world unworthy of creation is not a computational matter. It is rejected even before considerations of variety and order are brought to bear.

Adam, as Leibniz liked to put it, but another Adam, very like ours, yet not numerically the same one.[6]

This thought naturally extends to worlds themselves. If we think of worlds as maximal sets of compossible substances, they will have the identity conditions of sets, and in consequence will be identified in terms of their actual or possible members. So we could not envisage our world containing fewer members than it does, by the omission, say, of the Pyramids, for two distinct reasons. First, the reduced world would not be constituted of the same set of things as that contained in the larger world. Then, in addition, since the things that would be members of the reduced world would all possess different relational properties than those things in the larger world that are spatio-temporally related to the Pyramids, nothing in the reduced world could (by the new version of the 'complete concept' thesis) be a member of the larger world. In the absence of the Pyramids the world itself would be an entirely novel one and not merely a diminished version of our own. It is a consequence of this that any collection of monads would constitute a fully replete world, since no addition to it that preserved any of its original members would be logically possible. In that case, if God's attention is engaged by any replete world and he applies the Principle of the Best to select the one that displays the greatest possible perfection, that principle has to operate far more actively in God's reckonings than I have suggested. There can be no wholesale elimination of swathes of possibilities before consideration of Sufficient Reason comes into play in the course of the calculative process.

Support for this idea can certainly be found in Leibnizian texts, and I have no reason to think that Leibniz ever distanced himself from this use of the complete concept doctrine. Nevertheless, I propose to set it aside because it implausibly encourages us to see any set of compossible monads as a maximal world – even singletons, whose sole members are solipsistic items not acting in a world beyond

---

6 'It follows also that he would not have been our Adam, but another, if different things had happened to him, for nothing prevents our saying that he would be another' (Correspondence with Arnauld, in Parkinson (ed.), 56). For another famous statement of the thesis, see sections 414–17 of *Theodicy*.

themselves. Then also I ignore it because the doctrine would make it impossible for us to act in ways other than we in fact do and thus would undermine our free choice, the importance of which for Leibniz will surface in the final, ethically centred, sections of the work. To abstract from this extravagant version of the doctrine, which makes all truths about monads necessary truths (and so is entirely against the spirit of §36) does nothing to impugn the more modest version generated by Leibniz's commitment to Excluded Middle, which leaves ample room for the contingencies that Leibniz presumes he can and should preserve.

Worlds that engage God's attention at the point of creation, then, can only be maximal sets of compossible monads. One may pause here to ask, as I have said we should, how this leaves room for multiple possibilities among which God comes to choose. It could well appear that just as every *actual* individual is compossible with whatever else exists, so too every *possible* individual might also be compossible with whatever the earth actually harbours.[7] If Leibniz brings us to accept that this world is indeed one to which no further individuals could be added, our world would then already contain all the possibilities that there are, and so be the only world possible.

What is needed at this point is an account of how different monads (or collections of monads) could fail to coexist, how some fully specified monads might not be compossible with others. To make the demand more urgent, and perhaps more taxing, it is useful to insist on one notable feature of what we are looking for and not confuse it with another. There is no difficulty at all in envisaging incompatible possible worlds if we think of any situation that diverged from the actual one in terms of a possible world. Thus one possible world is the actual one in which my eyes are brown; and any situation in which my eyes are other than brown would, on this way of speaking, belong to a possible world other than the actual one. The world in which my eyes are brown is incompatible with the world in which my eyes are blue just because they cannot be both at once.

---

7   Not counting 'different' Adams as distinct possible individuals here, but merely as possibilities concerning actual individuals that are excluded by the way things happen to be. Meant are possible individuals distinct from any actual ones.

This is just the sort of incompatibility that is irrelevant to the present question, since in the way I have just envisaged we should be focusing on incompatibilities that arise out of suppositions we make about situations involving the same individuals and not between subjects that belong to different Leibnizian world systems altogether. Equally, while it is true that Simon is taller than Peter, Peter cannot be the same height as Simon, but such relational incompatibilities only concern suppositons about members of the same world, and we need something different from that if we are going to introduce Leibniz's idea of a world in a way that gives rise to incompatibilities between different worlds' members.

What is taxing about the demand is that it looks initially as if it cannot be fulfilled: incompatibilities arise because we are inclined to predicate F and not-F of the same individual or because we are thinking of the same individuals as standing in inconsistent relations to one another. Neither of these eventualities can be realized when we select individuals from different Leibnizian worlds. If we think of the non-relational properties that monads have, then it would seem that just as every truth in this world is compatible with every other, every monadic state in this world is compatible with any non-relational state of affairs that would hold if any other possible world were actual. No truth about me could conflict with any truth about a monad that belongs to some world other than this one. Nor could any relational truth in this world conflict with possible relational truths about monads in different worlds. So how can it be that there are limits on what a world can contain that are statable in terms of incompossibility? With no answer to the question, the idea of a Leibnizian world lacks content.

One obvious seeming answer is given by appeal to the complete concept doctrine in its extreme form, and if it were fully coherent and there were no alternative, that would be a reason to revise my cursory dismissal of it. The thought would be that once the identity of an individual is fixed by the properties it is envisaged by God as having, no situation which involves a change in those properties could be a situation involving that same possible individual. In that situation, a given individual that God considers together with others as a possible member of some set of things he contemplates creating would be excluded from any other set of *possibilia* just because, if it were not, it would then be envisaged as coming to stand in some novel relation to individuals outside its own world, and that would involve supposing it to have precisely the properties it was originally thought of as having and then, in addition, having some other ones. That situation is not tenable; hence one might think a notion of cross-world incompatibility has been introduced, which is just what we were looking for.

However, apart from the already-noted unwelcome features of the complete concept doctrine, the proposal is unsatisfactory because it is advanced on the back of an implicit assumption that the totalities of possibilities that make up a world are already delimited simply by God's having them and nothing else in mind. But as I have talked in the earlier pages of this chapter, and as Leibniz himself thinks, a set of possibilities has a unity as a world whether God considers it or not.[8] It may be, as Leibniz says (§43), that the reality there is in possibilities presupposes the existence of God, but it must also be true that the possibilities God recognizes are themselves possibilities independently of his doing so. The same must be true of the sets of compossibles that make up a world. The present proposal, however, gives us no way of identifying such sets. It merely observes that when we have done so incompatibilities would arise with any attempt to augment them. The crucial question is thus entirely begged since the Leibnizian idea of identifying a world in terms of the compossibility relations that hold between its members is taken for granted and passed over in silence. An altogether different approach is called for.

A far more promising idea than this is supplied by the notion of order that is built into Leibniz's notion of 'the best' and on which I have drawn in setting out why, from his point of view, it must be a mistake to suppose that there might have been more herring in the sea than in fact there are. It is also a notion that has implicitly underlain the idea of a monad's activity, just because that idea supposes an ordered world in which free action can be entertained and reliably

---

8 Cf. *Theodicy*, section 225: 'The infinity of possibles, however great it may be, is no greater than that of the wisdom of God, who knows all possibles.' God's knowledge is clearly thought of as answering to the possibilities there are, not constituting them.

executed. What I have in mind is that our world, and in particular the composite or aggregative physical world, is subject to natural laws. That this is Leibniz's considered view is confirmed by §79 where he says: 'Souls act according to the laws of final causation, through appetition, ends and means. Bodies obey the laws of efficient causation or of motion.'

As far as simple substances go, I have already suggested that their psychology, like God's, is dominated by the principle (loosely, the law, though we do not need insist on that) that they strive by their lights for the best. More closely relevant to the present issue is Leibniz's thought that bodies are governed by mechanical laws. It was a particular application of this idea that enabled me to say that had the order of the world been other than in fact it is, whatever different individuals it might have contained they would not have been *herring*. For something to be a salt-water fish, as the herring is, the world needed to be stocked with salt and to have evolved in such a way as our world in fact has evolved. Disruptions to this order, in particular disruptions to the laws by which it is ordered, would ensure that whatever constitution its creatures had – even if they had the outward appearance of familiar animals – they would not have belonged to our actual terrestrial species.

Once we allow that a world of active simple substances cannot but generate aggregates, in our case bodies of one kind or another, that are subject to laws, it is plain how the existence of some composites may be incompatible with the existence of other perfectly possible ones. Even though there will be no formal contradictions among conjunctions of atomic propositions specifying the properties of different individuals that belong to different worlds – no contradiction, because different properties are attributed to different individuals – it cannot be the case that in some one world x is a herring and y a unicorn (say) because the laws that make it possible for herring to exist exclude the presence of unicorns. (I use the term 'unicorn' here as a mere dummy, envisaged as not applying to anything that might fall under those natural laws that hold of our own familiar species of things such as lions or alligators.)

The suggestion this leads to, the properly Leibnizian suggestion, I think, is that worlds are maximal sets of monads generating composites that are subject to uniform bodies of laws.[9] These sets are incompatible with one another in that nothing composite that belongs to one set could coexist with anything that belongs to another set and which is ordered by different laws than those in accordance with which members of the first set develop and unfold. The collection of worlds that seriously competed for God's creative attention will have been the set of such maximal sets, sets which all have their particular unity independently of whether God considers them or not. Our world, as it happens, was just the most favoured member of that grand set judged by the variety permitted by its governing order and falling within the overarching consideration of its capacity to reflect God's perfections on the finite scale.

These remarks have been geared primarily to composite substances. However, they also have their application when we turn our attention to the simples that compose those aggregates, despite the fact that the internal principle I have identified as guiding their changes of state is the same from world to world and looks unsuited to generating constraints that would prevent the possible monads populating one world from participating in another. This notwith-standing, a development of the last thought that Leibniz would endorse makes the perceptions and desires we have far less flexible than seems at first sight possible, and that without derogating from the freedom Leibniz is anxious to retain for simple spirits. This arises from his belief, to be discussed below, that each simple monad is bound to a particular body through which it perceives what it does of the world and through which it realizes the desires that are its. The simple monad's organic body, as Leibniz calls it, is one that the monad cannot lose and to which it is joined throughout the whole span of its existence. It will follow that the possibility just mooted cannot arise. Since a physical body is identified as the sort of body it is (animal, rock, crystal, etc.) by reference to the laws that govern its behaviour, the sorts of desires and perceptions that individual monads can have

---

9 Textual support is provided in the Correspondence with Arnauld (Parkinson (ed.), 54): 'For as there is an infinity of possible worlds, there is also an infinity of laws, some proper to one world, others to another; and each possible indi-vidual of any world includes in its notion the laws of its world.'

as they realize their 'internal principle' are fairly narrowly circum-scribed by the laws governing the organic bodies to which they are bound. Given that such bodies could not belong to any world other than the world they in fact belong to, neither could the simple monadic subjects which are bound to them as to their own particular bodies.

I have in this last way secured something that Leibniz finds natural, namely plurality in the possibilities among which God chooses in coming to his ultimate decision about the nature of his creation, and we can see how systematically Leibniz can in this matter set himself apart from Spinoza, for whom the actual world is the only possible world. However, it really is no empty question just how many possible worlds there are and whether Leibniz can declare as he does that their number is infinite (§53). To recognize the uncertainty of the answer should reveal something about the subtlety of the system that Leibniz has erected.

Taking a step back for the moment, it looks as though we can say that as far as the Principle of Contradiction goes Leibniz is perfectly entitled to say that there are indefinitely many, perhaps infinitely many, constellations of possible things. These need not be completely specified or replete in the way I have elaborated. Then, in addition, one may suppose there are all sorts of replete and completely speci-fied worlds that run under sets of unified laws which we, not having the necessary conceptual resources, are not competent to grasp in our thought, though which the omniscient creating God most certainly can. There we might be tempted to leave it, thinking that these last worlds are differentiated among themselves not just by the differences of the laws that their constituting monads obey, but by their being strictly ranked on a progressive scale according to the values of variety and orderliness that they manifest. That is indeed what we would be encouraged to do if all that God takes into account in his calculations are the two values of variety and order officially announced at §58.

Yet we have seen already that the concern with orderly variety is itself subordinate to a broader *a priori* aim on God's part that inclines him – even, maybe, necessitates him, however much Leibniz would deprecate the suggestion – to select a world that mirrors his own perfection, and thus create a world in which his power, his knowledge and his goodness are realized as extensively as is possible. At several points in earlier pages this theme has either surfaced explicitly or else made its nearby presence felt. Substances, we should remind ourselves, are essentially active, and to be that they need to enjoy perception and appetition. Perception is presented as giving them knowledge of their world, and in that they begin to reflect God's own possession of omniscient knowledge. Their activity, manifest in the satisfaction of their desires, also intimates their proximity to God, for thereby they exercize power over their world, however limited it may be. In addition, their activity is governed by an internal principle, which I have suggested must be a this-worldly version of the Principle of the Best, and in that they manifest something approximating to divine benevolence. If their identification of the best is sufficiently perspicacious, they then display something approximating to God's wisdom, and if it is sufficiently effective they display something approximating to God's goodness.

Once this additional overarching concern on God's part is given prominence and considerations of variety and orderliness subordinated to it, the range of possible worlds among which God has a reasonable choice to make rapidly shrinks. Indeed it might be thought even to reduce sharply the range of worlds that are licensed by the Principle of Contradiction alone. If God has no choice under that principle but to select worlds whose members are truly real, possible worlds can only be worlds of substances. If substances are essentially active then Contradiction alone rules out worlds in which there is no reflection of his knowledge, power and benevolence. It may be that we are still left with an indefinitely large panoply of worlds to choose among, but even so the spread of possibilities is certainly taking on a different hue. Can the line of reflection be taken further?

Maybe it can. Perception and desire are formal notions in their way, but they are nonetheless notions of ours. So while they place no limits on what is perceived and what is desired, the systems that enact them must be comparable to ours. In particular, they require that active monads – and that is all of them – should have compound bodies through which their perceptions and appetitions are realized, and from our last reflections we can say that the worlds they inhabit must be governed by laws that allow this to take place. It would certainly be rash to conclude here that the only unified set of laws that would allow such a thing is precisely the set of laws that our actual world obeys, and hence that, all appearances to the contrary, there is only one possible world that God could have created. That would be to proceed too quickly. We just cannot know whether other laws than those which govern our world would permit the existence of minds enjoying perception and appetition through the possession of organic bodies (cf. §63), but the constraints on worlds that consist of fully active god-like finite substances are beginning to look quite formidable.[10] They will be all the more so as we stress God's *a priori* concern that the chosen world should imitate his perfections *as far as possible*, but I shall not insist further on that.

With an eye to the looming threat that there should only be one possible world after all – a threat which arises quite independently of the recurrent suspicion that if God has to choose the best world and our world is the best, then our world is the sole world possible[11] – one might be inclined to insist that there are hosts of possible worlds quite unlike our own that operate according to mechanical laws much like those that govern this world. Fiction and science-fiction offer ample proof, in the one case of worlds distinct from ours yet obeying the same laws, in the other of distinct worlds obeying different laws but which are nonetheless rife with perception and appetition. This temptation must be resisted.[12]

---

10 We should not forget such truths as that if gravity had been stronger only a small world could exist in which there would be no time for biological evolution. If atomic nuclei were to bind together more tightly than they actually do, the chemistry of nuclear processes in stars would not generate even helium; if less tightly, hydrogen could not survive the initial Big Bang. It may even lie within the bounds of reasonable speculation that matter itself should have to obey precisely those laws that actually obtain.

11 It should be noted that when Leibniz talks of a possible world he always means a world that harbours no internal contradiction. Worlds that God could not create just on account of his being necessitated to choose the best would still count as possible ones for Leibniz. It would be their imperfection that ruled them out, not their incoherence.

12 Leibniz himself did not always resist it. In 'On Freedom' (1689) he wrote:

The reason is simple. Even if there is no contradiction in supposing such worlds to be possible, they are ruled out by pre-computational application of Sufficient Reason. In the case of ordinary fictions, if they had been real possibilities for our world, the events and persons they describe would have to be thought of as possible additions to the world we have or as possible replacements for actual elements of our world. The former is not a possibility, for we know that our world is the maximal set of compossibles, and fictional characters do not belong to that set. If the latter, then we are considering a variant of our world, but a variant that we know is not the richest set, since again, if it had been, those fictional characters would have been real ones. Since God's calculations set in at the point at which he has to compare maximal sets under different laws and not earlier, the elimination of these variants has already taken place automatically before that point is reached.

As for the fantasies of science-fiction, there we like to think we are considering alternative possibilities to our world system or significant variants thereof. Too often, though, they mask contradictions, or are merely fanciful variants on our world. So it is not at all safe to use that example to secure a real possibility that God might have selected in preference to his actual choice as a matter of calculation. The trouble here is that one thinks one can imagine something without thinking it through in detail, but when we take the detail seriously, the detail of how perception and desire and its satisfaction are handled, the thought that we have to do with worlds very different from our own is barely sustainable. It would be surprising if it were, since the ability to get others, our friends and readers, to share what we imagine for their

---

> It cannot be denied that many stories, especially those we call novels, may be regarded as possible, even if they do not actually take place in this particular sequence of the universe which God has chosen – unless someone imagines that there are certain poetic regions in the infinite extent of space and time where we might see wandering over the earth King Arthur etc …
>
> (Ariew and Garber (eds), 94)

Here Leibniz is envisaging the novelist as imagining a way our world might have been, not a different world altogether (nor an otherwise unoccupied location in the actual world).

entertainment and edification depends on our calling on shared conceptual resources to do so, yet our shared resources are of concepts which have their application in the very world we share with those friends and readers. Not even in imagination can we really take a holiday from the world from which we set out. In that case science-fiction will be just another case of ordinary fiction, and then ruled out for the same reason as it.

Where does this leave us? Well, as before, and having to say that the metaphysics leaves the matter open. Once worlds are identified with maximal sets of simples governed by bodies of laws, any room for God's choice as a result of calculation will have to be made between maximal sets of such finite individuals existing under different laws yet fully endowed with a capacity for god-like action and appetition. As far as I can see there is nothing of substance in the Leibnizian system that allows us to assert confidently that there is more than one such possibility. Equally, there is nothing in the system that forces us to deny it. This must be a point at which Leibniz's rationalistic trust in reason to penetrate far to the bottom of our universe comes upon its natural limits. However, the location of this limit is one that reason can identify. As I said much earlier, in the monadological system it is penetrable to understanding how penetrable to understanding things are.

At the start of the chapter I said that Leibniz's notion of a world is limited by the requirement that every monad must reflect every other. This is stated (§56) as the claim that each monad is 'a perpetual living mirror of the universe', and is textually derived from the thought that in his selection of this world for creation God has chosen a set of monads all of which harmonize with one another. This systematic harmonization of things is itself what Leibniz relies on positively to account for efficient causation once the 'transitive' conception has been rejected, as it was in §§7 and 11, and it will be a matter for later on. Without taking that up now, I can still bring this discussion of worlds to a close by asking what the mirror thesis comes to and how widely it applies.

At the point of the claim's introduction it looks as if this world is especially favoured in having its monadic elements sensitive to each other, and that other, more chaotic, worlds might be less privileged. If that were all there is to it, then the mirror thesis would be little more than an exemplification of God's preference for orderliness. However, on occasion Leibniz speaks of monads reflecting one another so fully that it would be possible for a fully informed mind to construct a map of the whole universe on the basis of the information encoded by any single monad,[13] and just to say that in this world or in some other the simple elements are sensitive to each other does not sound as if they need to carry information about each other. To adapt an illustration of Leibniz's own, one could perfectly well envisage four string players individually practising the parts of one of Haydn's Apponyi Quartets, say, each one playing in ignorance of what the others were doing.[14] Yet as it happens their playing is harmonized and the studio engineer, with simultaneous access to all four of them, hears fine ensemble playing. Harmony without mirroring seems quite possible.

A very different idea, and something closer to what Leibniz seems to be thinking of, is derivable from the idea that monads have complete concepts. That will be true even when we decline to accept the thesis in the version that sets limits to the properties that individual monads could have had. It supposes that an exhaustive account of any individual will be given only when all its properties, *including its relational ones*, are taken into account. Since every monad has a fully determinate nature, how it stands in relation to all other items in the universe is part of the whole truth about it. So it makes good sense to say that if one knew the whole truth about any one individual in the world, one would *eo ipso* know the whole truth about all the others. Put like this the mirror thesis begins to earn its name.

Not only does it earn its name, but it does so in a way that holds as a matter of necessity in all worlds, not just as a favour in this one. It is

---

13 Cf. *Discourse on Metaphysics*, §9; *Theodicy*, section 360.

14 Leibniz to Arnauld (*GP* II, 95):

> This universal concomitance ... it is like several bands of musicians or choirs separately taking up their parts and placed in such a way that they neither see nor hear one another, though they nevertheless agree perfectly in following their notes, each one his own, in such a way that he who hears the whole finds in it a wonderful harmony much more surprising than if there were a connection among the performers.

as true of worlds that God rejects as of the one that he finally chooses to create that each of their individual members stands in many relations to every other member of that same world and that a true and full description of one individual would involve true and full descriptions of all the others in that world. This is as much the case in chaotic worlds as in orderly ones, and so cannot be taken as illustrative of God's concern for order and for law. Nonetheless there is something unsatisfactory about this reading, which deprives the idea of monads as mirrors of each other of all its peculiarly Leibnizian flavour. Since nothing at all could escape the fact that it can be truly described in terms of anything else, to say that one substance reflects another says nothing particularly informative at all about them, and that would surely leave Leibniz dissatisfied. We need to find another way of taking it, consistent of course with this anodyne truth that must be left in place.

The obvious adjustment that is called for is that the extensional thesis just canvassed should be read intentionally. That is, Leibniz must have in mind that it belongs to the *perceptions* of each monad that it reflects other monads in its world, not just that it stands in their various non-perceptual relations to them. Not, of course, that each monad is clearly and consciously aware of how things stand with the rest of the universe – that privilege belongs to God alone – but at least dimly and uncertainly each monad perceives whatever is going on around it and is also perceptively sensitive to the most insignificant disturbances in any part of the world. Information about the whole universe is encoded as it were in each monad's perceptual state, and indeed encoded in its perceptual flow at any moment.

Here we have a claim that is anything but anodyne. So little so, in fact, that we might wonder not whether it holds in every world, as does its extensional counterpart, but even whether there is any reason to suppose that it holds here in the actual world. Once it is not held in place by thoughts about the harmony of things, mentioned above, its seeming falsehood at the level of phenomenology (I seem not to possess information about what is going on at the North Pole now, and I doubt whether things are very different for you) suggests that the metaphysical backing is underpowered. Is there anything at all that Leibniz can say in its favour?

One thought to which he could have been responsive results from putting together the undeniable and anodyne thesis with the metaphysical thesis, already long in place, to the effect that the properties monads have can only be perceptions. The anodyne and extensional truth must hold, and it must hold within the very perceptions that make up the properties that monads can have. In that case, it will hardly be surprising that all monads reflect each other perceptively. Nor, on reflection, will it be surprising that this is bound to be the case in all possible worlds, and not in ours alone. That phenomenology does not confirm it is neither here nor there, since phenomenology can only capture apperception and thought that lies within the borders of consciousness, and Leibniz is quite clear that mental life extends much further than that. It is only to be expected that our sensitivity to the far off and the very small and close to hand should fall below the threshold of consciousness.[15] If there is a surprise at all it must be that all monads necessarily perceive everything in their world, and that this is a condition of their nature as perceiving substances and the trivial truth that everything is related to everything.

A rather different way of generating the mirror thesis would be to say that it is what must hold in any world that reflects God's omniscience as far as is finitely possible. At §83 Leibniz reminds his reader that 'souls are quite generally [i.e. any monads whatever] living mirrors or images of the universe of created things', and he distinguishes among them minds, which are 'images of God Himself.... capable of understanding the system of the universe and of imitating it in some measure through constructive exemplars, each mind being like a small divinity in its own sphere'. The suggestion might then be that the thesis is supported by Sufficient Reason rather than by the Principle of Contradiction, and that in consequence it ranges no wider than our world and others that have a serious claim on God's calculative attention.

---

15 Although the *Monadology* makes no allusion to the subject, it is here that what Leibniz has to say touches significantly on a recurrent theme in his thought – the way in which gross perceptual awareness results from the imperceptible *petites perceptions* imprinted on the mind. See in particular *NE*, 53–8, (Parkinson (ed.), 155–9).

There is something right about this, and something wrong. What is right, to go by the quotation from §83, is that the clarity with which souls mirror the universe is a differential matter, differing from soul to soul. In this world, where there are minds, the mirroring sometimes rises to consciousness, as, say, in our pursuit of scientific knowledge, and there we do something to imitate God's omniscience in consciousness. That is clearly what sets us apart from less favoured monads in our world, and also from monads in other possible worlds that are not similarly endowed. So as far as Sufficient Reason is concerned, that bears upon the apperceptive realization of the mirror thesis. What is wrong about it is that it suggests that there might be worlds in which the mirror thesis fails to hold at all, and that I think is ruled out by the considerations that hold its intentional version in place wherever there are minds – that is, in all possible worlds whatever.

By way of summary, it can be said that the possible constellations of things from among which God selects one at the moment of creation are thought of as fully determinate unaugmentable sets of monads coexisting under unified sets of laws. How many such worlds there are is uncertain. Perhaps they are infinite in number, perhaps not; Leibniz's metaphysics does not supply an answer. It is a further truth about such worlds, however many there might be, that each of their constitutive simple substances has exhaustive perceptual sensitivity to all the other monads of its own world. This sensitivity, though, is differentially clear and apperceptive from world to world, and in any one world is liable to be unequally clear and distinct among its members. This fact will have an important bearing on the way in which monads aggregate to form matter, and that is the concern of the next chapter.

Further reading

Russell, Chapter 5, 'Possibility and Compossibility'; Rutherford, Chapter 2, 'The Maximization of Perfection and Harmony'; Benson Mates, 'Leibniz on Possible Worlds', in Rooteslaar and Staal (eds) *Logic, Methodology and Philosophy of Science III* (Amsterdam, 1968); H. Ishiguro, 'Contingent Truths and Possible Worlds', in R. Woolhouse (ed.); David Wiggins, 'The Concept of the Subject

Contains the Concept of the Predicate', in J. J. Thompson (ed.) *On Being and Saying: Essays for Richard L. Cartwright* (Bradford, 1987), 263–84.

Chapter 7

Matter (§§ 2, 57)

Each soul knows the infinite, knows everything, but confusedly.

(PNG, §13)

The later sections of the *Monadology*, particularly §§63–79, are largely given over to discussion of the world as it presents itself to us in our experience, the world of living organisms obeying mechanical laws and influencing one another in familiar and unfamiliar ways. The metaphysical vision Leibniz offers of it is bizarre enough at first sight, but as we follow his thought through much that is strange can be seen to result from the fundamental principles in ways that should now be familiar. What is immediately pressing as we move to the philosophical description of the experienced world is to confront a problem that has lain in the background for some time and which occupied Leibniz over a period of years. This is the question of how the metaphysic of monads, of his 'atoms of substance', can so much as permit the existence of the material world. Its members are spatially extended bodies, yet the ultimate realities of God's creation have no extension, and the spatial continuum cannot be compounded of extensionless parts since putting one extensionless and immaterial thing together with another cannot result in anything but an extensionless and immaterial whole. The problem looks intractable.

The *Monadology* itself is unforthcoming in this respect. We know that bodies or 'compounds', as Leibniz refers to them in §2, are 'nothing other than a mass or aggregate of simples', but how we are to understand the construction of extended composites is not addressed. Nor is there any full discussion of the topic in Leibniz's other later writings. It is noteworthy, too, that the *Monadology* makes no allusion whatever to the view that Leibniz had long held to be the key to the problem, to his often repeated view, that is, that bodies are properly speaking just phenomena, well-founded phenomena it is true, but phenomena nonetheless. Even though he keeps silent about it here – perhaps he considered the popular nature of his treatise made it unsuitable for such disturbing, or at least highly contestable, ideas – other texts from the same period leave us in no doubt that, whatever it amounts to, that did remain his view at the time of the *Monadology*'s composition. His silence on the subject in the body of the text is no evidence for his having changed his mind. So our task is to make the best sense we can of his somewhat scattered remarks about the relationship between monads, phenomena and the material world, and with the caveat that my own attempts are perforce somewhat speculative that is what I shall try to do. To make matters easier I divide the discussion into two sections. In this chapter I concentrate on the construction of extended matter fundamental to the notion of corporeal things in general, and only in the next do I take up the theme of composite substances and their organic bodies. Moving in this way allows us to set aside for the time being all questions about the individuation of bodies and the reality that Leibniz accords them, be they animals or plants or artefacts of our making, and to focus on the anterior question of how to find room within the monadological system for the existence of the matter of which they are made up.

Consider a small clod of mud picked up on my boots as I cross the sodden garden path in the early morning. It has fairly determinate spatial extension, it obeys well-understood physical laws, it displays some resistance to pressure and exerts a degree of force (e.g. gravitational force) on its surroundings. These are features that for Leibniz qualify it as fully material. Further, without itself being a well-defined individual thing – it is as much a quantity of stuff as anything else – my small clod contains within itself all sorts of individuals – many kinds of seed, a crushed beetle or two, numerous grains of sand and the like. All of these individuals are themselves material, of course, so the issue that faces Leibniz is how any such material stuff and any such individuals can come to exist if what God is metaphysically bound to create are simple substances, and all the simples he can create are immaterial ones. Certainly it is not open to Leibniz to think we should write off our beliefs in the existence of the material world as illusory, if only because so much of the knowledge that we have is precisely knowledge *about* it, and to downgrade that would be to downgrade God's ability to make us in his image, not omniscient to be sure, but knowledgeable enough in our limited way.

Interpretation and speculation here will be guided by a number of fixed points, quite apart from such textual pointers as we find throughout Leibniz's writings:

(a) We must respect as far as possible the claim of §2 of the *Monadology* that bodies are *compounds* or *aggregates* of simples. That is, in some unequivocal way truths about matter must clearly be answerable to truths about collectivities of monads.
(b) We must make something of the contrast Leibniz draws between collections of substances and the phenomena they give rise to. In particular, we should be guided by his repeated use of the rainbow as a paradigm of something that is in its way real, but nonetheless phenomenal.[1]
(c) We should remember that by the time he wrote the *Monadology* Leibniz had encountered Berkeley's writings, and that while he found the Irishman's thought too paradoxical for his taste he did recognize that it was not without some measure of good sense.

---

1 Cf. to Arnauld (*GP* II, 77, 119, 435; *NE*, 146).

We should therefore expect there to be some community and some divergence between the two thinkers on the subject of matter.

(d) We need to achieve some sense of how the individual subject (the monad) can be so related to the material world that action is possible. Monads are necessarily active, and without engagement with the corporeal world plans and deeds aiming at the satisfaction of their desires would be impossible.

These various points of course do nothing of themselves to tell us how Leibniz thought he could resolve the extension problem, but they will prove helpful in assessing the merits of the various alternative strategies open to him. Of these, I find three that deserve particular attention.

First attempt

Although I did not say so at the end of the last chapter, the mirror thesis of §56 has as a consequence that as far as the content of its perceptions goes every monad has the same representations as every other. If every monad represents the whole universe and nothing else, then every monad must represent just what every other one does. They differ only in clarity with respect to detail, God's knowledge alone being clear in all its detail. §57 may be read as teaching us that the organized clarity of a monad's representations is manifested in terms of the individual's particular *prise de conscience* of the world. Thus my perspective on things presents me with the façade of the house opposite, but not its rear. You, by contrast, looking out onto the back of the house from your own point of view, have no conscious awareness of its façade. Nevertheless, each of us represents that same house to ourselves both from the front and from the rear.[2] It is just that I am not consciously (*apperceptively*, in Leibniz's terminology) aware of my representation of the rear, nor you of yours of the façade. The

---

2 The identity of the house we represent is secured by our representations being full ones. We saw that the complete concept doctrine, outlined in the last chapter, ensured that each such representation can match only one compliant.

differing distinctness of our perceptions is what makes it true that I have the particular perspective I do onto the house and likewise gives you yours. We are emphatically not to think that it is our respective points of view (i.e. spatial situations) that generate the distinctness or clarity of our perceptions; rather, our points of view derive precisely from the distinctness with which our representations of things are systematically arranged. In this light we should understand what Leibniz tells us at §60:

> It is not in regard to the objects of their knowledge that monads are restricted so much as in the manner of that knowledge. Monads reach out confusedly to infinity, to everything, but they are restricted and distinguished from each other by the degrees of distinctness of their perceptions.

The differential clarity of monads' perceptions is evidently forced onto Leibniz to allow him to distinguish between world-reflecting monads, subjects which would otherwise be reduced to one by the Identity of Indiscernibles.[3] For later reference we should note that the clarity of a representation is best understood adverbially, as a modification of the representing that the individual monad does. Only thus can the 'point of view' onto the world that differentiates one monad from another be understood as a property of the individual and one that is unique to it at any one time. By contrast, what it is that the monad represents (the world, the whole universe) is itself neither clear nor obscure. It simply is.[4]

Taking the mirror thesis of §56, discussed in the last chapter as our starting-point, then, the construction of matter may be assayed in a

---

3 If one tried saying that they could nonetheless have different appetitions while having the same perceptions one would have to know how they could differ. Our desires grow out of our perception of our situation, so it would seem that some difference of perception is basic here. That will be provided by the perspective we have on the world, which is a function of the clarity of our individual vision of it, and differing as it does from one subject to the next.

4 Though *what* it contains are of course subjects enjoying differential clarity of their perceptions, which itself bears on how the world presents itself to us in our confused experience of it.

first way by saying that it will be true that there is a clod of earth stuck to my boot just in case all monads represent this as being so – whether or not their individual perceptions of that state of affairs are distinct or confused and however clear or confused they may be. Fundamentally, truths about the material world, truths of any kind whatever about things that are not themselves monads, will be constituted by such conformity among the perceptions of all actual monads. Furthermore, since it is a metaphysical truth that monads are active and thus able to satisfy their appetites, it is natural to think that any possible world has to be a world of material things. Hence, on this view, all possible worlds would have to be constituted by monads agreeing with one another in representing spatially extended things that exert force on and offer resistance to one another.

In the actual world the writing desk in my study is made of a quantity of oak, and on this reading of Leibniz's view that is true just in virtue of all actual monads representing the desk there and perceiving it as being made of oak. The table in the dining room next door is also made of oak, and that too is so because of the way I (dimly and confusedly) represent that room and its contents along with every other monad (some more, some less dimly than I, according to their particular constitutions). The fact that I am in my study and not next door is neither here nor there in the matter, for my location does not determine what I can represent – for example, that I can represent how things are here but not upstairs – rather, what I represent clearly (this desk and its surroundings) determines where I am located, namely at the point of origin of my view onto things. The same, of course, is true of you and anyone else. What it is that we living mirrors of the universe represent, though, is exactly the same.

The beauty of this interpretation of Leibniz is that it handles the vexing extension problem in a particularly smooth way. Extended matter exists in that statements concerning it are true and what makes them true is nothing other than that all monads represent it as being the case that this or that quantity of extended matter is thus and so, that there is a clod of earth on my boot, that there is still some wine left in that bottle and so on. Here the existence of matter is secured without it even beginning to look as if we are attempting to construct the continuum out of unextended monadic parts. True, matter would not exist unless individual monads existed, but the collection of monads on which the mud's or the oak's or the wine's existence depends – the totality of monads, that is – is not identified with the mud or the oak or the wine, and no part of the mud or the oak or the wine is itself a monad or any collection of monads. Material things do of course have parts, but those are just other extended things (cf. the seeds, the crushed beetles and the grains of sand that are all parts of my small clod of earth).

While the *Monadology* offers neither confirmation nor disconfirmation of this highly phenomenalistic reading of the relationship between simples and composites, there are two passages from Leibniz's later writings that could be seen as offering encouragement. Since one of these is contained in a letter of July 1714, which Leibniz had prepared for Nicolas Remond to accompany the *Monadology* on its way to Prince Eugène and in which he offers some brief commentary of his own on the work, one might suppose the encouragement is substantial enough. The relevant passage runs thus:

> We must not conceive of monads as moving and pushing or touching each other like points in a real space; it is enough that the phenomena make it appear so, and this appearance is true to the extent that these phenomena are founded, that is, are in agreement (*consentans*). Movement and interaction (*les concours*) is only appearance, but appearance that is well founded and which is never belied, like exact and long-lasting (*exactes et perseverans*) dreams. Movement is the appearance of change through time and place, body is the phenomenon that changes.... There are no actions in substances but their perceptions and appetitions. All other actions are phenomena, as are all other acting things. Plato seems to have seen something of this since he thought that material things had little reality, and the Academics doubted whether they exist outside us, which can be reasonably explained by saying that they are nothing other than perceptions and that they have their reality through the agreement of the perceptions of conscious substances.

> (*GP* III, 623)

While this passage says nothing about just what form of agreement makes appearances 'well founded', the phenomenalistic strain seems undeniable. How else could one understand the assertion that 'appearance is true to the extent that the appearances are founded, that is, in agreement' or that appearances are well-founded which are never belied and are 'like exact and long-lasting dreams'?

The negative answer suggested by my rhetorical question would appear to be reinforced by another late passage bearing on this issue, from the *New Essays*. There Leibniz says he had shown an earlier correspondent (the Abbé Foucher) 'that the truth about sensible things consists only in the linking together of phenomena, this linking (for which there must be a reason) being what distinguished sensible things from dreams'. Later in the same paragraph he writes:

> I believe that where objects of the senses are concerned the true *criterion* is the linking together of phenomena, i.e. the connected-ness of what happens at different times and places and the experiences of different men – with men themselves being phenomena to one another.
>
> (*NE*, 375)

We should be on our guard, however. The *New Essays* passage is taken from a context that is entirely epistemic in tenor, and Leibniz's use of the term 'criterion' – meaning *way of telling* – makes this plain. So what he is saying there is that the agreement of appearances is what we rely on to judge truly that sensible things are as they seem. He is precisely *not* saying that agreement in appearances is what sensible things being so and so consists in. Once this epistemic orientation of his thought is brought out it is open to us to wonder whether the Remond letter may not also be more concerned with epistemology than ontology, and then the textual evidence I have offered for an out-and-out phenomenalistic reading of the *Monadology* would be nugatory.

To be sure, I am here contemplating reading the later passage in the light of the earlier one, and there is no imperative textual reason to do that. However, the passage from the *New Essays* goes on to observe that it is a metaphysical possibility that there should be well-ordered and long-lasting dreams – as long as a man's life even – but that it would be contrary to reason to suppose that to be our situation. Here it is evident that Leibniz views the envisaged 'well-ordered dream' to be a sort of illusion, misleading us about the truth of things, so it is highly unlikely that in the Remond letter he should be recommending an ontological stance he has already firmly rejected (presumably because God could have no reason for selecting that sort of dream-world in favour of one in which beliefs attain to genuine knowledge and enable his creatures to imitate him). At the very least we should not take the Remond letter as settling the extension problem by recourse to phenomenalism, and if we are moved by the force of the passage from the *New Essays* we may well think we have good reason to reject such a reading of it and therefore of the *Monadology* too.

These textual matters aside, the phenomenalistic proposal does not fare well by any of the four benchmarks I mentioned. I have already pointed out how strained a reading of the *Monadology*'s §2 it forces on us. More than that, not only do material composites fail to be aggregates of simples, but perhaps even more striking, to the extent that we are prepared to speak of the phenomenalistic dependence of matter on (the experiences of) monads in terms of aggregation at all, every single piece of matter becomes an 'aggregate' of every single monad. The reason is just that what makes any statement about matter true is the agreement of *all* monads, and that I think stretches the notion of aggregation too far.

The phenomenalistic reading does have the virtue of honouring Leibniz's concern to account for body in terms of phenomena. That cannot be denied, but we may doubt whether it does so in the right way. If we allow ourselves to be guided by the rainbow analogy that he affected we shall have grounds to think it does not. If matter is to monads as rainbows are to raindrops, we have to be able to think of matter in ways that allow there to be a distinction between a shared illusion of a pool of water (as in a mirage, say) and a real pool of water, just as we can make the conceptual distinction between an illusory rainbow and a real rainbow. But if the reality of things is nothing other than agreement in monads' experiences this distinction will be lost. So we should look for another way of handling 'well founded phenomena', one that makes well-foundedness depend on agreement, as the Remond letter insists, but which augments that with something else so that the resources are put in place to distinguish between reality and widely shared illusion.

Next, this first attempt on the extension problem aligns Leibniz very closely indeed with Berkeley's immaterialism and makes it hard to explain what Leibniz would have found to be too paradoxical in that philosophy. Finally, constructing matter and body out of monads' representations makes it very difficult to see ourselves as genuinely embodied, as Leibniz wants us to do. How we might satisfy our desires and appetites through voluntary control of the physical world in which we ourselves are situated is a testing issue for monado-logical theory at the best of times, but on its phenomenalistic interpretation a testing issue becomes an impenetrable mystery, and Leibniz's contempt for those has already been remarked.

Second attempt

The difference between a shared illusion of a rainbow and genuine rainbow must depend on the causal origin of the experience in the two cases. The real rainbow is a phenomenon produced by diffraction of the sun's light through raindrops; the common illusion might be no more than the appearance as of a rainbow brought about in us at the same time by some fortuitous and simultaneous perturbation of our brains and nervous systems. With this thought in mind, we might look again at the claim that composites are aggregates of simples and take Leibniz to be saying that matter consists of aggregates of monads that produce certain material effects, just as sunlight and raindrops produce the effect of the real rainbow. So it might be suggested that just as a rainbow or a sound or a hologram is distinct from whatever it is that causes these things (raindrops, perturbations of the air, etc.), and distinct also from any particular experiences we might have of them (the rainbow exists whether or not anyone sees it), so matter – clods of earth, volumes of liquid and the like – is distinct both from the monads that supply its foundation and distinct from any partic-ular representations that perceiving subjects have of it. Here, I think, we are getting closer to Leibniz's own intentions and closer to a more plausible derivation of matter from the mandatory monadic base.

As before, the extension problem is handled with a satisfying degree of smoothness. The properties that matter has are explained in terms of the ways in which relevant aggregates of monads impinge on other monads in their experience of the world. The world has been so organized at its start that infinite numbers of monads are liable to affect others as having such and such an extension, weight, colour and the like, and for this to be so does not require that we think of the collections of monads that give rise to the phenomena as themselves extended any more than they have to be coloured or have a certain weight to generate those effects. All these material properties of things are here construed as effects that aggregates of monads are liable to have on suitably well-placed and properly attuned perceivers.

Conclusive textual support for this suggestion is not to be had. However, an early passage, from the *Principles of Nature and Grace*, makes it much more attractive than the proposal I have just dismissed. At §3 of that essay Leibniz states: 'Each distinct simple substance or monad ... is surrounded by a mass composed of an infinity of other monads, which constitute the body belonging to this central monad, through whose properties the monad represents the things outside it, similarly to the way a centre does.' Here at least he does explicitly narrow down the groups of monads to which the existence of any single quantity of matter is answerable. There is no question of the clod of mud being an 'aggregate' of *all* monads' perceptions.

Then, too, although we cannot strictly say that my clod is constituted of the monads that give rise to the phenomenal clodlike effects, adherence to the image of the rainbow might discourage us from struggling too hard to do that. After all, if the relation of matter to its monadic base is to run in parallel with the relation of the rainbow to the relevant collection of raindrops, we may think it right to resist the idea that matter is an aggregate of monads just as we hesitate to say that a rainbow is truly a collection of raindrops. Drawing, as we should, on the thought that it is at most in a sense highlighted by scare-quotes that an aggregation of raindrops 'constitutes' a rainbow, so it can seem appealing to suggest that it is in some such attenuated way too that Leibniz may hold that compounds are 'aggregates' of simples.

Although it is a clear improvement on the first attempt, we cannot have done well enough here to satisfy Leibniz. Not only is the 'well founded phenomena' thesis left to sit uneasily together with the aggregation doctrine, but matter itself comes to be too precariously placed between our representational experiences and the monadic realm that gives rise to them. By this I mean that Leibniz is represented as thinking of rainbows as something distinct both from our experience of them and from the drops that 'constitute' them. As a result, it looks as if the material nature of things is effectively being reduced in a roundabout way to monads' (actual or possible) experiences or representations, ones having a particular monadic genesis just as on this model rainbows are thought of as experiences, actual or possible, that are causally answerable in the right way to rain and sunlight. Matter and monads are just too detached from one another, and the background phenomenalistic flavour of the construction is unwholesomely intrusive.

Third attempt

What is needed is an adjustment or two that builds on the advantages promised by the last proposal. To make the aggregation doctrine and the well-founded phenomena thesis work in harness I suggest that as a first step we contemplate a treatment of the topic in two steps. First we should concentrate on a bare quantity of matter itself and deal with its spatial character. Then we can turn to the gross perceptible properties it has, such as displaying a certain passive resistance and active force and so on, in virtue of which we have to do with a lump of mud, or a quantity of wine or a block of oak. In this manner we should be seeking to identify the matter with a certain group of monads along the lines of *PNG* §3, read quite literally, and subsequently to understand the sensible properties it has in line with the phenomenal properties of the rainbow (leaving it open for the nonce just how that is to be taken). In that way, any volume of matter will be an aggregate of monads taken *au pied de la lettre*, and the features matter displays in our experience will be well-founded phenomena on account of their being causally anchored to the underlying monads that generate them. This strategy of divide and rule may promise Leibniz the best of both worlds.

Success or failure of the proposal will depend on the details, though, and before measuring it up against our benchmarks something more must to be said about each of the two strands of this approach. First, let me deal with the identification of a given quantity of matter with a particular set of its monadic constituents, for we have at all costs to make sure that the extension problem does not irrupt again with all its original force. Evidently, the material mass or the bodily individual that has the properties it does must be of a type to bear them. Yet once we identify the mass with some collection of unextended simples whose mere concatenation cannot constitute it an extended whole it must seem that any resultant qualities it should come to possess cannot be qualities of anything material nor any composite individual a physical body. In that case we should be back where we started and the original problem unanswered.

Distinguish here two ways in which a group of monads might be supposed to compose an extended mass. That which Leibniz clearly excludes is composition by the *concatenation* of minute elements as happens when a long rope is constituted by the intertwining of overlapping short strands. To achieve a rope of any length the strands themselves must possess dimension, however short. In the case of monads that is not so much as possible since *ab origine* monads do not even have spatial position, let alone spatial dimension, as basic and underived properties. In the words of the Remond letter, 'We must not conceive of monads as moving and pushing or touching each other like points in a real space'. As far as their 'original' qualities go, monads are nowhere. Nevertheless, Leibniz wants to say, monads *do* have a position, a *derived* position as I shall put it, derived, that is, from their perceptions, and it is this that we may be able to draw on to explain how they can come to constitute an extended mass, not by concatenation, but derivatively, by giving rise to it.

The individual monad acquires a spatial position derivatively from the particular distribution of clarity of its representations of the world that presents itself to the subject as its (presumably) conscious perspective onto things. My view of the world is as from a particular point in the world I represent, namely the point from which it seems to me that I represent it; your point of view is as from another such point. So we might understand Leibniz to suggest when, in the 'New

System' of 1695, he says that monads 'might be called *metaphysical points*; there is about them *something vital* and a kind of *perception*, and *mathematical points* are their *points of view* for expressing the universe'.[5]

It is important for the construction of matter now afoot that the unextended mathematical points in question should be thought of as points of view in a *single* space, even though they are derived from the perceptions of monads that have no original community with one another other than that of being members of the same maximal set of compossible substances. This may look a tall order since, as we usually think of it, your representation of the world is one representation and mine another, and what makes it true that they are representations of a common world is that our perceptions give us access to and arise causally out of a realm of objects that are themselves underivedly spatial and make their impact on us both. Yet, in Leibniz's case we have only our representations to go on, and while they may be isomorphic to one another, that by itself looks quite inadequate to ground the claim that they are representations of one and the same common space in which each of us has our own position and point of view.

To make headway we need to insist on the distinction I alluded to above between what it is that the single monad represents and the way in which it does so. *What* it represents is its world, having the contents that it does. *How* it represents it is a matter (*inter alia*) of the differential clarity or confusion of its representation of its world at different points and at different times (as it changes its point of view and as the world that it views itself changes). Now, we have seen already that there have to be differences in how monads view the world lest the monads whose representations they are should fail to be numerically distinct from one another. But given the mirror thesis and abstracting from all considerations of *how* the monads represent the universe, as far as its content goes *what* one monad represents is exactly similar to what any other monad represents. Consequently, because of their indiscernibility their represented worlds can only be a single world, and not a number of distinct worlds each one private to its representing

---

5 Parkinson (ed.), 121.

subject and just subjectively parallel to one another.[6] Monads' representations, then, are necessarily of a shared world. Hence if a given monad acquires a derived position by reason of *how* it represents its world, its derived position locates it in the very same spatial world as any other monad compossible with it. The Identity of Indiscernibles precludes any other possibility.

As far as the comprehension of material extension goes, the crucial feature must be its three-dimensionality or its spatial continuity. Continuity in a dimension may be expressed by the thought that between any two arbitrarily chosen points in the dimension there is another point. And that facet of the material world is derivably capturable in Leibniz's system if among the monads a world contains there are infinities that have points of view generating continuities in length, breadth and depth. In this way, from the existence of an infinity of monads, each one of which derives its own position from its perception of a three-dimensional world, is generated an occupied three-dimensional spatial volume in that world.

Given that a totality of monads has to constitute a material mass it is important that what is derived in this way should not be a volume of empty space but an occupied spatial volume. That is secured not just by the Leibnizian thought that empty space would be an incoherent idea – how could there be distinguishable parts of empty space? – but more directly by the thought that the mathematical point that is defined by a monad's point of view and allows us to assign the monad a position is itself a point that is occupied by the monad whose point of view it is. So, as we come to construct an extended volume in space, that volume, constituted by an infinite mass of monads, is itself inevitably occupied by that mass. And that mass, being derivably continuous in three dimensions is an extended mass. The extension problem thus seems soluble in the derivative mode without any appeal to phenomena akin to rainbows, be they well founded or not. This is a notable improvement over the first two attempts on the problem since it opens up the possibility of finding a place for materially constituted

6   There is no illegitimate quantification into an intensional context here. Leibniz's terms 'represent' and 'perceive' are meant extensionally. The perceived spatial world is real enough even if not 'originally' so.

things in the very world that God creates, the world of monads. The best that the phenomenalistic interpretations could do was to say that the world of matter lies beyond the world of monads even if is causally dependent on it; only that best, I suggested, was not good enough.

With space-occupying matter now in place, we can turn to the second strand of the construction, that which concerns itself with the nature of the extended matter derivatively occupying the space taken up by myriad extensionless monads. Here it is that the Leibnizian notion of well-founded phenomena must operate and the analogy with the relationship between a rainbow and its physical base find its place. To get this right it will be useful to spend another moment with the rainbow itself, which I have already briefly considered twice. To understand that simply as a kind of shared experience or 'phenomenon' was found unsatisfactory because it did not distinguish between real rainbows and illusory ones. To improve the situation by making the shared experience answerable to a particular causal base – raindrops and diffracted sunlight – and thus thinking of it as a 'well founded phenomenon' was none too happy either, for while the real rainbow is well-enough distinguished from the illusory one, that is done at the price of leaving it and its material base too detached from one another. We have two things rather than one, and to insist on that aspect of the analogy divorces the world of monads from the world of material things, leaving them related, to be sure, but not with the intimacy of a true marriage. We need an altogether different understanding of the rainbow.

The obvious alternative to the two already tried is to see that when we talk of rainbows we are picking out a body of raindrops and nothing else, but according to the way in which such things typically appear to us when seen in appropriately falling sunlight, that is, as Leibniz would say, 'confusedly'. The rainbow and the drops are one, only those drops are experienced and presented in language and thought as a rainbow. It isn't that the raindrops are one thing (a certain changing body of water) and the bow another; rather the rainbow is nothing other than the body of rain that appears to us in the peculiar way rain does when refracting sunlight. We might put it by saying that when we talk of rainbows we are reifying certain properties of raindrops, namely the way in which they typically appear to us when light passes through them, but that does not mean that what we experience is not what has those qualities, namely the body of drops. By focusing on the appearance, our way of talking serves to bring home that we do not see the drops distinctly as drops, but 'confusedly' as that familiar and quite predictable bow in the sky. Nonetheless, what we see are the drops, and they are the bow.

Reading Leibniz's analogy in this way gives us a suitably non-phenomenalistic way of thinking about quantities of matter, such as my clod of mud and individual bodily things like my writing desk, and makes it plain why Leibniz should so often find it natural to talk of them as well-founded phenomena. Our commerce with bodies is primarily in our experience of them, but for Leibniz our perceptual experience of them is always and inevitably confused. In perception we are stimulated by hosts of monads, but we are not ever consciously aware of the individual simple substance making its contribution to our sensory awareness. Our total experience results from our subliminal experience of the individuals, from our *petites perceptions*, as Leibniz calls them, and in those circumstances it is very natural that our grosser experience of the simples that impinge upon us should be articulated in the terms of the way in which they present themselves to us.[7] So, given that we are unconscious of the details and just confusedly aware of the whole, there is no surprise that the ways in which we talk encapsulate that confusion. As we speak of clods of earth, or quantities of wine or blocks of oak, so we are indeed experiencing and picking out different collections of monads, but picking them out in the light of the way in which they present themselves to us, *as* lumps of mud, *as* blocks of oak and so on. That is one reason why Leibniz calls bodies 'phenomena'. It is less a term of reference picking out something distinct from, though causally related to, the real simple substances responsible for the appearances than one that introduces those same simple substances under their inevitably confused modes of presentation.[8] Those phenomena are well founded, not just in

---

7   The theme of 'petites perceptions' is most fully set out in the Preface to the *New Essays* (*NE*, 54–8; Parkinson (ed.), 155–9).

8   Inevitable, that is, in our human situation. In *New Essays* Theophilus says: 'we have *petites perceptions* of which we are not consciously aware in our actual

being causally related to a monadic base, but also because their confused modes of appearance are systematically correlated with the nature of the human perceptual system as well.

Enough said about the rainbow. As we try to use the analogy understood in this new way and apply it to quantities of stuff and their perceptible properties we have to face two puzzles. The first is how Leibniz can suppose that the confused terms which are apt to capture the nature of our experience can possibly be applied truly to the monadic world that our experience is experience of. The second is how the confused terms we use can apply to the world rather than to our experience itself. Bluntly, how can the monads that make up the charcoal in the grate be truly hot and how can the heat we experience be in the fire rather than in the eye or hand that perceives it? Without adequate answers to these queries, our third attempt on the problem of matter must fail. Fortunately, Leibniz is sure he knows how to respond on both counts.

The first issue is resolved by a claim he makes to the effect that all the standard ways we have of talking about the world, be it in primary quality terms or in secondary or others, involve confusion. They all have a certain relativity to the human perspective on things,[9] so that what it is for something to be hot, say, is for it (the relevant group of monads) to strike us in the large confusedly as being hot. Understood like that, such 'denominations', as Leibniz calls our ways of speaking, are true of groups of monads providing those groups do strike us as hot when we view them in appropriate circumstances and when the humours of the body are not deranged.[10] As we experience the world we perceive it from our human point of view – through the mediation of our organic bodies (cf. §63) – and there is no very great surprise that the descriptions we give of our experience reflect that. Still this does not prevent us from speaking truly of the things we perceive in such

---

state. However we could be aware of them and make them the subject of our thought if we were not distracted by their number which confuses the mind, or if they were not obscured by grosser ones' (NE,134).

9 Cf. NE, 131–2.
10 Ibid., 132–3.

confused terms.[11] Material things are indeed just such as to bring it about that we perceive them as hot or cold, coloured or not, sticky and weighty, and since those things are constellations of monads, those constellations must be correctly described as we use such terms. Once we see that the language we use to articulate experience has a built-in relativity to our own constitution there is no reason to think that the 'confusion' that Leibniz holds it to embody is at odds with the straightforward truth of what we say.

Turn now to the thought that these confused experiential terms properly apply to the bodies we apply them to rather than to our experiences themselves or to our ideas, as Berkeley thought they did, and as Locke sometimes said.[12] Leibniz is quite definite about this. In calling something hot, we are in fact referring to some feature of the mass that we do not perceive distinctly and that our confused experience represents to us *as* hot. Thus he says

> the pain I feel does not resemble the movements of the pin, but it may well resemble the movements that the pin causes in my body. Likewise the light is in the fire because there are in the fire movements which are not perceptible by themselves, but whose confusion or conjunction is sensible and is represented to us in our experience of light.[13]

Put rather more generally, the ways we have of talking about the perceptible features of the world apply to it rather than to our perception itself just because the objects we perceive have the capacity to

---

11 Leibniz's term 'confused' is explained in 'Of Universal Synthesis and Analysis' as applying to concepts which are understood through themselves, but which we have to introduce by ostension, 'which we cannot explain to another except by pointing' (Parkinson (ed.), 11). Lockean secondary qualities would be prime examples, though Leibniz tells us (*NE*, 130, 132) that in this respect primary and secondary qualities are not to be distinguished. Nor are they to be distinguished, as Locke believes, by the resemblance there is between primary qualities and our ideas of them and the failure of resemblance in the secondary quality case (cf. *Essay*, II. viii. 15). Leibniz acutely observes that there is 'resemblance' (or, better, systematic correlation) in both cases (ibid.).

12 Cf. *Essay*, II. viii. 19 for the most egregious example.

13 *NE*, 131–2.

produce the various sorts of perceptual experience in us, and that is what we are saying about them when we call them 'hot' or, 'rhomboid' or 'heavy' or 'solid' and so on. So Leibniz has answers to the pressing residual questions to which the last attempt on the construction of matter from its inescapable monadic base gives rise, and that encourages me to think that he would find in it much to approve of. To test this optimism, let us now review the merits of the proposal by asking how well it fares by our leading benchmark tests.

First, it does not jar badly with the texts that bear on the subject. Matter is indeed composed of aggregates of monads, as §2 of the *Monadology* insists. Thinking of it as I have just been doing allows us to see why Leibniz should say that each monad is surrounded by a mass composed of an infinity of others (*PNG* §3). It also allows us to employ the language of spatiality and extension in regard to that mass consistently with his denial in the Remond letter that monads have 'real' (i.e. underived) spatial position.

Second, we have found a way of handling the extension problem without making monads themselves atoms of matter. Further, this has been done in a way that preserves the rainbow analogy once that is given a slightly unexpected reading. It also makes sense of Leibniz's speaking of the world of our experience as a well-founded phenomenon. Then, too, a way has been found of locating the individual monad, most notably the self in the case of rational souls, within the physical world in which it seeks the satisfaction of its desires. The demand that simple substances be genuinely active members of the world we know and love seems, in prospect at least, to be one that lies well within Leibniz's grasp.

Finally, we saw that Leibniz finds something to approve of in Berkeley and something to deplore. If we decline the phenomenalistic understanding of matter it could look as if there is not much left to approve of. Only this is not true. The underived realities of the world are all minds, and in an underived fashion nothing else exists at all. In a derived fashion, though, matter exists as well; it results (as Leibniz puts it) from monads and their perceptions, and in this Berkeley and Leibniz are at one. Where they diverge is that there is room in Leibniz's system, as there is not in Berkeley's, for causal interaction between derived material masses and the minds that perceive them.

There is also for Leibniz, though not for Berkeley, the metaphysical possibility (never in fact realized) that matter should exist without ever being consciously perceived.[14] In sum, where they agree, they do so in thinking that the material world has to be explained in terms of minds and their perceptions, and where they disagree it is because Berkeley holds that matter can be directly reduced to the conscious perceptions of minds (i.e. 'ideas'), whereas Leibniz holds that matter results from or, as we would put it, depends on or supervenes on the collections of minds that God decided to create.

Further reading

Montgomery Furth, 'Monadology', *Philosophical Review* (1967), 169–200, reprinted in Frankfurt (ed.), presents the classic phenomenalistic reading; see also R. M. Adams, 'Phenomenalism and Corporeal Substance in Leibniz', *Midwestern Studies in Philosophy VIII* (Minnesota, 1983), 217–57; also Adams, Chapter 9, 'Leibniz's Phenomenalism'; M. D. Wilson, 'The "Phenomenalisms" of Leibniz and Berkeley', in *Ideas and Mechanism: Essays on Early Modern Philosophy* (Princeton, NJ, 1999), 306–21. The relation between Leibniz's metaphysics and his philosophy of science is discussed by Gerd Buchdahl's 'Leibniz: Science and Metaphysics', in *Metaphysics and the Philosophy of Science* (Oxford, 1969), 388–469; Rutherford, Chapter 9, 'Dynamics and the Reality of Matter'; M. D. Wilson,'Confused Ideas', in *Ideas and Mechanism* (Princeton, NJ, 1999); Ishiguro, Chapter 4, 'Ideas of Sensible Qualities'.

---

14   We should not forget that Berkeleyan ideas would, in Leibnizian terms, all be apperceptions. He has no room for a mental life of which its subjects are not consciously aware.

Chapter 8

Organic bodies and composite substances (§§60–77)

In the last chapter we saw how monads compound to form matter, space-occupying stuff that exerts force and displays resistance. From our earlier discussion we know also that monads are bound to do so in ways that obey strict mechanical laws. Even if we are driven to say that matter is a derived and not an original existence, the reserve that that brings with it is fairly minimal and does nothing to impugn the reality that matter enjoys where it exists. We know of course that in our world, the actual world, there is matter, but what may come as a surprise is that the same is equally true in any other possible world as well. It will come as a further surprise that the way in which all worlds must incorporate matter ensures that they all contain individual composite substances despite the fact that these are not 'original' realities. What these claims amount to and how they arise within the monadological system is the concern of this chapter.

Leibniz's introduction of matter into the discussion occurs in §§60–2, where the mechanical influence of one material thing upon all others, and ultimately upon each single monad, is adduced as an explanation of how the mirror thesis of §56 can be realized in giving each simple substance perceptual access to the whole universe. As he presents it, monads or souls can perceive only what is represented within themselves, and to be perceptually aware of everything, everything has to come to be imprinted on their souls.[1] Since what monads represent is a material world, the way this must happen is through each material event or state impressing itself on every other material thing, so that each one records the full truth about the universe. To bridge the gap between what is imprinted mechanically on each material element of the world and what the soul reads within itself, Leibniz supposes that each monad must have a body of its own, 'one that belongs to it in a particular way'. Since the whole truth about the universe is imprinted on everything the universe contains, it is imprinted on every body, so on any monad's own body. Thence it comes to be imprinted on every monad's soul.

If this were all that could be said, it would be fair to observe that it might at least go some way to explaining how monads could have perceptual knowledge of a world that was through and through a material one. It throws light on how in our world the mirror thesis is realized, but if we think that other possible worlds may be notably different from our own, in particular by lacking the material element that is such a pervasive feature of ours, then it will be quite mysterious how the mirror thesis can hold in them too, as I said at the end of Chapter 6 that it must. Determined deployment of the tools of Leibniz's workshop will assure us that we need not fear mystery and will make the reflections of these important sections look less local in character than the actual argumentation would suggest.

Of necessity, substances are both passive and active. Their passivity essentially expresses itself in receptive perception of their world; their activity, in their search for satisfaction of desire, in appetition. For a monad to be capable either of perception or of appetition

---

1   To talk of 'imprinting' as I do here emphasizes the mechanical nature of the operation. However, it carries no implication whatever for its analysis. In particular, the particular way in which physical states of things come to be imprinted on the soul is here left blank. Chapter 9 discusses the detail.

Leibniz wants to say it has to have a body of its own. Furthermore, its perception and its appetition must be directed towards other bodies. Since these two ideas are quite general conditions on perception and desire, all possible monads must have bodies and be directed towards bodies. Since bodies are essentially material things, any world that God might have reason to create must incorporate matter within it, even if as a derived rather than an original reality. The speculation about other non-material worlds is therefore idle and could have no application. So the model for the mirror thesis' realization is general and not local at all. An argument to this effect that should meet with Leibniz's approval can be mounted from either direction.

Consider first the side of passivity. The perceptions that make up a monad's principal properties or states cannot just be any old representations that this or that is the case, representations *as of* such and such being thus and so. If they were that, the truth or adequacy of a monad's representations to the world would be neither here nor there. We have seen, though, partly as a consequence of the mirror thesis itself, and then deriving ultimately from the theological considerations lying in the background, that a monad's representations must fundamentally be instances of knowledge. This will standardly be knowledge possessed by the individual of its surrounding world, and so the monad's representations need to be of a kind that will render this possible. For this purpose what is needed is a way of distinguishing knowledge-conveying representations from other records of the way the world may be, and that can be done by insisting that these representations be genuinely perceptual ones, and not simply representations of some other sort which, even if they were true to the world, would not provide knowledge of it. Such, for example, would be the case of true imaginings about the world's contents. The upshot of this is that Leibniz's identification of monads' properties at §14 as *perceptions* is best understood in a quite specific way rather than a broad one that is indifferent between one kind of representation and another. 'Perception', we might say, means *perception*.

This commitment to perception proper is brought out reasonably clearly in §62, where Leibniz first introduces the idea of bodily things and says that 'as this body expresses the whole universe through the interconnection of all matter in the plenum, the soul too represents the whole universe in representing that body, which belongs to it in a special way'. The idea is important enough to be repeated in the very next section, where he puts it by saying that 'since every monad is in its own way a mirror of the universe and the universe is regulated in a perfectly orderly way, there must be order in the representer, and so also in the body through which it represents the universe' (§63).

Both passages manifest Leibniz's concern with the mechanism of the perceptual representation of the whole. The soul has to represent the wider world through representing a body which is its. One train of thought that may well be guiding Leibniz here is that we may distinguish veridical perception which delivers empirical knowledge of the world from true imaginings which do not do so by insisting that our representations have the appropriate causal history. That history, Leibniz may have supposed, must involve the soul (or, more generally, the monad) being sensitive to the way in which the things it comes to know have impressed themselves on a particular body, namely on a body which is the knowing monad's own. Since whatever happens at some place in the universe is, by the mirror thesis, reflected everywhere else in the universe by mechanical means, it is through its sensitivity to what happens in its own body that the monad can reach out in thought to touch such other bodies as exist beyond its own very local one. We are aware of the world around us in being aware of a body that is ours, and without a body that is our own belonging to us 'in a special way' extensive empirical knowledge of our world would be denied us. More generally, since other monads must have their bodies too, bodies which provide them with their outlook onto the world and are their source of information about it, when I perceive something through representing my body, the mirror thesis assures me that what I perceive will be other bodies, in particular the bodies of others. Our passive and receptive nature as expressed in perception thus requires that the world contain material things.

It may appear to be an unsatisfactory feature of this chain of reasoning that the introduction of a monad's own body seems rather weakly motivated, relying as it does on what could seem to be contingent features of our own make-up, and that if he were thinking of making a metaphysical claim to the effect that bodies must find their place in all worlds Leibniz would be smuggling in the assumption of materiality too easily. To this it can be replied that representations that did not causally involve stimulation of the perceiver's sensory mechanisms, and hence of the body, would not be instances of *perception*. That is central to what perception is. Without involvement of a sensory system, a representation would not be properly speaking a perceptual one, and sensory systems are necessarily material ones.

The nearest that Leibniz comes to offering a general argument to this effect is in the reflections of §§61 and 62 which arise from his conception of perception itself. In a nutshell, his view is that strictly speaking what the soul is aware of can only be what lies within itself[2] – its perceptual experience – but that does give us knowledge of the world around us provided that our experience is caused by the object we loosely say is perceived. The idea of direct and unmediated intellectual intuition of things apart from ourselves may not be incoherent, but it can only apply to God's knowledge of the world[3] and not to that of finite beings such as ourselves. So when we have perceptual knowledge of things that are distinct from us, there needs to be some causal mechanism that serves the purpose and provides the necessary mediation.

Why though does the introduction of a causal relation between the external perceived object and the perceptual experience enjoyed by the perceiving subject require that subject to have a body? The answer is that what I am distinctly aware of in perception has to be of something close to me and it is only if distant things can make an impact on the near to hand that it will be possible for the subject to perceive them with any sharpness. So Leibniz draws the picture (§61) of one distant thing making its impact on another, by mechanical impression, and eventually by a transitive process making itself felt through the impression it eventually produces in the perceiver's own near to hand body, which is all that the mind is *immediately* sensitive to in its surroundings. It is thus that 'the soul too represents the whole universe in representing that body which belongs to it in a special way'.

We could put it by saying that the very nature of perception

---

2   Cf. *NE*, 135 and 145.
3   Cf. *PNG*, §13: 'God alone has distinct knowledge of everything ... everything is present to him immediately.'

requires that the perceiver enjoy experience that is causally sensitive to something in the world that is both distinct from its mind and also closely enough related to it to make further transitive mediation unnecessary. The chain of causes has to terminate, and that will only happen if each monadic perceiver has a body to which it is directly sensitive. Since all monads are perceivers, all monads must have a body to which they are so sensitive, and the mirror thesis of §56 is realized through the way in which each such body not only makes the universe known to its associated mind but makes itself known to other minds through the way in which it leaves traces or impressions on other bodies, directly or indirectly as the case may be.

Such is the somewhat tortuous route from a monad's passivity to its world necessarily enjoying a material constitution. The route to that same conclusion from consideration of monadic *activity* is quicker, although it is hardly independent of the pathway already traversed. To be properly active, Leibnizian substances must be capable of engineering changes in their perceptual states in answer to the sorts of desires that it is their nature to have. A banal example is provided by my response to thirst. My desire for water prompts me to search for it, to move my body so that I become able to drink and as a result no longer suffer the desire. By the mechanism just described, my body is involved in finding and perceptually recognizing the means to quench my thirst. It is also involved in the satisfaction of the desire itself, a state of the body (satiation) which is then recorded, or transduced, in the soul. If I am thirsty, it will not help me if someone else finds water and drinks it instead of me. Even if, as may be, my desire is momentarily rendered inert when that happens – by surprise or outrage, say – my thirst has not been quenched, and the change in my state of mind is not that of satisfaction, but merely one in which desire is suspended or otherwise momentarily inhibited. So just as in the case of perception, we cannot attribute activity to a monad unless there are bodies upon which it leaves its mark in its pursuit of the satisfaction of its desires; equally it cannot satisfy its desires except through changes in the states of a body that is its own, causally sensitive to the changes it produces in the world around it as it seeks its satisfaction. Activity, like passivity, requires the monad's world to be a world of bodies, hence a material world.

Both lines of thought rely on the idea in the monad's soul needing to be the direct awareness it has of some sort of mark made by external things on a body which is uniquely its own. Perception and desire each require direct and unmediated awareness of states of that body. However, absolutely nothing is said in the sections under discussion about how this might be, and that is an issue that we can take up later. For the time being I restrict attention to the topic of the body and leave its connection with the mind for the next chapter.

If we ask ourselves what Leibnizian bodies are, the answer seems to be that they are masses of monads that enjoy a certain kind of unity. Particular masses of simple substances impress themselves on our notice as being distinct from others, and the ways in which we distinguish them from others may depend on their displaying behaviour that we find useful to mark with a name as we come to make sense of the world we perceive and in which we pursue our goals. So, for example, we pick out certain masses of matter as heaps of stones, and distinguish one such heap from another. Similarly with flocks of sheep, and armies of men and slabs of marble, all of which, like the heap of stones, are examples of Leibniz's own. A term like 'slab of marble' then applies to a material monadic mass as long as it displays the right sort of organizational structure and it marks out that mass as distinct from other masses displaying a similar structure and also from other masses displaying different kinds of structure, such as a statue made from the marble block.

Examples like these are all paradigms of what Leibniz calls unities by aggregation. They are compounds arising, as §2 has it, from 'a mass or aggregate of simples'. However, Leibniz makes it clear that such bodily compounds are not identical with the masses of monads from which they arise just because the very same body is liable to be made up of different simple parts at different times. As he puts it (§71), 'all bodies are in perpetual flux like rivers, and parts are continually entering and leaving them', and just because bodies are not identical with material masses of simples we might be inclined to think that monadological theory must be committed to the existence of a third sort of thing apart from simple substances and the monadic masses that go to make up individual monad's bodies, namely those bodies themselves. That, however, would be a mistake.

The heap of stones, the flock of sheep and the slab of marble are, for Leibniz, shifting masses of monads that display a relatively stable pattern, be it structural (the slab), or behavioural (the flock) or social (the army). For him these patterns are not natural unities but merely reflections of our interests and habits of discrimination. Their existence is in one way or another conventional, and for that reason they 'have their unity only in our minds'.[4] It is on this account, as well as on that already discussed, that Leibniz finds it illuminating to call such aggregative things 'phenomena', reflecting the fact that the concepts we make use of in dividing up the masses of monads that confront us into bodies of one kind or another involve ideas of unity of our devising rather than match any pre-existing realities.[5] As far as pre-existing realities go, all that there are are simple substances, and much that we dignify with the name of *individual* is a merely phenomenal or conventional aggregation of simples which have no closer metaphysical connection to each other than 'a cheese filled with worms'.[6]

While the examples I have cited all lend themselves to this 'phenomenal' treatment, they are also quite atypical examples of the sort of material thing in which Leibniz is primarily interested, namely the animals and plants and other organic entities that populate the world. These surely are bodily unities whose existence is naturally determined and not a conventional matter at all. Their bodies are also precisely of the sort that is needed to allow monads the capacity for perception and appetition, and so it must seem either that I have misrepresented Leibniz's thought by generalizing too recklessly from the bodily aggregates he likes to call 'phenomena', or else that he himself is inconsistent in his treatment of the material world. Once we direct our attention to the bodies that are said (§63) to be peculiarly bound up with the simple monads, we seem to have lit upon ineliminable compounds that do not fit into the dichotomous division between simple substances and (phenomenal) aggregates which seems to be offered to us by §2.

---

4   To Arnauld, 30 April 1687 (*GP* II, 96).

5   This is a completely different use of the term from that discussed in Chapter 7, though sometimes Leibniz is inclined to run them together (as he does at *NE*, 146).

6   *GP* II, 197 (1699).

In the case of *living things* and *animals*, Leibniz says, we have to do with unities that are formed of a simple monad *together with* its perception-and-appetition-facilitating body. The difference between a mere living thing and an animal is a matter of the nature of the principal monads involved. At the simplest level the perceptions and desires of the living thing are fairly minimal, and Leibniz (§18) calls their monadic subjects mere *entelechies* (meaning roughly: things striving for their perfection). The bodies that are required to meet their needs are correspondingly simple, and so the whole thing – a plant, maybe – is just a living organism. Monads having a more complicated structure of perception and desire are more than mere entelechies: they are *souls*, and as such need a correspondingly complex body to realize them. Such wholes as these are *animals*. Men are more complex again, for their dominant monads are *rational intelligences* and their mental life can only be expressed through bodies that are notably different from those in the rest of the animal kingdom.

I shall come back to the hierarchical structure of the natural world in a while, but for now I shall use the way Leibniz has set things up to answer the immediate query about the place of natural organic bodies in his metaphysical scheme. In each of the three kinds of case just mentioned, plants, animals and men – and even in that of angels and other superhuman (though still embodied) creatures (if such there be (cf. §72)) – we want to know how we are to think of the unity that consists of the principal or dominant monad and its organic body, and also how to think of its body apart from that dominant monadic element. The answer that Leibniz is led to is that in the first case we have to do with genuinely unified compound substances, and in the second that we are concerned with no more than phenomenal material aggregates. There is indeed a dichotomy between natural things and phenomena, and it coincides with the dichotomy between substances and aggregates. Only among substances there is the further division between the simple and the compound. About these latter we have as yet heard nothing, and strangely the *Monadology* is silent on the subject. Readers have to do their own work here, but when the work is done they will understand that the existence of natural compound substances is ubiquitous and, indeed, ubiquitous in any world that God might have created.

The body that is a monad's own is made up of a mass of monads which, like the slab of marble or the wormy cheese, enjoys a certain kind of unity. But in these central cases the unity is supplied not by our interests and classificatory habits but by the natural world itself, by the monads, that is, whose perceptions and desires are realized through a particular shifting mass of monads being naturally distinct and distinguishable from those that surround them. The dominant monad is itself what lends unity to this mass of other monads making up its body, and its body is precisely whatever mass it is through which that dominant monad's perceptions and desires are expressed. That our desires and perceptions are expressed through a given material mass is a fact about the world and holds whether we recognize it or not, independently of our habits of mind and our classificatory interests.

If we try to think of that mass as enjoying any unity apart from that of its dominant monad, as we do when we consider a corpse once the life that animated it has left,[7] we are bound to fail. Because of the shifting pattern of its constituent simples the cadaver is not the very same collection of monads as made up the living body in its last stages, and other than that it has no unity beyond the somewhat rough-and-ready one we use to distinguish it from the earth to which it will soon return. So, as Leibniz puts it to Arnauld, a cadaver is very much an aggregative being, an *ens per aggregationem*, one with the heap of stones, the flock of sheep or the army of men, and quite unlike a genuine substance having a unity *per se*. Indeed, the temptation we have to talk of the monad's body apart from its dominant monad does not really make coherent sense. The body we have in mind can only be identified in terms of a unity that is supplied by that dominant monad, so abstracting from that monad cannot leave us with anything rightly thought of as the same body at all. All we really have in such a case is a mass of monads with a history that once involved a dominant monad, and that is not a natural unity at all.

Things are entirely different, however, when we consider the monad *together with* its body. We have seen that as long as the monad exists and is capable of perception and appetition, as all monads are,

---

7   Cf. to Arnauld, 8 December 1686 (Parkinson (ed.), 64).

it has to have its appropriately ordered organic body. What is more, since it is the monad itself that supplies the unity to the mass of monads that constitute that body, and since it can have only a single such mass, absolutely any total mass that it comes to dominate will constitute the selfsame living body, or, in the case of more developed monads, the same animal body, or human, or angelic one. In this way, the unity of the whole is a truly unbreakable one, and just as with simple substances this fact allows us to say that the whole composite organism is everlasting, is ungenerable and is imperishable. It is these claims that are defended in the exuberant and extravagant-sounding passages of §§71–7 and which can now be integrated into the systematic whole.

Monadology §77 reminds us of the natural indestructibility of the soul that we were introduced to earlier, in §4. To that is here added the natural indestructibility of the animal, which should now be fully comprehensible. No soul can perish; all souls have a body of their own as long as they last, and thus wherever there is an everlasting soul there there will be an everlasting unity of soul-cum-organic-body. Since all souls are necessarily everlasting, there could be no such composite unity that was anything less than everlasting.

Against this background Leibniz is understandably sensitive to the need to explain the nature of our mortal passage. The generation and decay of natural organisms is constantly with us. He is sure that to do so without mental discomfort we need only keep a clear head and not be misled by appearances. In the first place, the Heracleitean conception of bodies as being in constant flux serves to block the idea that for souls or monads to persist over time the body they have must consist of a stable mass of matter permanently attached to them. Identity of the composite whole is supplied not by the identity of the elements of the whole but by the continuity of the appropriate functioning of whatever subordinate monads from time to time serve as any dominant monad's body. Such continuous functioning directed by the dominant monad will readily allow it to annex to its service at different times quite different quantities of matter (§71). The appearance of death or destruction of the whole is no more than the reverse of this. When the dominant monad changes the manner of its activity, the matter that functionally subserves it also changes, and many of the monads that previously made up its body no longer do so. For all that, they do not cease to be. They are left behind much as the matter of the chrysalis is left behind when the butterfly emerges from it or when the snake sloughs off its skin. Only by force of habit and unclarity of mind we are inclined to identify the man with his living body and to think that when we come upon the dead body the man himself must have perished. However, for the reasons already given, this cannot be, so seeing things aright we are obliged say that the man or animal continues to exist despite the change that it has undergone. The truth is that the corpse is just a mass of matter that once functioned as the man's organic integument but which has now has been cast off (§77) and no longer functions as it did before. The compound substance that is the man himself lives on.

Considerations of the very same order apply to the phenomena of generation and birth. There, too, there can be no coming into existence of a naturally compounded whole, since the dominant monad of the whole we newly come upon has always existed and has always had its organic body. What is new is our coming upon the thing, not what it is we come upon. At a child's birth, the dominant monad's body takes on a new conformation, but the creature must have preexisted the material organization that is appropriate to its appetitive and perceptive activity at this new stage of its existence. Leibniz tells us that at conception all that happens is that the already existing animal 'became disposed to undergo a large transformation into an animal of a different kind' (§74), and he compares this situation to the transformations of worms (maggots, I suppose) into flies and of caterpillars into butterflies. Whether we agree with him or not, we can see now why he is led to say these strange-sounding things, and as long as we regard his speaking of an organic whole's 'becoming a new kind of animal' as no more than a way of referring to its entering another phase of a certain natural sort of life, the coherence of his view is unimpeachable.

To tidy up the detail of these dense sections we need only pick up the rejection of metempsychosis (§72) which accompanies the acceptance of metamorphosis that the Heracleitean view of body has prepared the way for. Metempsychosis, or the migration of the soul from body to body, such as is envisaged in Locke's tale of the cobbler and the prince (*Essay,* II. xxvii. 15), would require the soul to domi-nate at one time a body that was originally its own and then at another time one that was originally the body peculiarly bound to some other soul or body-dominating monad. This is impossible though, since as we have already seen we cannot identify the body that a soul domi-nates as anything other than its own. It cannot lose its own body to another monad, for its continuing existence demands that it retain its body. What can happen is that a certain quantity of matter that at one stage served as the organic body of one given dominant monad should become available to serve as the body of another. That situa-tion though is not the situation of metempsychosis. It is merely the case of a certain development and growth on the part of one organic whole and the envelopment and diminution of another with a one-way exchange of matter between them. The transmigration of souls is an absolute metaphysical impossibility.[8]

Animals and plants and men, then, are organic wholes that enjoy a real unity. On that account they qualify as substances even though they are compound ones. They also qualify by being active, for that idea is no more than the idea of being the spontaneous source of their changes of state. The body, it is true, is responsive to the desires and perceptions of its dominant monad, but those desires and perceptions are themselves formed in the light of the nature that the dominant monad has and the body with which that nature equips it. The activity of the whole can thus often be explained by reference to a concern for its own well-being, and in that it is no different from simple substances themselves and their activity. The only remaining hesita-tion I can see that Leibniz might have about thinking of such composites as genuine substances is that their material constitution is derivative and not original in the way the last chapter set out. However, I have said that to acknowledge that is not to deny them reality but merely to describe the reality that is theirs. So even if we find ourselves saying that the reality of wholes composed of simple substances and their organic bodies are themselves derived realities,

---

8 Leibniz gives a full discussion of the topic in *New Essays*. See especially *NE*, 232–5.

they are still real, they still enjoy a genuine unity *per se* and they are still fully capable of spontaneous activity.

Earlier on I asserted, maybe surprisingly, that compound substances are ubiquitously present in every world. We have everything in hand now to see why this must be. Whatever world God creates must consist of an infinite number of simple substances. Being capable of action and having perception of its world each monad is necessarily endowed with its own organic body and thus, by the argument I have just been rehearsing, enters into a composite substance. So every world contains infinite numbers of composite substances. Since every matter-containing world has to be a spatial world, and since the idea of empty space is a nonsense (cf. §68), all points in any world that God might come to create would have to be occupied, and indeed be occupied by monads that enter into material organic wholes. On the entirely reasonable assumption that the place occupied by a composite substance cannot exclude the point occupied by its dominant monad, every place in the world will be occupied by a compound substance. Compound substances, then, are not merely locally present in any world that might have come to exist: they would have been ubiquitously present in any such world.

To complete this discussion of the material world, I want to bring out two ways in which it is highly stratified. The first is a simple consequence of each monad being dominant over its own body. Let us take it that the relation of dominance is an extensional relation so that if monad *a* dominates *b* it dominates it no matter how it is described or referred to. Let us also assume that if *a* dominates *b* and also dominates *c*, it dominates the composite (*b* and *c*). We may also assume the transitivity of dominance, so that if *a* dominates *b*, and *b* dominates *c*, *a* dominates *c*. Given that bodies consist of an infinity of monads, each simple monadic substance dominates an infinity of others. Since each of these has its own body, which together with it constitutes a composite substance, every single monad must dominate an infinity of other compound substances. It will follow that in the least portion of space there is an infinity of living things or organisms. This is what we are told at §§67–8, though it is not at all clear in those sections how rigorous Leibniz sees his derivation as being. His saying in §67 that 'every portion of matter may be thought of as a garden full of plants or like a pond full of fishes' and that 'every branch of every plant, each limb of each animal, and every drop of its liquid humours is another such garden, another such pond' sounds as if it is the sort of thing that is suggested by observations made with Leeuwenhoek's microscopes and thus fully empirical. Also, of course, the reference to fish, ponds and plants has a very local ring to it. However, we should easily be able to see now that as long as we speak in terms of composite substances in general and do not attempt to specify them further, the general thought that Leibniz offers here is purely *a priori* and does not record empirical truths at all. So we may think that when (§76) he says that these '*a posteriori* reflections based on experience accord perfectly with the principles established above *a priori*', the reference is not only to the immediately preceding assertions about generation and decay, which I have already discussed, but may stretch back as far as the infinite complexities of things that are the subject of §66–7.

We can perhaps tease out just a little more from the general truth that one composite substance consists of a host of others, each one of which consists of a further such host, and this is that the desires and perceptions that animate each substance must enable it spontaneously to serve those monads which most immediately dominate it. In serving them it enables them in their turn to serve those other monads which most immediately dominate them. In this conception of the world we have something akin to a system of natural machines (cf. §64) having parts designed to keep the whole system working and whose parts are themselves designed with the specific function of maintaining the operation of the machine's principal parts. Thus if we take the human being as an example, we would expect to find it containing principal organs, such as the heart, so structured that while the heart keeps the man alive it has muscles and tissue of a kind whose proper medical understanding will show how they serve to keep the heart regularly beating and lead us to expect that the cells of blood that come to be dominated by the heart operate under its dominance to keep its muscles and tissue in good order.

This sort of structure is a better guide to the kind of stratified system that must abound in any world whatever than the rather fanciful picture Leibniz offers us (§67) of fish within fish within fish, which is hardly systematically underpinned in its detail.[9] Furthermore, it is highly suggestive about the direction in which it would be sensible to pursue empirical research into the workings of the world, because it sets out some formal constraints on the sorts of theory that we should expect to be true and which Leibniz is convinced are confirmed by observation and experiment. At the same time, we should also notice that because all bodies are in constant flux, the composite wholes that serve as hearts or blood cells and so on at any given time can be expected to change their functions as they come under the domination of different monads in the course of the development and growth or the envelopment and diminution that they undergo and which Leibniz mentions in §73. So even if the human being is bound to have a heart throughout its life we should not assume that the masses of monads that realize this function will always belong to the same higher-level composite substance. At one moment it may be that one mass of compound substances plays that cardiac role (the constant heart) and at a later time that role is taken over by a different such mass. Our tendency is to say that the man has the same heart through his life, and that is right enough when the heart is understood as a functioning part of the organism, but Leibniz would warn us against identifying whatever plays a standing and essential function in the service of a high-level organism with any given mass of lower-level compound substances which at some particular time constitutes that organism's body. He would also warn us against thinking of the functioning parts of an organism, such as the heart, as themselves being compound substances, even if compound substances are what ultimately they are made up of.[10]

The other sort of hierarchy that Leibniz talks about is the hierarchy of kinds of monad and the organic wholes that they enter into, of entelechies, souls and rational intelligences on the one hand and living things, animals and men on the other. It is a hierarchy that may

---

9 Unless this is taken diachronically, each monad being 'big with the future' (cf. *Discourse of Metaphysics* §13), though that is not how the passage reads.

10 If the heart were itself a composite substance, its dominant monad would be bound to that of the animal it served, and so on down the chain, thus making stranger composite substances than any that Leibniz envisages.

perhaps extend further to various sorts of angelic intelligence and their organic bodies and finally to God himself – who alone 'is altogether detached from body' (§72). This hierarchy of beings is quite distinct from the one I have just been discussing, since there is no *a priori* reason to assume that we men have organic bodies whose functional parts are themselves animals, or that our parts' functional parts are living things, or that we humans are dominated by organic wholes that are angels. So we can ask whether Leibniz thinks that the kind of class structure among monads he envisages reflects a reality merely of our world or whether it would be mirrored in other worlds that might have engaged God's attention in choosing which universe to create.

This question is itself ambiguous, ambiguous between whether there has to be a class structure at all and whether in other possible worlds there need be the very same kind of class structure among monads as is exemplified here. In the actual world, governed by those physical laws that obtain, it is reasonable to explain the monadic class structure in a way complementary to the explanation offered of the hierarchical functioning of compound substances themselves. There we saw that a material substance had to be composed of other substances that enabled it to realize its desires and provide it with perceptions of an appropriate kind. Now we can say that monads and the organic wholes that come with them are not self-sufficient and so depend for their well-being on the material support without which it would be impossible for them to exist and function as they do. It makes good sense therefore to suppose that, given that rational intelligences exist in the first place, there should exist also animals of one sort or another, and that for there to exist animal life there must be plant life too, and so on down a chain of species members of which are not parts of members of the higher species but do still facilitate their existence.

Given that any world God might create has to be a material world, it is natural enough to suppose that if other such worlds were to contain rational intelligences in the way ours does the physical laws that reign there could hardly be all that different from the laws that prevail here. In that case there would have to be a hierarchy of facilitating species in those other possible worlds too, in the absence of which rational intelligences and their organic bodies would fail to enjoy the sort of presence and permanence that Leibniz's metaphysics guarantees to be theirs.

If those other worlds were to contain rational intelligences ... But one might think there is absolutely no reason to suppose that every possible world is like ours in this respect. Some may surely be richer and some poorer, and in impoverished but nonetheless possible worlds there may be no class system of the kind we see here, but just a sort of basic monadic brew (consisting, of course, of complex substances, but of the very most basic sort). So one might suppose – only to think that is to think of other possible worlds as being constrained just by the Principle of Contradiction and to forget that the range of real possibilities offering themselves to God as appealing ones is subject also to Sufficient Reason. Remembering the latter principle enables us to see the matter in a quite different light.

First of all, we know from §58 that God's choice is guided by a concern for order and variety, so it looks as though a classless world will fare badly on that score in the creation stakes. However, the argument is of uncertain weight just because, for all we know, there may be other ways in which a significant degree of order and variety could be obtained under physical laws rather like ours but without the operation of a hierarchical system among species. So let us mark this reflection with a question mark. Is there anything else to which Leibniz might appeal?

We have seen the requirement that possible worlds be material to turn in part on theological considerations that Leibniz thought reason forces upon us, and we have seen too that among these is the belief that God's perfection guides his choice among logically possible worlds. One of his perfections is the desire for the best, and that the best can only be the replication as far as possible of God's own perfections – his omnipotence, his omniscience and his benevolence. The moral implications of this I can leave over to the final chapter, but this metaphysically guaranteed drive for God to replicate his own perfection in his creation will ensure that a world that failed to contain rational intelligence must be considered as a poor starter, no matter how much variety and order it might otherwise display. And there we have it, for if any world acceptable to God is bound to contain rational intelligences, then it must contain also kinds of things that make the existence and flourishing of such intelligences possible, as in our world animals and plants and lesser creatures do. So the metaphysics that is driven by the initial two Great Principles will lead us to think that all other interesting possible worlds share a hierarchically stratified structure in common with this one. Yet again we see at work the operation of what Leibniz called the fundamental maxim governing his whole philosophy and which I set at the head of Chapter 1: 'The foundations are everywhere the same'.

Further reading

Adams, Chapter 10, 'Corporeal Substance'; Rutherford, Chapter 8, 'Monads, Matter and Organisms'.

Chapter 9

Mind and body (§§78–81 and §17)

In §§78–81 Leibniz turns to the outstanding issues concerning the relation between mind and body. The situation that faces him is one he has inherited from Descartes, and he is anxious both to correct errors he sees in his predecessor's teaching and to find a way of embedding within the monadological framework such truths as Descartes himself had discerned or had come close to discerning. To understand what Leibniz proposes we should first remind ourselves of the Cartesian background.

For both philosophers there are two fundamental questions. How are mind and body united? How do mind and body interact? The answer Descartes implicitly offers to the first of these is that the union is more phenomenological than real. His answer to the second is that if they interact at all they do so by influx. Leibniz finds both of these suggestions objectionable. Consider first the issue of union. This poses an insuperable problem for Descartes. To his way of thinking, truths about the world can only be expressed by sentences predicating properties of substances that fall into two mutually exclusive classes, the class of material things and that of mental things. Any quality a material thing possesses must be some modification of the attribute *extension*; any quality a mental substance has can only be a modification of the attribute *thought*. So the body moves, weighs a few stones, exerts pressure on other bodies and bears the imprint of things that press upon it, but it does not dream, work out how to beat the traffic or ponder the ills of the world. The mind, or the thinking subject, is immaterial, weighs nothing and takes up no room, but it does reflect, harbour desire, enjoy sensation and suffer the passions. Yet all this is quite at odds with our lives as we live them. The feelings and sentiments we have are spread through the body itself so pervasively that mind and body present themselves to us as inextricably intertwined, and the interplay of the two is so intimate that we find ourselves unable to deny that together they constitute 'a substantial unity' (*Meditation* VI), a genuine whole. The trouble for Descartes is that genuine wholes are substances, and they must consequently be either minds or bodies. There is no other possibility. So any talk of a real substantial union between mind and body will be flawed at the outset. Whatever the phenomenology, the conception of the matter that Descartes is forced to, quite against his inclination, is that in relation to the body the soul or mind can in truth function in no other way than as a pilot or helmsman to the vessel he is steering to port. The ship is something utterly distinct from the pilot, who is merely a temporary and adventitious passenger aboard. Metaphysically speaking, there is and could be no union between them.

We need to appreciate how much of this story Leibniz accepts. For him, true sentences must indeed be about substances, simple or compound, or if they are not (as when we talk about human artefacts or masses of matter like the corpse of the last chapter) they will ultimately depend upon truths about substances, viz. simple ones.[1] Simple substances are thinking things, souls or minds, which have no

---

1 This will of course be true also when we speak of aggregates of compound substances, the regiment or the team or the flock of sheep. Just as the roar of the sea that we hear results from our minute perceptions of the individual waves (cf. *NE*, 54).

physical properties. Here Leibniz is in perfect agreement with Descartes. With Descartes he holds too that the organic bodies of compound substances and other physical aggregates that we encounter are extended things, which can have only physical properties and not mental ones. Only, as we know, these things are not substances, and in this he is set against Descartes. Then, as a further and most notable contrast, Leibniz recognizes the existence of compound substances that have both physical and mental properties, those living things, animals and men and so on which are the topic of §§63–77 and which I have just been discussing. So while we find endorsement of Cartesian dualism in the sharp division Leibniz makes between minds, or souls and bodies, there is at the same time a rejection of it in his recognition of utterly ubiquitous genuine substantial unities that possess both physical and mental features. Without injustice to either party we may speak of Descartes' stance as full-bloodedly dualistic and of its Leibnizian revision as mitigatedly so.

Refashioning the Cartesian story in this way gives Leibniz room to combine the phenomenological claim that pressed on Descartes with a metaphysic that allows our experience to record truths. That this should be possible is important for both thinkers, since for Descartes it must be a grave embarrassment that the clarity of the phenomenology represents a metaphysical falsehood rather than a truth. How can God be so deceitful? As for Leibniz, cast as he is in God's image, the experience that he and we have of the world must reveal it to us as it is, else we could not in our small way mirror God's omniscience. Consequently, there must indeed be a genuine union between a mind and its body. Together they comprise one real thing in that they form an unbreakable substantial compound, one that at the same time is made up of a dominant mind and a non-substantial shifting bodily aggregate of infinitely many monads in the way outlined above. Within this metaphysical framework there is nothing to stop Leibniz taking the phenomenology of experience at face value.

Emending Descartes' views in this way permits Leibniz to point out how ill-suited is the nautical simile of the pilot and his ship to express the true metaphysical position. It fails on at least four counts. First, we know from earlier discussion that the substantial body cannot even exist without a controlling mind, nor the mind without its organic body. Ships only need pilots on rare occasions, and even then the need may arise from considerations of industrial rather than metaphysical relations. If Descartes' 'pilot' is meant to be the helmsman, as is probable, the same observation will hold. The ship has to be steered, but the automatic pilot can often do the job well enough. Second, the pilot or helmsman can move freely from vessel to vessel, and the same vessel may be served by different pilots at different times. Leibniz's rejection of metempsychosis at §72 makes the point that mind and body are not so free. Third, and this comes close to the spot at which Descartes finds his own image chafing,[2] the soul's awareness of its own body must be immediate and intuitive and largely uninferred from the state it sees or feels its body to be in. Descartes himself remarks that if the image were completely apt, we would know we were wounded, not by feeling pain but by the understanding, as when the pilot sees from its erratic behaviour that something must be wrong with his ship. Leibniz would concur, and add that this is no small detail but of the very essence. The monad's knowledge of its body is necessarily direct and intuitive (cf. §62). Lastly, to be in his ship, the pilot needs to have a location, yet to Descartes' way of thinking that entails he is no more than a material thing, whereas the mind the pilot stands for in the analogy cannot be so placed. The image is inconsistent with the metaphysical position it is meant to illustrate. Nevertheless, generous as he always was to those with whom he disagreed, Leibniz might have conceded that there really is something appropriate about the simile. Two chapters back, we saw that monads must be assigned a position in a public world, namely the position in that world that defines their point of view, and that position will regularly fall within the spatial limits of their organic body. So the mind is indeed in its way in the body, like the pilot in his ship, but even so there is still this difference: Descartes' pilot has the position he does contingently; Leibniz's souls or minds are fixed within their bodies of necessity.

---

2 People sometimes forget Descartes' own words: 'Nature teaches me by these feelings of pain, hunger, thirst etc., that I am not just lodged in my body like a pilot in his ship, but besides, that I am very closely conjoined with it and so mixed up with it that together with it I form a single whole.'

Although Leibniz glancingly alludes to the topic of the unity of mind and body in §78, the anti-Cartesian stance I have just outlined is really no more than the upshot of §§62–73. What he is primarily concerned with in the present sections is not that so much as the conformity of the two, by which he means the capacity they have to interact. This is the second topic to which Descartes had an unsatisfactory response, one whose deficiency is masked by the picture of the pilot that he used to illustrate his thought. The pilot obviously enough uses physical means to direct his vessel, just as does the rider (cf. *Theodicy*, section 60) who controls his mount with reins, bridle, bit and spur. Since the Cartesian soul cannot avail itself of anything of such a material order to do its work, it is a mystery how the parts of a Cartesian 'union' can work together. Leibniz has to improve on the Cartesian story since his compound substances clearly possess functionally interactive parts, and the improvement he offers is precisely the famous doctrine of pre-established harmony that is presented to us in §§78–81. We are led there by reflecting on just what is amiss with Descartes' own proposal.

When Descartes considered the way we move our bodies, and thereby move physical things in the world beyond, he hypothesized a power of the will to change the direction of movement of the little understood, seemingly functionless, pineal gland buried deep within the skull. The will's effect on the gland radiates out through the whirling vortices of material globules that constitute the body and brings about changes of the kind that are to be explained. Obviously there is a danger of regress here. How does the will exert its immaterial power over the material gland? By its control of the 'animal spirits'. But are those 'spirits' material or immaterial? If the latter, how do they affect the material gland? If the former, how does the will control them? Leibniz does not press the issue of regress, though, since he has a farther-reaching objection, which he states at §80. Behind that objection lies yet another which prepares the way for his own answer to the question.

For Descartes, one attraction of the pineal gland explanation was that as well as finding a credible function for the mysterious bodily organ it appeared to answer the methodological need to respect physical conservation laws. When I decide to stand up and walk about the room, it might look as though by the exercise of my will I inject movement into the world that was not previously present. That Descartes thinks is impossible, since the quantity of motion that the world contains is constant. The pineal gland, however, does incessantly wave about, and on Descartes' understanding of things the way the will impinges upon it is by harnessing the direction of its movement to bring about changes in the body down the line. So quantity of movement is left unchanged; only its direction is altered. Leibniz's explicit criticism in §80 is that while Descartes' heart is in the right place he is simply mistaken in thinking that his explanation does respect the ruling conservation laws. The truth is that in the physical world both quantity and direction of movement are conserved, so that the picture of the will controlling the direction of the gland's waving is as intolerable as Decartes knew its producing changes in the quantity of movement would be. Given his methodological soundness, Descartes would not have stuck to his story if he had got his science right.

We need not pause over the detail of Leibniz's science here because it is plain that what underlies Descartes' struggle with the problem is a twofold conceptual error that no amount of good physics could dispel. The first is that in the name of causal efficacy something (be it quantity or direction of movement, or even something quite different) is being passed over from mind (in the guise of Will) to body (in the guise of Gland), and that is not possible even within the mitigated form of dualism that Leibniz embraces, let alone in Descartes' own full-blooded version. Nothing can be passed from mind to body any more than properties can be passed from one thing to another anyway.[3] In the Cartesian story the nonsense is compounded by the fact that the players involved are constitutionally incapable of receiving the only kind of property that the other party can possess. The pineal gland story is patently at odds with the metaphysics that Descartes espouses.

---

3 This is not to deny that material things can gain and lose parts from one another. Parts and properties are not the same, and Leibniz's animadversions against 'transitive' causation bear on the transfer of properties, not of parts, though of course where we are concerned with simples a transfer of parts will be impossible anyway.

That last point is merely *ad hominem*. It tells against Descartes, but it does not tell against Leibniz or against the mitigated dualism that is his. What is really wrong with it is not that Descartes is supposing there to be causal interaction between substances of different kinds, but that the interaction there really is effected by the transfer of properties from one party to the other. This is the second of the conceptual errors mentioned above. We have already seen in discussion of §7 that monads have no windows and doors and that any 'transitive' conception of causation is an out-and-out nonsense (see Chapter 4 above). If only that muddle can be avoided it will be possible to find a place for mind–body interaction, and indeed find room for it within a mitigatedly dualistic metaphysics like that of the *Monadology*. The pre-established harmony of §§78–81, so often seen as a metaphysical rabbit extracted from the magician's hat, really arises from the need to avoid any such rubbish as this and, as Leibniz says, if Descartes had only seen what was wrong with his own proposal, meaning thereby not just the way his appeal to the pineal gland flouted the going conservation laws but indeed the incoherence of his conception of causation, he would easily have found his own way to it.

All that we have been told about causation in earlier sections, however, has been negative in character. A 'transitive' account of causation is incoherent, and occasionalistic appeal to God's miraculous interference in the detailed working of things is unreasonable. The present sections, discussing the harmony between the realms of mind and matter, provide the positive doctrine that we have been waiting for. Once the other two options have been ruled out, the solution here proposed is all that remains. In point of fact Leibniz is scarcely forthcoming at this juncture. All he explicitly tells his reader is that when we say one event causes another, the monads involved are doing no more than developing according to their natures and in such a way that there is harmony between them. As the 'New System' put it:

> God first created the soul, and every other real unity, in such a
> way that everything in it must spring from within itself, by a
> perfect *spontaneity* with regard to itself, and yet in a perfect
> *conformity* with things outside.... It follows from this that ...
> there will be a perfect agreement between all these substances,

producing the same effect as would occur if they communicated with one another by means of a transmission of species or qualities, as the common run of philosophers maintain.[4]

Although the corresponding passage of the *Monadology* is concerned with mind–body interaction and speaks of a harmony between the two realms, we see here that Leibniz is proposing a quite general account of interaction between substances of whatever kind, between derived realities as much as between simples and also between simple substances and derived realities. So the question of causation between mind and body is no more than a special case of the general theory. That is an added reason not to view the appeal to pre-established harmony as an *ad hoc* device designed merely to deal with a troubling issue in the philosophy of mind.

This is not the place to discuss the merits of regularity accounts of causation, of which Leibniz's is one of the first (pre-dating Hume's by fifty years or more). Apart from anything else, the very sketchiness of Leibniz's offering makes that unprofitable. However, we do glean enough from his texts to see how well the general theory lends itself to incorporation within the general metaphysic and how, once incorporated there, it smoothly handles the problem of mind–body interaction and their mutual conformity, which it is introduced at §78 to handle. What we do have to do here, though, is to persuade ourselves that the doctrine of pre-established harmony is not inconsistent with the overall aspirations of monadological theory.

One worry we may have is this. If causal relations are ultimately no more than instances of harmonious regularities between monads as they develop according to God-given laws, should we not say that these relations are symmetrical rather than asymmetrical or nonsymmetrical, as we tend to think? If the truth of '*A* causes *B*' depends on the harmonious co-ordination of monads, then because the *B*-constituting individuals are as harmoniously co-ordinated with the *A*-constituting ones as the other way round, we have no better reason to say *A* causes *B* than that *B* causes *A*. This question is entirely general, but it has a particular importance in its application to

---

4 Parkinson (ed.), 122–3.

Leibniz's philosophy of mind since, if correct, it would encourage him to say that the domination of the body by the mind, as attested in our power of action, is no better grounded than domination of the mind by the body. That is, the organic structure of compound substances which marks such an advance over the Cartesian conception of the natural world appears to be in danger of collapsing into a phenomenology that is at odds with reality itself. No philosophy could face a more bitter defeat than that.

The problem did not go unnoticed by Leibniz. At different times he has different responses to it. In a draft letter to Arnauld of December 1686, he simply accepts the symmetry point and says that when we consider a phenomenon like a moving ship's wake 'in strict metaphysical precision we have no more reason to say that the ship pushes the water to produce the large number of circles which serve to fill up the place of the ship than to say that the water is caused to produce all those circles and that it causes the ship to move accordingly'.[5] Just because God's decisions about what happens in the world are not made with respect to particulars but only in regard of the whole, just because he does not, say, create Eve in order to supply Adam with help meet for him, failing which poor Adam would be comfortless, but instead chooses a whole universe containing both comforted Adam and comforting Eve, no unidirectional causal dependencies make sense. Rather we have to explain our willingness to discern causal asymmetries in terms of our ability to provide simple explanations for the phenomena we observe. Thus it is that we tend to project our own biased sensitivities to dependencies between things onto the world itself in ways that misrepresent it. As Leibniz puts it in another paper of the same period: 'Causes are assumed, not from a real influx, but from the need to give an explanation.'[6]

Ten years later, though, he appears to have changed his mind, and so much the better for the project of matching the phenomenology of mind to the underlying reality. In the 'New System' we are told that

---

5   Ibid., 64.
6   'A Specimen of Discoveries about Marvellous Secrets' (c. 1686), in Parkinson (ed.), 79.

[w]hen we find the particular disposition of a given substance is the explanation of a change taking place in an intelligible manner, so that we can infer that it is to this substance that the others have been adjusted in this regard from the beginning, in accordance with the order of the decrees of God, then that substance ought to be conceived of as *acting* on the others.[7]

This passage plainly supposes that when we find an explanation of B in terms of A satisfying on account of its power and simplicity then there is some truth about the created monads that that reflects and that we do not just have to do with a misleading projection of our minds onto the world. Thus the directionality of causation is preserved not as a projection but as a reality that the mind is often enough well able to recognize. For the preservation of the dominance of mind over body, this is all to the good, but we have to ask whether it really commits Leibniz to giving up his conception of the holistic nature of God's creative choice. Certainly he thought it had that consequence when he wrote to Arnauld, but maybe that was not forced upon him.

At heart, the proposal that Leibniz can be seen to make here is that A causes B when A and B are instances of regularities among monads of a kind such that if A had not occurred B would not have occurred. If the only source of anxiety about the proposal is that it involves God in indecorous concern for the fate of individual monads and as making adjustments to the system so that the favoured few are privileged at the expense of others – as when Adam is supplied with Eve to the detriment of his rib because otherwise things would just have got out of hand – then Leibniz need not worry. Perhaps he sees that he need not worry, since in the earlier period he would not have asserted the counterfactual. After all, it is perfectly consistent with God's making a choice of a whole world at the moment of creation that the totalities that are most satisfactory from the point of view of variety and orderliness (cf. §58) should be worlds which display asymmetrical dependencies. To choose a world in which regularities hold of kinds that make it true that if A had not happened B would not have

---

7   Parkinson (ed.), 124–5.

happened, but not vice versa, is not to choose a world in which God has to intervene occasionalistically from time to time to keep things on the rails or to rectify what would otherwise be an unfortunate oversight. Unidirectional causal dependencies can obtain throughout worlds which present themselves as fully specific possibilities for God's selection or rejection when the crucial decision is made about which world to create. To recognize this is to make way for the possibility of the domination of mind over body being a metaphysical reality as well as a phenomenological one. A major disaster is thus averted.

To be content with this way of handling the issue we have to be sure also that it allows Leibniz to say, as he does at §81, that 'bodies act as if there were (*per impossibile*) no souls, and that souls act as if there were no bodies, and both act as if the one influenced the other'. If we suppose him to hold that when *A* causes *B*, *B* would not have occurred but for *A*, can he also claim that *B* would have happened spontaneously in the working out of its nature even if *A* had not existed? Paradoxical though it may appear, the answer is 'Yes'. All that §81 is claiming is that the various states that *A* and *B* display are rooted in their own nature, so that all change comes from within and not by any so derided 'influx'. This insistence on the spontaneity of change is simply made graphic by saying that (in the case of mind–body interaction) it is *as if* (my emphasis) the body were unaccompanied by the soul. But what is put in this graphic and hypothetical way is not inconsistent with the claim that in actuality the spontaneous development of monads *A* and *B* is such that if the change in *A* had not come about there would have been no change in *B*. That second thought, captured in our everyday speech by saying that *A* causes *B*, records a certain order among the spontaneous development of individual monads. Spontaneity of development and harmonious co-ordination fit happily together. This is precisely the virtue of the system of pre-established harmony, and one sure source of Leibniz's understandable pride in it.

A second hesitation arising out of the application of the harmony proposal to the mind–body issue is that in the case of different monads perceiving the same event – and we know from §56 that this is a universal phenomenon – it would seem that the relation that holds between the representation in the mind of *A* is as much caused by what happens in the body of *B* as it is by what happens in its own body. That is, *A* wouldn't have had the perception it did unless its own body had been affected as it was, but then neither would it have had that perception unless *B*'s body were affected as it was. If this is right, then it will appear that the harmony between my soul and my body is no closer than that between my soul and others' bodies, and that Leibniz's contention at §62 that each soul has a body that is peculiarly its own is under threat, and with it the union of mind and body that he had putatively saved from the Cartesian abyss.

By now we shall expect the Leibnizian response to draw on the differential clarity that affects monads' several perceptions of the same thing. From your point of view a perceived event presents itself rather differently than it presents itself to me or to any other monad. So it might be thought that while there is a regular harmony between my perceptual representations and the impressions made on my body by the perceived world, there is not the same harmony between my representations and the impact made by the represented events on your body. But whether or not there is the same harmony, isn't there a harmony all the same, and is not that enough? Won't it be that unless there is the impression made on *B*'s body *A* won't represent the event in question? The answer must be that *that* indeed is true enough. Given that things are as they are, there is no way that monad *A* can represent to itself a perceived event without that event impinging both on its body and the body of its friend, monad *B*. Only it does not follow from this that *A* would only have represented that event if *B* had been affected, for that supposes that *B* would have represented the event in question (and have represented it just as it did) no matter what things had been like, and given Leibniz's concern (cf. §33) to allow for the occurrence of contingent truths of fact, he can well point out that there might have been situations in which *A* would have perceived the event but *B* would not, or else would have perceived it more or less distinctly than in fact he did. *B* might not have existed after all, or have been blind, or have perceived the event from such a great distance that it would have presented him with a very different representation than in fact it did. So Leibniz can quite happily deny the counterfactual that is suggested and insist that this is consistent with our accepting the mirror thesis of §56. All that thesis commits him to is that any event will impinge on the organic bodies of all monads with the degree of clarity that their nature and point of view in fact determine. There is ample room there to envisage possible circumstances in which *A* represents a perceived event as it does without the event impinging on *B*'s body as it in fact does. The doctrine of pre-established harmony can coexist with the mirror thesis without threatening the activity of the monad at the point at which that impinges on the mind–body issue.

With these remarks made about Leibniz's positive account of causation and the conformity of the two realms of final and efficient causes – the realms, that is, of mind and matter – we can look back and see how monadological theory supplies answers to pressing questions both about the union of soul and body and about their conformity that cannot but leave Cartesians perplexed. I pick out four in particular, two on each count.

1   Arising out of the material about substantial union, there is no question of the mind being just contingently situated within the body. By this I mean not just that every mind has to be conjoined with a body, but that this *I* (cf. §30) has to be conjoined with *this* very body. Nothing could be done (even by God) to unite this mind with another body, nor to supply this body with a different mind. But care must be taken: for the latter impossibility does not exclude the mass of monads that served the dominant monad that is me at one moment coming to serve a dominant monad which is you at another. In such a situation the strong temptation would be to think that we have there the same body now serving two different masters. However, we have seen that for Leibniz this is ruled out by the fact that the identity of the body is given by its dominant monad, so when the same bodily mass of monads comes to serve you instead of serving me it no longer makes up the same body, as before, even if it is just the same collection of simple substances (cf. the same collection of cells). Likewise, when a person is supplied with replacement body parts, enabling him to regain clear perception or some other bodily function, he won't have acquired a new body (no matter how extensive the prosthetic surgery may be). What will have happened is that his original body remains, but

augmented by the adjunction of new matter.

2   Descartes would not be able to say why a person might not have several bodies either at once, or serially. If the soul is just contingently connected to its body then it is contingent that it is not connected to several. For Leibniz this cannot be, because any body that serves me is mine, and no matter how spread around its constituents are, they can make up only one. If we ask Leibniz why I might not compete with you for the same body of matter, as the Cartesian self might do, his answer will be that a material mass of monads could constitute your organic body and mine only if they were controlled immediately from two different points of view (however minimal the difference between them). That, however, would be enough to ensure that different quantities of matter were in question, which the supposition excludes. The same reflection provides further grounds for Leibniz to deny the possibility of my having two distinct functioning bodies, for to direct them from a point of view that makes them immediately dominated by me I would have to enjoy several different positions at the same time. Of course I can *indirectly* control different bodies at the same time – think of the general of an army or the captain of a cricket team – but what is in question here is not that but whether I could control two bodies directly and immediately. There the Leibnizian answer must be 'No', and in this case, as in the others, it is the Leibnizian answer that marches with our intuitions.

3   Drawing now on the reflections about the conformity of mind and body, Leibniz can raise the question where the limits of my body lie. His answer will most probably be that they fall (roughly) at the point at which I no longer have direct control of it. Whatever adjustment may be needed to the suggestion, it is plain that it derives from his overall conception of compound substances. For their activity is of their essence, and activity requires spontaneous control. Even if Descartes were to say the same thing, for him that could be no more than an empirical observation. For Leibniz its roots lie deep in the metaphysic.

Some adjustment to the suggestion is needed, though, since we want to count our blood or our hair as part of our body, and our control of these parts of ourselves is indirect rather than immediate. One option available to Leibniz is to say that, direct control on one side, these bodily parts will belong to the body as long as the monads that go to make them up systematically serve the well-being of the dominant monad, the self. Of course, we are liable to make mistakes about just what body of matter does serve the soul from time to time, so here he can acknowledge that it may not be easy to use the suggestion in making accurate fine cuts. We are ignorant maybe, but that does not prevent the suggestion from providing the framework of a good answer where the Cartesian philosophy has none.

4   A final question to which Descartes would have no reply is why it should be that the body we have has the configuration that it does. The pilot in his vessel has no influence over the configuration of the vessel it is his job to steer to port. For Leibniz it must be quite other: the mass of monads that each of us dominates takes the form it does just because of the appetitions and perceptions that we are liable to have as a matter of our nature. We see the world as we are bound to do, and seeing it in that way is already to see it through the eyes of a body of a certain kind. We have learnt from the *Monadology*'s early sections that the way we see the world and the sorts of desires we have are matters for the spontaneously developing nature of a particular dominant monad – so having those perceptions and desires requires that we have the sort of body that we do. Moreover, as our perceptions and desires change and develop, so our body changes and develops too. That is the process of enlargement and shrinking of which Leibniz speaks at §73.

Is it necessary that we have the type of body that we do? Perhaps not, for Leibniz does sometimes envisage the possibility of our mental lives being other than in fact they are. However, that is not the most interesting point: rather it is, given that we have desires and perceptions of the sorts we do, that we are bound to have the kinds of body that we do. There is even a point in *New Essays* at which Leibniz comments on the science-fiction of his day and reflects that about other worlds 'one could say, more or less, that as in Harlequin's lunar empire, it is "just like here"'.[8] In particular, given that we are (for some stretch of time at least) intelligent souls, then we must have human bodies, for it is they and they alone that express the rational function of the mind in a world subject to those physical laws that govern the material world that is ours. Possibly in other worlds, where the lesser monads have different sorts of bodies than do the simple entelechies of our world, intelligent souls could within narrow limits take on a different bodily form. After all, we should not expect visitors from other galaxies or different planetary systems to be like us in all respects. So, perhaps Leibniz should say that whatever they are like, we must expect them to be similar to us in having bodies that express their intellectual capacities. Textually, §63 makes the point that having a body with a given form brings with it mental capacities. It is line with this thought that Leibniz tells us that the physical conception of the human being is the expression of a change of status of the pre-existing soul (cf. §74), and thus we 'are elevated to the rank of reason and to the prerogative of minds' (§82). At the moment of the body's conception the soul comes to have an executive and mental capacity that previously it did not possess. Not that Leibniz would suppose the soul could already recite its multiplication tables in the womb, but that as the whole that has then come to be conceived grows and develops it will have capacities of the sort that would be needed to perform that modest task and which, prior to its acquisition of the new bodily form it has taken on, it used to lack. Such ideas, which cannot but put us admiringly in mind of Wittgenstein's observation that the human body is the best picture of the human soul (cf. *Philosophical Investigations* II, iv), would have been quite beyond the range of Cartesian thought.

At the heart of our modern dissatisfaction with the erection of Cartesian dualism lies its unargued and entirely question-begging

---

8   *NE*, 472. The reference is to a comedy by Nolant de Fatouville, *Arlequin, empereur de la lune* (1693). One scene retails various details of human customs and has the moon's inhabitants comment each time: 'Just like here'.

assumption that no subject can possess both physical and mental features. Descartes does not propose this as a truth of logic, and the claim certainly is not an analytic one, true in virtue of the meaning of the words used to state it. For him, it holds as a metaphysical necessity, yet of that no untendentious proof is ever offered. Not unnaturally, when we turn to Leibniz's philosophy of mind we want to know whether he does any better than Descartes at this point, not of course in arguing that nothing can possess features of both kinds but in his assumption that material things cannot think except through the agency of the simple monadic substances that dominate them (when they do). Even if we were prepared to accept the existence of simple substances of the Leibnizian variety, we might still want to ask why there should not also be bodies of matter that had perception and desire much as monads themselves do.

The nearest Leibniz comes to addressing that issue is in §17, where he argues that perception could not be explained mechanically and that it – and, one takes it, any other sort of mental activity – could not be accounted for in terms of figure and movement. We are brought to see this by reflecting that there is a sort of absurdity in imagining a large machine such as a windmill that is driven by mechanical processes and yet which thinks and feels and perceives. Its workings could easily and completely be surveyed by someone who entered the machine and inspected what was going on, but from the observations he or she made there would not be the slightest reason to suppose that the machine had a mental life. Similarly with the brain.

The passage is revealing. It does not purport to show, as the Cartesians would have it, that there is a contradiction in the idea of thinking matter. On that topic Leibniz is quite explicit in the Preface to the *New Essays*, that God could 'by miracle' add thought to bare matter should he choose to do so. But in doing that he would be abandoning reason, since he would be imposing superfluous change on a world that he already had the best of reasons to create and thus to regard as incapable of improvement in the state in which it is.

The underlying assumption here appears to be that the properties things have under the reign of Sufficient Reason they are bound to have naturally and without the need for occasional divine interference, and that the test for naturalness is that the possession of these

203

properties should be derivable from the laws under which the objects fall, together with an adequate understanding (a clear idea) of the things in question. Having that clear idea and knowing the laws, if we are so fortunate, will enable us to bring them under those laws and thus provide an explanation of their being as they are. If they did not fit within this pattern, we should fall short of the understanding and knowledge that our small-scale likeness to God guarantees us.

How does this bear on the question whether matter can think? The answer is that, according to Leibniz, we are assured of two things which rule that out as a natural possibility. The first is that the laws that govern the material world are known by us to be mechanical laws. I have suggested even that they are laws that for Leibniz define the very notion of what matter is. Second, we have a clear enough idea of concepts such as *perception* and *appetition* and *feeling* to appreciate that they cannot be distinctly grasped in such a way as to bring them under mechanical laws. Hence matter cannot naturally think. Such would be a fully Leibnizian way of handling the topic, and one that we find revealed most plainly at the end of the Preface to the *New Essays*, in a passage I quoted at the end of Chapter 1. However little it might satisfy us today, it will at least impress us by providing an answer to the question that Descartes simply begged in this area and providing it in a way that is fully integrated within Leibniz's theologico-metaphysical system.

Without pausing over the more obvious weaknesses – we know the laws of matter are not those of classical mechanics, more likely approaching the schemata of quantum electro-dynamics; we don't expect every feature of the physical world to admit of conceptualization that brings it directly under the prevailing natural laws – it is reasonable to ask whether the train of thought I have outlined does really allow Leibniz to escape the charge that he, no less than Descartes, has ultimately begged the crucial question in his own favour. One way in which it might be supposed he has done so is in the confidence he has that the phenomena of thought cannot be reduced to 'figures or motions' (or whatever we find to replace them, at the end of the day). Now it is certainly true that beyond saying (§17) that going into the imaginary windmill or robot we should not see anything that would explain a perception Leibniz says nothing to the point. But it would be quite natural for him to draw upon the thought that is already in play, that simple imperishable and unextended substances do think, desire and feel and that it is of their essential nature not to fall within physical laws that govern the behaviour of the extended world. Once we have the unextended simples in place, which is presupposed by the existence of aggregates, there is an *a priori* route to the unamenability of thought to recruitment to whatever laws apply to the extended material world.

Suppose someone were to object that that only tells us about the thought processes of simples. Nothing whatever rules out the possibility that there should be thought of a different kind, distinctly and clearly understandable in ways that make it attributable to material aggregates. It is simply question-begging for Leibniz to close his eyes to such a possibility or to rule it out by pointing to a species of mental phenomenon which is obviously at odds with that. In reply, Leibniz could say that by 'thought' we mean *thought*, and that the whole *Monadology* has made it plain that what we bring under that term is the thought of simples. That phenomenon cannot attach to aggregates, and when we apply the idea to compound substances we do so entirely derivatively from its application to their simple dominant monads. Whether other phenomena than perception, desire and feeling might apply to aggregates and bear some resemblance to thought proper is an open question, maybe; but in our world there is no reason to think that such a phenomenon exists, and even if it did that would not give us any reason to suppose that matter might naturally *think* .

But, one might ask, is not the question begged even further back? Is it not begged at the point at which Leibniz has seen fit to make the existence of matter itself dependent on thinking immaterial substances? It may not be fair to say that the question is begged, but at all events Leibniz has everything that he might need to be able to raise it once more in a way that runs quite counter to the line of thought that he had pursued over many years. The crucial issue can be put in terms of one further reflection about the Cartesian image of the pilot and his ship.

Consider the observation, made in Leibniz's name some pages back, that the pilot can serve many vessels, whereas the mind must constantly dominate one and the same body. It might have occurred to the reader that the objection would not have arisen if the pilot were taken not so much as the individual man employed to steer the ship safely to port as a *role* that has to be performed in the good conduct of an operating ship. For each ship something must play the role of pilot or steersman, and there is no question that the role can be detached from the ship and moved around from one vessel to another like the shipping company's employees.

In all likelihood Leibniz would not have thought that this idea could serve him, since its employment to help us think about the mind would involve us in treating the dominant monads of compound substances as functions that organize bare matter, and then it would seem to him that the basic unities out of which matter has been constructed would be lost. But is this really so? The ultimate need for simple immaterial unities arose from the need to introduce things that are truly *one*, and hence truly exist. *Ens et unum convertuntur* was the predominant marching song, for reasons made out in Chapter 3. Yet in the last two chapters we have seen how true unity is possessed not only by simple substances but by organic compounds. So Leibniz ought to be able to ask himself whether the dominant monads of those compounds might not be treated as irreducible functions in terms of which a body of matter finds its unity. Thus, for example, a living thing is a body of matter that so functions as to regulate itself for the sake of preserving a particular kind of active existence; a thermostat is a body of matter so organized to keep a body of matter within a selected range of temperatures, and so on. In cases like these, the unity of the whole is supplied not by a dominant monad but by the function that organizes the behaviour of the matter involved and determines what material can and what can not be incorporated in the unity that it provides.

Pursued to the very end, the suggestion is nothing other than that once Leibniz has seen how to make room for composite substances in a way that does justice to the world as he and we know it, he has everything in hand to abandon the assumption that seems so natural at §2 – the assumption that there must be simple substances because there are compounds. Of course, he did not abandon it, but we can surely say that if he had taken full advantage of the thought that allows him to recognize compounds, he could well have gone on to ask whether the unity that is allegedly provided by their dominant monads is at base anything more than the unity they enjoy in virtue of their matter functioning in a particular way.[9] At that point, the question whether matter can think takes on a lease of life that Leibniz believed it could not have.[10] Perhaps not taking that final step is not exactly to have begged the burning question, but at the very least by not taking it Leibniz prevented himself from asking it in a way that invites what must appear to be an entirely unexpected answer.

Further reading

Russell, Chapter 12, 'Soul and Body'; Rutherford, Chapter 10, 'Corporeal Substance and Soul–Body Union'; Hidé Ishiguro, 'Pre-established Harmony *versus* Constant Conjunction: A Reconsideration of the Distinction between Rationalism and Empiricism', in A. Kenny (ed.) *Rationalism, Empiricism and Idealism* (OUP, 1986), 61–85.

---

9 Certainly the construction of matter itself then needs to be reconsidered, but if compound substances were to move centre-stage and play the role that Leibniz thought could only fall to the lot of monads, matter could itself be introduced early on as that of which the true unities of the world are made up. In a way, the idea is not quite as alien to Leibniz as it might seem, since on his view the organs of the body should be identified in terms of functions that are fulfilled by a constantly shifting pattern of monads together with their organic bodies. It is little more than a reversal of this same idea to suppose that the dominant monad itself is a function that gives unity to a gross corporeal substance composed of a changing body of cellular elements.

10 If we distinguish sharply between the question 'What does this mass of matter do?' (the question of function) and 'How does it do it?' (the question of execution), Leibniz's insistence on assimilating all matter-involving concepts to determinations of figure and motion in the pursuit of distinctness of our ideas must be rejected. Function is not to be reduced to execution.

Chapter 10

Spirits and the moral order (§§82–90)

Until we reach the last few sections of the *Monadology* the world that God creates is presented in terms that are morally quite neutral.[1] Although we know it is as perfect as can be given the inevitable limitations of its finitude, the relevant idea of perfection has been officially rehearsed as a simple maximization of variety and order (§58). The realization of such a maximum is just an engineering problem, albeit a complicated one. Not for nothing is God spoken of as the divine architect or 'architect of the machine of the universe' (§§84, 87, 89) and his creation thought of as a sort of gigantic artefact. What is entirely lacking is any thought that in his choice of a perfect world God might have made special provision for the well-being of its constituent substances, in particular for the well-being of those that attain to the rank of spirits—intelligent creatures capable of self-conscious reflection and of reason. In the light

---

1 Though the world's creation is a matter of God's goodness, not just his wisdom (cf. *Theodicy*, section 228).

of material discussed so far, Leibniz's doctrine that ours is the best world there could have been might encourage us to admire and hold in awe God's ingenuity in engineering the harmonious and lawlike interplay between the realms of mind and body, but also to reprove his apparent lack of concern for the way his rich and varied choice bears upon the spirits he has brought into existence. War, dearth, age, agues, tyrannies, despair, law and chance all slay mercilessly, and when the accusation is raised that these are hardly the works of a caring God it is scarcely satisfactory to be told that they nonetheless add to the order and variety of things and are living proof of the creator's wonderful wisdom (*scilicet*, his admirable engineering skill).

The final sections of the *Monadology* address the issue. They do so in a seemingly conventional way, but while this may disappoint the hasty reader who will find them rather piously appended to the rest, for Leibniz himself they grow naturally out of the metaphysic already in place and are anything but superficially tacked on to the foundational material. For him they are the culmination of the whole and that to which the rest has been leading. Seeing the apparently conventional ethical thought as an integral part of the rest gives it a weight and an impact that it could not have by itself. In this final chapter I concentrate on the studied continuity between the metaphysics and the moral theology. As we go along I try to show that a purely conventional reading of these passages does not do best justice to Leibniz's thought.

We know by now that no possible world could contain only bare monadic substances. There have to be compound substances too, and in any world that might be a serious candidate for God's creative choice among them must be embodied spirits, that is, creatures having the powers of reason and reflection. In the previous chapter I envisaged the argument being taken further than this. Given that the hierarchical structure of the world was driven by the orthodox theological idea that in his creation God replicates his own perfections, Leibniz can conclude that there may well be an orderly sequence of spirits that approximate more and more closely to God in character, an order of beings in which we humans are merely one of the more lowly kinds. The *Principles of Nature and Grace* speaks of 'minds, whether of men or superhuman spirits'[2], even if the *Monadology* makes no mention of any such created beings.

There is no particular difficulty about fitting the higher spirits, if such there be, into the systematic framework. We may locate them in parts of the world to which we have no access (for Leibniz, the moon, the sun and so forth); alternatively, we can think of them as earthly beings standing to us and our organic bodies in the very same relation in which we stand to the monadic aggregates of which we humans are the dominant and super-dominant monads. The dominated aggregates have reasonably clear knowledge of their own organic bodies (even superhuman spirits could not do without them: cf §72), but little or no (conscious) awareness of the substances that are hierarchically superior to them. Analogously, we may be dominated by higher spirits and even be parts of their organic bodies without being clearly aware of them as long as we remain human and do not pursue a course of existence that takes us to a position higher in the hierarchy than that which we now occupy. Leibniz does not need to be specific here, merely to allow for such a possibility lying beyond our ken. But he does have to say something about how spirits, human or superhuman, come to be, and that is the theme he addresses at §82, picking up the earlier discussion at §§74–5, which I touched on briefly before.

The problem Leibniz faces is that we are liable to see the generation of spirits and human minds as new creations. That seems to threaten the idea that God's unique miraculous work lies at the original creation of the world and that the substances he then elected for existence, be they simple or compound, are everlasting. Everything else that happens lies within the natural order. Accordingly, souls of whatever nature have existed from the beginning, in which case the conception of the child cannot be the physical manifestation of a new spiritual existence. The solution to the problem that is proposed at §82, and on which I commented above, is that some souls – which were up to a certain moment merely low-caste, 'sensitive', beings – acquire at some pre-ordained time the power to reason and to be self-conscious. Correspondingly, their already existing organic bodies take on a new form to give these novel powers expression. In our case, the

---

2   At §15 of *PNG* (Parkinson (ed.), 202).

form is that of the human body; in the case of yet higher spirits, we can't say just what form they will take, but in principle the same can be said of them as of us. Whatever it is like, the new shape the body takes on will arise quite naturally from the mingling of monadic material (say, at the moment of physical conception) in the usual Heracleitean way we have come to expect.

At §74 Leibniz mentions, without explicitly endorsing, the contemporary scientific idea, suggested by observations made with microscopes, that seeds contain seeds within them. How otherwise could the seed give rise to the tree that bears fruit? This, he says, suggests that the animal itself is present before conception, and that that event merely prepares it to become a different kind of animal. However, that picture does not really fit what he must think goes on. If we are talking about the soul, that cannot contain anything (let alone another soul), for it is simple and has no parts. If we are concerned with the organic body, that will indeed at any given time contain other organic bodies (indeed, even whole living animals, organic bodies together with their souls), but there is no good reason to think that the animals and other living things my body contains at any time must be my progeniture. The Heracleitean nature of things may involve animals moving from one body through a series of others in the course of their history. Since 'the animal and the soul begin with the world itself' (§82), it is not clear just what the notion of 'progeniture' comes to anyway. At best we would be talking about the source of the material out of which the organic body of a monad comes to consist when that monad attains the rank of spirit (*mutatis mutandis* for the progeniture of lesser animals). Certainly, if we follow Leibniz's thought through in all consistency we must abandon the notion that our parents are the true creators of a new spirit and that they produce a body that did not exist before their intercourse. The monad that is me or you has always existed and has always had its own body.

One may want to ask whether a monad that has attained to the rank of spirit can ever forfeit that status, as a man may be stripped of his knighthood or other honorific title. There is no contradiction in this idea as long as the monad persists and still perceives and is active. Empirically speaking, it certainly looks as if Leibniz should say that monads change their bodies in ways that render them incapable of exercizing the spiritual powers they once had, and that they then sink back to the state of souls or even bare monads. That is not mandatory, though, and it may be contrary to divine wisdom to choose a world in which a monad having once attained the status of spirit is then deprived of it. The loss to the world of some spirit is a loss of some small perfection, and the presumption is that that would be a retrograde step unless the loss were made good elsewhere by something that gave rise to greater overall gain. While the *Monadology* says nothing to the point, a letter to Arnauld in October 1687 is explicit that minds must 'keep their personality and their moral qualities to the end that the City of God may not lose any person'.[3] If that doctrine is underwritten by Sufficient Reason, as it seems to be, we can expect it to hold in any world that might be a serious candidate for God's creative choice, and not just in ours.

Once this last point is built into the system it will follow that not all monads can become spirits. For any spirit must have an organic body naturally adapted to it, and in the case of the lowest order of spirits in this world, human beings, their organic bodies are largely made up of mere souls or bare monads. So however close one gets to the end of time there will be monads that have never been spirits. That seems to be a condition of the existence of the spiritual hierarchy itself, and one might wonder whether this does not introduce an unacceptable injustice into the system. At §75 Leibniz goes so far as to speak of there being relatively few, just the elect, who 'play a greater role' (meaning, I take it, as minds and therefore members of the community of spirits, the City of God), and it may seem as though the notion of gratuitous election involves some unfairness in granting to some monads a boon that is gratuitously withheld from others. If that were the right way to view it, then it would be a little hazardous for Leibniz to view the City of God as 'the most perfect state possible, under the most perfect of monarchs' (§85).

That conclusion is not forced on him, however, although maybe the term 'elect' (*Elûs*) that he uses to speak of spirits is not the happiest choice of expression. God chooses the best world he can: it contains only so many spirits, monads having the path of intellect

---

3   Parkinson (ed.), 74 (*GP* II, 125).

inscribed upon them. Of no monad that conforms to another pattern can we ask why did it not fall to it to have different powers from the ones bestowed on it. On one quite Leibnizian way of thinking, its very identity is given by the powers it has, so the supposition that it might have been chosen to be a spirit, but in fact was not so chosen, makes no sense. But, to the extent that Leibniz is prepared to entertain such counterfactual questions as 'Why wasn't I created with other powers than the ones I actually have?',[4] the answer is given in terms of the subordination of the individual to the interests of the whole. If the whole is better for the individual having just those properties that it does have, however personally unsatisfactory that might be for the individual concerned, then there is no rational source of grief even to the individual himself (cf. §90). No injustice accrues to him by a dispensation that produces a better overall result than would another, more favourable, dispensation for the individual which left the whole worse off. (Having grown up in a more egalitarian age than Leibniz's, we would probably disagree: for the sake of justice between individuals we may think it proper to forgo some overall maximization of welfare distribution that leaves some people grossly disadvantaged in comparison with their fellows.) Of course, if monads could lose their status as spirits as well as gain it, then there would be no reason in logic why each one should not eventually have its turn, and in that case the question of injustice in the election of some, but not of others, to the rank of spirits need not arise.

At §83 Leibniz contrasts minds with mere souls. These latter mirror the created universe in ways I have already discussed in connection with the mirror thesis of §56, primarily, though not exclusively, in ways that are unconscious or unclear, obscure and confused. Minds, however, do so apperceptively, and they are in addition themselves creators within the small world they inhabit. We exert our intellectual powers in the pursuit of knowledge in science, in the construction of artefacts (engineering and art) and in the devising of political and

---

4 Section 103 of *Theodicy* supplies an instance, one in which Leibniz allows that God could always have placed any sinner in more salutary circumstances and have given him internal and external aids that would have enabled him to vanquish even the most vicious nature that a soul might have.

social organizations for the orderliness of our lives. In this exercise of power, knowledge, wisdom and spiritual goodness we imitate God, 'each mind being like a small divinity in its own sphere' (§83).

This thought is drawn on at §84 to introduce God's concern for spirits. For the first time a specifically ethical element of God's nature and his creative calculations makes an appearance. The structural likeness of spirits to God functions as the hinge that makes his interest in spirits not just that of a curious and distant observer, but that of a concerned prince for his subjects or of a loving father for his children. This is no arbitrary matter conveniently serving the moral optimism of the *Monadology*'s last few sections, but has been carefully prepared for from the start and held in reserve until the appropriate moment. God's absolute perfection has been secured at §41, and we are assured that this includes absolute goodness by the reflection (§42) that the limited goodness we have as a perfection must be derived from God's own. If God is endowed with goodness, it has to be deployed and expressed somewhere, since an unexploited perfection makes no sense, and in the hierarchy of beings those that approximate to God by being spirits are the likeliest candidates for its deployment. After all, if we ourselves are most closely tied in our affective concerns to our own children, whom we see as our own creation, how could God, in whose image we are made, not be similarly closely tied to his?

Building on the intellectual powers of spirits, in particular on their intellectual ability to penetrate the system of the universe and, one supposes, on their capacity to know necessary and eternal truths (not least of which must be theological truths – see §29), Leibniz concludes that the assemblage of spirits makes up the City of God, a unified community under the governance of God, a community whose well-being is at the centre of his interest and concern. Drawing on the uncontentious perfection of God's goodness, Leibniz straightway concludes (§85) that this City or community is the most perfect possible state under the most perfect of monarchs. However uncertain we may be about the exact content of the claim, it is obvious that the conception of the best possible world (a phrase, incidentally, not used in the *Monadology*) as understood in terms of variety and order (cf. §58) has now acquired a further moral dimension tied specifically to the interests of spirits. I take care here not to say the interests of human beings, since the point is not a narrowly local one. Whatever world God might have chosen in conformity with Sufficient Reason would have been a world embracing a City of God. In this world that City contains humans among its members, though in other possible worlds humans would be absent. In the world where we humans do exist we can conclude on quite general grounds that our interests have been given as much weight as possible in the balance of competing claims among spirits.

Quite what content we can give to Leibniz's very loosely specified conception of the City of God, that most perfect of possible states, is uncertain. It gains some specificity, though, from his constant determination to present us with a metaphysics that is naturalistic in tenor. By this I mean that we have time and again seen what initially appear to be assertions of fantasy engaging with a natural world subject to natural laws and leaving next to no room for inexplicable or unintelligible miracle or whim. Time and again I have stressed the intellectual pressure that Leibniz feels to insist on the naturalistic character of his thought, best exemplified perhaps by the relatively late appearance, at §78, of the pre-established harmony between the kingdom of final causes and the kingdom of natural law. This is a pressure that is maintained and reinforced at §87, where the initial harmony between the two natural realms is mirrored by a harmony between the physical kingdom of nature and the moral kingdom of grace. This further harmony has consequences for the ethical conclusions we can draw from the closing passages of the work.

Spirits belong to the kingdom of grace as a matter of natural fact. It belongs to their nature as finite likenesses of God to be inclined to strive for the good (as they see it, of course). To have that inclination is not something they acquire as a matter of their own free choice, since we do not choose what nature to have, and so do not choose to desire the good.[5] Thus at section 98 of *Theodicy* Leibniz says: 'It depends on

---

5   They do, however, choose the good freely. It was to preserve this freedom that I avoided a reading of Leibniz's 'complete concept' doctrine of substances in Chapter 6 which would have rendered that freedom incoherent, making it strictly impossible for any monad to act otherwise than it in fact acts.

God to give them [sinners lacking good will] this good will. He is the master of desires, the hearts of kings and of other men are in his hands' (see also *Theodicy*, sections 99 and 301). Leibniz tells us that an inclination towards the good is the grace spirits receive from God (*Theodicy*, section 99), but we must be careful not to understand this as a gratuitous gift that he might have withheld from them. Rather it is part of their essential nature as spirits, something that supplies the framework within which they exercize their intelligence and understanding in the course of practical action and which binds them together in community with each other and with God himself.

The harmony between the physical realm of nature and the moral realm requires that 'things lead to grace even by the ways of nature' (§88), so that we should see the perfect state of God's devising as a natural state and not one that is imagined to obtain only in the far-off beyond. That could not be the way to understand it, since the state of grace must be a state of the created world and its naturally imperishable spiritual members. So their ultimate good must either be a final natural state, as Leibniz seems to have in mind when alluding to the Last Judgement – he speaks in §88 of the ultimate destruction and repair of this earthly globe – or, as seems more in harmony with the naturalized reading of his thought, a final account of a whole (phase of) life lived as spirit, which may come to an end even though the life of the relevant monad does not.

Let me enlarge a little on this last possibility. In the *Monadology*'s final passages, at §§88, 89 and 90, it becomes clear that Leibniz views the perfect state that God ordains as one in which good is rewarded and evil punished. By the harmony that reigns between the natural and the moral order, 'sins bring with them their punishment by the order of nature in virtue of the mechanical structure of things' (§89). So one must conclude that the good that we do, and the bad likewise, is rewarded and punished as a natural consequence of our actions. In our usual sense of 'punishment' and 'reward' there is some judge or other authority whose task it is to bestow prizes or impose forfeits, but placing Leibniz's moral reflections in their naturalized context and declining to see them as a purely theologico-legal matter or to take God himself as some magisterial Heavenly Arbiter, we are bound to understand these ideas in terms of the consequences of our actions.

This can make very good sense, for if it is natural for us to aim at the good (though often failing to achieve it) and likewise natural for us to identify the good correctly, it would scarcely be possible for the consequences of our good actions to be standardly bad ones or ones that had no bearing on our well-being. If our goals are good and energetically pursued, then the expectation must be that the consequences we shall reap will normally be good ones. In Leibniz's naturalistic sense they will be rewarded. Similarly for the bad that we do. So, for instance, it would be a plausible illustration of Leibniz's thought here to suppose that if we continue to burn down the forests and pour fossil fuels into our motorcars, as we now do, we shall have to pay for it, not perhaps immediately, but certainly in the long run, and the longer we shut our eyes to the harm we do the larger the bill will be in the natural course of things. Leibniz says as much of rewards for our noble deeds – they come by 'in mechanical ways as far as our bodies are concerned, although that cannot and should not happen immediately' (§89). The same will apply to our misdeeds, whether they arise from ill will or from downright stupidity, from surfeit of passion or sheer thoughtlessness .

Leibniz's reference at §85 to the perfect state instituted by God and to the subsequent rather legalistic notions of punishment and reward suggests that he wants to tie punishment to the individual wrong-doer and reward to the individual person of virtue. Section 90 speaks of there being no good action without reward, and asserts that 'everything shall serve the good of the righteous'. The 1697 paper 'On the Ultimate Origination of Things' is also explicit that 'just as in a well regulated commonwealth care is taken that as far as possible things shall be to the interest of the individual, in the same way the universe would not be sufficiently perfect unless, as far as can be done without upsetting universal harmony, the good of individual people is considered'.[6] This individualized notion of reward clearly goes beyond anything I have yet suggested, where the sorts of ill I cited are paid for less by those who perpetrate them than by their successors and the individual's socially virtuous deeds are no surer of gathering praise than of harvesting derision. Sometimes justice is done by history, but

---

6   Parkinson (ed.), 143.

I suspect that it is not that kind of thought that Leibniz would want to make use of, not even when married with the now-familiar claim that spirits are imperishable. Somehow the connection between good and reward, and ill and punishment, effected in this way is too unreliable to be of much general service. What Leibniz needs is a closer internal link between individual action and reward than this can provide. The question is whether there is any such link to be had and which might be said to be effected 'in mechanical ways as far as our bodies are concerned' (§89).

When Voltaire portrays Dr Pangloss riddled with the pox after his lessons in experimental physics with Paquette in the park of the most beautiful and most agreeable of all possible castles he may have supposed he had come as close as may be to what Leibniz had in mind, and in satirizing it to have shown it up for worthless. But an older philosophical tradition offers something more hopeful, namely a close connection between the nature of actions performed and the individual agent's happiness, mediated by conscience and self-knowledge. Learning that he has killed his father and committed incest with his mother Oedipus puts out his eyes. But the wound he inflicts on himself is not itself his punishment, but merely a symbolic representation of it, for what he really suffers is the knowledge of his wrong-doing and his consequent inability to face himself. Socrates dies happy drinking the hemlock in the knowledge that he has done right in abiding by the sentence of the law and knowing that he 'cannot be justly blamed for anything', as would have been the case if he had accepted his friends' offer of escape. In either case, reward and punishment of the individual for his deeds is effected by the liability of the subject's acknowledgement of them to impinge on the way he views himself. In this, the individual's happiness or misery is inevitably affected. I know of no text in which Leibniz explicitly endorses such a view,[7] but I see no reason to deny that it is just what the naturalizing tendency of the *Monadology*'s morality leads to.

It is a central feature of spirits that they have self-consciousness and memory. Without those they would be impervious to moral

---

7 Though see note 8 and notice the connection Leibniz makes between the good and the praiseworthy man who 'cannot be justly blamed for anything'.

reflection. (Leibniz is clear about this at *NE*, 236–7.) He can say then that men are liable to be aware that they have acted well or badly when they have done so. What has to be made out is that the thought that one has acted ill impinges on one's happiness for the worse as Leibniz conceives of that, and equally that the consciously virtuous person's action enlarges his happiness. There is every reason to think that how one perceives oneself cannot but be a central element in whether a life is a happy one, and that is something one can say independently of any precise specification of what happiness consists in, a topic I shall continue to leave unexamined for the moment.

Someone of a Voltairean turn of mind might object that Leibniz's naturalization of reward and punishment is considered as far as the body is concerned, and that leads straight to the ridiculous moralization of the wretched Pangloss's misfortune, a moralization we have seen rehearsed in our own day in some of the more primitive responses to the appearance of the AIDS virus. That would be a mistake. In the first place, what is rewarded or punished is the activity of the subject, and that can only be the soul. So far as rewards and punishments for the soul go, the terms 'pleasure' and 'pain', which the eighteenth century affected, can be seen as crude expressions of something that reaches farther and deeper – satisfaction and dissatisfaction with the self. Leibniz's text allows us to read him in this light even while it does not oblige us to.[8]

Then, as far as the body goes, one thing to remark is that in so far as human virtues and vices have a bodily component, they are in part identified as goods and ills by the causal consequences they have for the body itself. Temperance is a virtue very largely on account of the damage done to the body by excessive intake of poison, be it in the form of tobacco, alcohol or drugs. It makes little sense to say of

---

8   At section 251 of *Theodicy* he comments on the ideas of pleasure and pain:

> We agree that physical ill is nothing other than dis-pleasure (*déplaisir*) and I understand that term to cover pain, sorrow, and all other sorts of distress (*incommodité*). But is what is physically good just pleasure? I think rather that it consists in a sort of intermediate state. We are well enough when there is nothing wrong with us. Not to be in the grip of passion is wisdom of a kind. Thus one is praiseworthy indeed when one cannot be justly blamed for anything.

someone that they are intemperate in their consumption of spring water, however much of it they drink. While Leibniz can perfectly well make some such observation as this,[9] he can also do rather better. Under the system of pre-established harmony, the lack of self-esteem that naturally follows the course of bad conscience has its expression in the physical world. Likewise with the reward of virtue. Accordingly, Leibniz is well able to say that we must expect the rewards of good and ill in the spiritual realm to find bodily expression, namely in the way in which we act and conduct our daily lives. There must be something correct about this, because how people view themselves cannot be divorced from the behaviour which allows us to interpret them as thinking about themselves in this way or that. That is something that is not just fortuitously manifest in their carriage and in their day-to-day comportment in the physical world.

Leibniz is well aware that he has to say something about those whose ill deeds do not catch up with them, living a life of Riley on the Costa del Sol. His tendency here is to appeal to the Last Judgement, as he envisages doing at §88. But pursuing the harmony of nature and grace he has the further option of saying that such people fall into two classes, those who in the end recognize the error of their ways and those who do not. Of those who do he can say that they suffer in recognizing that their life of Riley has been a wasted life. Of those who don't he can say that they are punished in wasting their lives without even having the clarity of mind to know it. In either case they may have escaped the law of man, but not the law of the Styx that they have called down upon themselves.[10]

---

9 *Theodicy*, section 112:

> One can say that the forbidden action brought those bad consequences with it as a natural result, and that was why God forbade it and not because of some arbitrary decree. Roughly put, that is why we forbid children the use of knives. If drunkards bred children given to that same vice as a natural consequence of what takes place in their bodies, that would be a punishment for the parents, though not a punishment decreed by the law. For the contemplation of God's wisdom inclines us to believe that the natural world serves the kingdom of grace.

10 'The law of the Styx is inescapable. We have to submit to it' (*Theodicy*, section

All this is well and good, but unless it is supplemented by a substantive conception of the good and the bad, the notion of a wasted life that I have used as a last resort is pretty empty. So far the *Monadology* has been silent on that score. The only hint it offers in its very last paragraph, about the good and the righteous, is that they are

> those who are not discontent in this great state, who trust in providence after having done their duty and who properly emulate and love the author of all good, delighting in the contemplation of His perfection with true pure love, which finds pleasure in the happiness of those we love.

We should not mistake the edifying tone of these lines as an empty substitute for genuine content.

We have been told at §86 that the community of minds, the City of God, is the most exalted of God's works, and that the 'glory of God consists in this, since it would be nothing were His goodness and greatness not recognized and adored by minds'. The good or righteous man then must be one who glorifies God, who knows and wonders at his goodness. But this way of putting it smacks of a somewhat passive conception of our duty towards God, as if one might sing his praises in church and make mayhem at home or on the streets. To suppose that would be to neglect the idea present in the quotation from §90 that our perfection consists in 'loving *and imitating* the author of all good', imitating him by cultivating those powers we have as spirits and which make each of us 'a small divinity in its own

---

121). In the same passage Leibniz responds to the query why God should permit there to be evil in the first place. Answer: 'His wisdom reveals to God the best possible exercise of his benevolence. After that, the evil that occurs is an indispensable consequence of the best. I would add something even stronger: to permit evil, as God does, is the greatest goodness. *Si mala sustulerat, non erat ille bonus*' (Had he removed the bad, he would not have been good).

sphere', to wit our powers of intelligence, reason and creative order, exercized, as is natural, in accordance with the fundamental will to the good which we all have as a matter of grace, and which I suggested before is that 'internal principle' from which our actions and perceptions are said to stem (§11).

From this reflection it follows that for Leibniz we glorify God not only passively but actively by imitating him as best we can through the exercise of our god-like faculties, those through which we grasp necessary truths (such as the metaphysical ones of the *Monadology*), understand the machine of the universe (through pursuit of the natural sciences) and strive to improve the world we inherit from our parents in our practical lives (by the exercise of our creative abilities). As we do these things we glorify God, for thus we imitate him and display 'true *pure love*'.

Offered these thoughts, the villain on the Costa might say: 'True, I do not pretend to be good or righteous in any of those ways, but my life of pleasure on the proceeds of crime is as happy as life could be. It is only envy and sour grapes that prevents you from admitting it.' To this Leibniz has a response. 'Happiness is the spiritual equivalent of perfection in other things' (*Discourse on Metaphysics*, §36). That is, there is an intimate connection between the good and our happiness, and it is a connection that once again goes through the self-awareness that is the prerogative of spirits. If I see that I am imperfect by a standard that I acknowledge (as does our imagined villain), I cannot fail to be discomforted and suffer pain from being so (see note 5). Consequently I cannot be genuinely happy. Like the villain, I can of course think I am happy, but my thought will be a false one, and it would be perfectly consonant with Leibnizian principles to think that my error adds to my imperfection a further imperfection, one which makes my 'punishment' and real unhappiness worse than it would otherwise be.

In the final sentences of §90 Leibniz brings us face to face with the evident imperfections of the world. He is quite clear that the ills it contains are not illusory, but is also sure that he has told us enough to recognize that in his choice of a world that is in accord with the Principle of Sufficient Reason God has had as much regard for the good of spirits in general and for the individual spirits in particular as was consistent with a world that is overall the most worthy of choice. If we have followed the path of the *Monadology* conscientiously we shall perceive that clearly and distinctly, and hence believe it.[11] Seeing that the ills that there are in the world could not have been avoided except at the cost of greater ill we have no cause to be dissatisfied with the world that is ours. This is of course no reason not to strive to make it better. In doing that we imitate God and aim to conform to his 'presumptive or antecedent will', which is the state he would have wished to bring about had the limitations of the finite nature of the world not prevented it. When we find that our efforts do not amount to much and that God's effective choice (his 'consequent and decisive will') is of an imperfect world we know that we have no grounds for discontent.

Although I have spoken in these last pages of ourselves and of the human lot, and of our perfection and happiness, it is noteworthy that the only explicit reference Leibniz makes to this world is at §88, in reference to the destruction of 'this earth' at the time of Last Judgement. It is doubtful whether that allusion is more than a sop to religious orthodoxy, and if my understanding of the *Monadology* is correct there is little place for it in Leibniz's metaphysical scheme. We know that God can annihilate the world (§6) just as he created it, but nothing that the *Monadology* envisages could offer him a sufficient reason for doing so. The thought articulated at §88 to the effect that such destruction will take place at the time demanded by the government of minds for the chastisement of some can only be taken allegorically once we naturalize Leibniz's ethical thinking in the way his harmony between the kingdom of grace and the kingdom of nature seems to require. Once we set aside this passing reference to our

---

11 See *Theodicy*, section 311: 'the clear and distinct perception of a truth contains in itself the affirmation of that truth: thus the understanding is necessitated by it'.

own situation,[12] we can take the whole of the last, ethically directed, section of the work to apply to any candidate world that aspires for God's favour. We know already that all such worlds must contain spirits made in the image of God. Now we know that their perfection consists in imitating him and loving him, and their happiness and misery must be achieved, as it is in our world, by the ways of nature alone. The ethical and moral truths Leibniz takes to govern our world are just those that reason shows us will apply in any world to which such reflection has application – that is, to any world that enjoys a spiritual dimension. That can only mean that they apply to any world whatever that might pass the test of the two Great Principles with which we began.

Further reading

David Blumenfeld, 'Perfection and Happiness in the Best Possible World', in Jolley (ed.); Gregory Brown, 'Leibniz's Moral Philosophy', ibid.; Rutherford, Chapter 3, 'Happiness and Virtue in the Best of All Possible Worlds'.

---

12 Although the expressions 'the assemblage of all minds' and 'this City of God' occurring in §§85 and 86 may appear to do so, on my reading they do not refer specifically to the assembly of minds that actually exists, but pick out such assemblages as would be bound to exist in any world God might reasonably have decided to create.

Appendix
Monadology

1 Monads, which are our concern here, are nothing other than simple substances. They are simple in that they have no parts. (*Theodicy*, section 10)

2 There must be simple substances because there are compounds, and a compound is nothing other than a mass or aggregate of simples.

3 Now where there are no parts, neither extension nor shape nor division is possible. These monads are the true atoms of nature. In a word, they are the elements of things.

4 For them there is no dissolution to be feared, nor is there any way in which we can conceive of simple substances perishing by natural means. (*Theodicy*, section 89)

5 For the same reason there is no natural way by which simple substances could come to be since they cannot be formed by composition.

6 So we can say that monads cannot begin or end save all at once. That is, they can only begin by way of Creation and end by way of Annihilation. By contrast, compounds begin and end by way of parts.

7 Nor is there any way of explaining how monads could be internally changed or altered by any other created beings. In them nothing permits of transposition, and one cannot conceive of any internal movement occurring in them that might be excited or directed or augmented or diminished as happens with compounds when there is change among their parts. Monads have no windows through which anything can come in or go out. Accidents cannot detach themselves from substances and wander about outside them, as the sensible species of the scholastics were said to do. So neither substances nor accidents can enter monads from without.

8 However, monads must have some qualities and undergo some changes, otherwise they would not be anything at all. If simple substances were nothing, composites too would be reduced to nothing. Monads are not mathematical points for those are only extremities, and lines cannot be composed of points. And if simple substances did not have different qualities from one another there would be no possibility of our being aware of changes in things. For what is found in compounds can only come from their simple ingredients. Being quite without qualities monads would be indistinguishable from one another because they would then also be quantitatively indistinguishable. Then too, supposing there to be no vacuum, each place would only receive the equivalent amount of motion as it had had in the past, and one state of affairs would be indistinguishable from any other. (*Theodicy*, Preface)

9 It is even necessary that each monad be different from every other. For in nature there are never two beings that are exactly alike and where one cannot find some internal difference between them or one that is founded on some intrinsic denomination.

10 I take it for granted that every created thing is subject to change. So that holds too for created monads. I assume too that this change is continuous in each one.

11 It follows from what we have just said that the natural changes that come about in monads derive from an internal principle, which one might call their 'active force', since external causes can have no influence on their inner constitution. One can say quite generally that force is nothing but the principle of change. (*Theodicy*, sections 396, 400)

12 Quite apart from this principle of change there must also be detailed complexity in what changes, which, so to speak, makes for the specification and the variety of simple substances.

13 This detailed complexity must embrace multiplicity in the one or in what is simple. All natural change being gradual, something always changes and something always remains. Consequently in simple substances there has to be a plurality of qualities and relations even though there are no parts.

14 The passing state that contains and represents a multitude in the one, or in the simple substance, is what is called perception. This must be distinguished from apperception or conscious awareness, as will be made plain below. The Cartesians have quite failed to see this and so entirely overlooked perceptions that we are not aware of. It is this that has led them to hold that the only monads are minds, and that animals have no souls and that there are no other sorts of entelechies. This is also why they have made the common mistake of confusing a long period of stupor with death in the strict sense of the word, and what has led them to accept the scholastic prejudice of souls completely separated [from the body (A.S.)] and what has encouraged some to embrace the misguided view that the soul is mortal.

15 The working of the internal principle that accounts for the transition from one perception to another may be called appetition. It is true that appetite [or desire (A.S.)] does not always completely attain what it strives for, but it always achieves something of it and so leads to new perceptions.

16 We ourselves experience multiplicity in the simple substance when we find that the least thought that we are aware of embodies variety in its object. So all those who recognize that the soul is a simple substance will acknowledge this inner multiplicity of the monad, and Monsieur Bayle should find no difficulty in accepting it, as he does in his *Dictionary* article 'Rorarius'.

17 Further, we must admit that perception and everything that depends on perception is inexplicable on mechanical principles, that is, in terms of shapes and movements. If we imagine a machine whose structure allowed it to think, to feel and to perceive, we can conceive of it as being enlarged while conserving its proportions and so permitting us to enter it as into a mill. Supposing that to be the case, on visiting its interior we should only come across parts exerting pressure on one another and never find anything that might explain perception. So we must look for that in simple substances and not in aggregates or machines. And that is all we shall find in simple substances, namely perceptions and their changes. The inner actions of simple substances can consist in nothing else.

18 One could give the name 'entelechy' to all simple substances or created monads, for they have within themselves a certain perfection (*echousi to enteles*). They enjoy a self-sufficiency (*autarkia*) that renders them the source of their internal actions and makes them, so to speak, incorporeal automata. (*Theodicy*, section 87)

19 If we were to call souls everything that has perception and appetition in the general way I have just explained, then all simple substances or created monads could be called souls. But since sensation is something more than simple perception, I think that the general terms 'monad' or 'entelechy' are more appropriate to simple substances that only have that, and that we should call 'souls' only those monads whose perceptions are more distinct and accompanied by memory.

20 We sometimes experience in ourselves states in which we remember nothing and have no distinct perceptions as when we fall into a faint or when we are overcome by a deep dreamless sleep. In such states our souls scarcely differ from those of bare monads. But since such states are of short duration and we emerge from them, souls are something more than they are.

21 It by no means follows that in those states simple substances are altogether without perceptions. For the reasons given above that could not be. They cannot perish, nor can they exist without possessing some qualities, and those are their perceptions. But when there is a great number of minute perceptions in which nothing is distinguished, then we are dazed as when we turn round constantly in the same direction a number of times and we suffer a vertigo which can make us faint and permits us to distinguish nothing. Death may produce such a state in animals for a time.

22 Just as every present state of a simple substance is the natural outcome of its preceding states, so the present is pregnant with the future. (*Theodicy*, section 360)

23 So since when we come to from our stupor we are conscious of our perceptions we must have had some immediately beforehand although we were not aware of them at the time. For a perception can only arise naturally from other perceptions, just as a movement can only come from another movement. (*Theodicy*, sections 401, 403)

24 We see from this that if there was nothing distinct or so to speak piquant and of a heightened flavour in our perceptions, we should always be in a state of stupor. Such is the condition of bare monads.

25 We can see too that nature has provided animals with heightened perceptions from the care she has taken to furnish them with bodily organs that collect many rays of light or many vibrations of the air so that in the mass they should be more effective. Something similar occurs with smell and taste and touch and perhaps with numerous other senses too of which we are ignorant. I shall shortly explain how what takes place in the soul represents what happens in our bodily organs.

26 Memory furnishes the soul with a sort of internal connectedness that is analogous to reason but which should be distinguished from it. Thus we see animals perceiving something that strikes them and which they have perceived once before and then in virtue of what their memory represents to them they expect the same thing as had previously been associated with their earlier perception and they are brought to have similar feelings as they had had before. For example when you show a dog a stick, it remembers the pain the stick had previously caused it and it whimpers and runs away.

27 And the power of the impressions that strike them and move them is due either to the intensity or the large quantity of their previous perceptions. Often a powerful impression produces the same effect at a stroke as a long-established habit or the repetition of many perceptions of only moderate power.

28 So long as their perceptions are only connected by their memories men act like animals. Then they resemble Empirical physicians of the trial and error school, whose practice is simple and uninformed by theory. We are empirics in three quarters of our actions. For example, when we expect there to be daylight tomorrow we do so as empirics because that has always happened in the past. Only the astronomer bases his judgement on reason. (*Theodicy*, Preliminary Discourse, section 65)

29 It is the knowledge of necessary and eternal truths that distinguishes us from mere animals and which gives us reason and the sciences, affording us knowledge of ourselves and of God. And this is what is called our rational soul or mind.

30 It is also through knowledge of necessary truths and by abstracting them from their background that we arrive at reflexive acts, acts by which we think of what is called 'I' [or the Self (A.S.)] and consider that this or that lies within us. So it is that in thinking of ourselves we reflect on being, on substance, on the simple and the complex, on what is immaterial and on God Himself, considering what is limited in us and what is in Him without limits. These reflexive acts provide our reasoning with its main topics. (*Theodicy*, Preface)

31 Our reasonings are founded on two Great Principles, that of Contradiction, whereby we judge to be false what contains a contradiction and to be true what is opposed to or contradicts the false. (*Theodicy*, sections 44, 169)

32 And that of Sufficient Reason, whereby we consider that no fact can hold or be real, and no proposition true, but there be a sufficient reason why it is so and not otherwise, even though for the most part these reasons cannot be known by us. (*Theodicy*, sections 44, 196)

33 There are two kinds of truths, those of reason and those of fact. Truths of reason are necessary, and their opposites are impossible. Those of fact are contingent and their opposites are possible. When a truth is necessary one can discover the reason why it holds by analysis, reducing it to simpler ideas and truths until one arrives at the primitive ones. (*Theodicy*, sections 170, 174, 189, 280–2, 367; Abridgement, obj. 3)

34 Thus it is in mathematics that speculative theorems and practical canons are reduced by analysis to definitions, axioms and postulates.

35 Ultimately one arrives at simple ideas that cannot be further defined. There are

also axioms and postulates, in a word primitive principles, which cannot be proved and stand in no need of it either. These are identical propositions, whose opposite contains an explicit contradiction.

36 But there must also be sufficient reason for contingent truths, or truths of fact, that is for the succession of things extended throughout the created universe, where their resolution into individual reasons would know no bounds on account of nature's vastness and the infinite divisibility of bodies. There is an infinity of shapes and movements both present and past that enters into the efficient cause of my present writing, and there is an infinity of minute inclinations and dispositions of my soul that enters into its final cause. (*Theodicy*, sections 36, 37, 44, 45, 52, 121, 122, 337, 340, 344)

37 And as all this detail just contains other preceding and more detailed contingencies, each of which requires a similar analysis to arrive at its reason, one is no further forward. The ultimate and sufficient reason must lie outside the succession of things or the series of detailed contingencies, however infinite it may be.

38 Thus it is that the ultimate reason for things must lie in a Necessary Substance, one in which the complex detail of all changes is contained merely eminently, as their source. This it is that we call God. (*Theodicy*, section 7)

39 Now since this substance is a sufficient reason for all this complex detail, which is also through and though interconnected, there is only one God, and this God is enough.

40 We may also infer that this Supreme Substance – which is unique, universal and necessary, having nothing beyond it that is independent of it, and existing as a simple consequence of being possible – must be incapable of being limited, and must contain as much reality as is possible.

41 From which it follows that God is absolutely perfect, perfection being nothing other than the amount of positive reality strictly understood, setting aside the limits or boundaries in the case of those things that have them. And where there are no limits, that is to say, in God, perfection is absolutely infinite. (*Theodicy*, Preface, section 22)

42 It also follows that the perfections that created things have are due to God's influence; their imperfections, though, are due to their own natures, incapable as they are of being without limits. It is in this that they are distinguished from God. This original imperfection that belongs to created things is manifest in the natural inertia of bodies.

43 It is true too that God is not just the origin of existing things, but also of essences in so far as they are real, or of what is real in possibilities. This is

because God's understanding is the region of eternal truths or of the ideas on which they depend. Without Him there would be nothing real in possibilities, not just nothing actual, but nothing possible either. (*Theodicy*, section 20)

44 For if there is any reality in essences or possibilities, or even in eternal truths, it must be founded on something existing and actual, and in consequence on the existence of the Necessary Being, whose essence comprehends its existence, and whose very possibility ensures its actuality.

45 So God alone, or the Necessary Being, has this privilege, that He must exist if He is possible. And since nothing can inhibit the possibility of what has no limits and no negation and so no contradiction, this by itself is enough to secure the existence of God *a priori*. We have also proved it through the reality of eternal truths. But we have just now proved it *a posteriori* as well, since contingent beings exist and their ultimate or sufficient reason can only be located in the Necessary Being that contains the reason for its own existence within itself.

46 One should not suppose, as some are wont to do, that eternal truths are dependent on God and that they are arbitrary and a matter for His will. Descartes seems to have thought this, and Monsieur Poiret too. That is only correct for contingent truths, the ground of which is their fittingness or God's choice of the best. By contrast, necessary truths depend only on His understanding and are its internal objects. (*Theodicy*, sections 180–4, 185, 335, 351, 380)

47 So God alone is the primary unity, or the original simple substance and the source of all created or derivative monads, which are born, as it were, by continual fulgurations of the divinity from moment to moment. They are bounded by their nature as created beings, things whose essence it is to be limited. (*Theodicy*, sections 382–91, 395, 398)

48 In God there is power, which is the source of everything; there is knowledge, which contains the complex detail of ideas; and finally there is will, which determines the production of things and their changes in accordance with the Principle of the Best. (*Theodicy*, sections 7, 48, 149, 150)

It is these attributes that correspond in God to what in the case of created monads is the subject or the basis, that is; the perceptive and the appetitive faculties. Only in God are these attributes absolutely infinite or perfect. In created monads or in entelechies [or *perfectihabies*, as Hermolous Barbarus rendered that word] in so far as there is perfection in them they are limitations. (*Theodicy*, sections 48, 87)

49 Created beings are said to act on others beyond themselves in so far as they possess perfection: and they are passively acted upon by others to the extent that they are imperfect. So we can attribute activity to monads in so far as their perceptions are distinct, and passivity in so far as they are confused. (*Theodicy*, sections 32, 66, 386)

50 And one created thing is more perfect than another when there is in the one what explains *a priori* what happens in the other. That is how the former is said to act upon the latter.

51 In the case of simple substances, one monad has no more than an ideal influence on another, and only achieves its effect through the intervention of God. This occurs by there being good reason for one monad to require that God take its nature into account in ordering other things from the very beginning. Since created monads cannot exercise any physical influence on the inner nature of others this is the only way that one of them can be dependent on another. (*Theodicy*, sections 9, 54, 65, 66, 201; Abridgement, obj. 3)

52 In this way among created beings activity and passivity are reciprocal. For in considering two simple substances God finds reasons in each one to accommodate the other to it. So what is in some respects active is passive from another point of view. It is active in that what is distinctly perceived in it explains what happens in the other, and passive in that what happens to it is distinctly perceived in the other. (*Theodicy*, section 66)

53 Now, as there is an infinity of possible universes in the ideas of God and because only one of them can be actual, there has to be a sufficient reason for God's choice which determines Him in favour of one rather than another. (*Theodicy*, sections 8, 10, 44, 173, 196–9, 225, 414–16)

54 And this reason can only be found in the fitness or in the degrees of perfection that these worlds contain, each one having as much right to claim existence as there is perfection in it. Hence nothing is entirely arbitrary. (*Theodicy*, sections 74, 130, 167, 201, 345–7, 350, 352, 354)

55 What brings about the existence of the best is that God's wisdom has Him recognize it, His goodness has Him choose it, and His power has Him create it. (*Theodicy*, sections 8, 78, 80, 84, 119, 204, 206, 208; Abridgement, objs 1 and 8)

56 Now this interconnection and accommodation of every created thing to every other, of all to each, gives every simple substance relations that express all the others so that each one is a perpetual living mirror of the universe. (*Theodicy*, sections 130, 360)

57 And just as the same town appears quite different as it is viewed from different sides and is, as it were, perspectivally multiplied, so it is that in virtue of the infinite multitude of simple substances it appears as if there are so many different universes, which in fact are nothing other than aspects of the same one according to the different points of view of each monad. (*Theodicy*, section 147)

58 And this is how as much variety as possible is achieved, though with the greatest

possible order, that is to say, it is the way of obtaining as much perfection as possible. (*Theodicy*, sections 129, 124, 214, 241–3, 275)

59 Moreover, no other hypothesis than this (which I venture to say is now established) is as capable of properly exalting the greatness of God. M. Bayle recognized as much when he raised objections to it in his *Dictionary* (article 'Rorarius'), going so far as to hold that I attributed too much to God, more even than is possible. Yet he was unable to produce any reason to suppose that this universal harmony that enables one substance to express all the others exactly is impossible.

60 From what I have just said one can see the *a priori* reasons why things could not be otherwise than as they are. This is because in regulating the whole God took account of each simple part, notably of each monad, whose very nature being representative makes it incapable of being restricted to representing only one part of things. It is true enough that their representations are confused when it comes to the fine detail of the universe, and that they are distinct only over a narrow range, that is, over what is closest to each one or what is largest in its vicinity. Otherwise each monad would be a divinity. It is not in regard to the objects of their knowledge that monads are restricted so much as in the manner of that knowledge. Monads reach out confusedly to infinity, to everything, but they are restricted and distinguished from each other by the degrees of distinctness of their perceptions.

61 In this compounds behave like simples. For the whole is a plenum, which makes all matter interconnected, and as in a plenum every movement has some effect on far off bodies depending on their distance from one another. In consequence every body is affected not just by those that touch it in one way or another, feeling everything that happens to them, but also through their mediation each one is sensitive to all those that touch the ones with which it is in direct contact.

It follows that this intercommunication stretches out as far as may be. Consequently every body is sensitive to everything in the universe, so that someone who saw everything could read in each thing what happens everywhere, even what has happened and what will come to be, noticing in what is nearest at hand what is furthest away, be it in time or in space. *Sympnoia panta* ('all things conspire' [AS]), Hippocrates said. But the soul can only discern what is represented within itself distinctly. It cannot unfold all at once the full detail of what it contains, for that extends *ad infinitum*.

62 Thus although each created monad represents the whole universe, it represents most clearly the body to which it is most particularly attached and whose entelechy it is, and which is always organic in nature so that the body should be an orderly one. And as this body expresses the whole universe through the interconnection of all matter in the plenum, the soul too represents the whole universe in representing that body which belongs to it in a special way.

63 The body that belongs to a monad that is its entelechy or its soul, together with

that entelechy, makes up what we can call a living being, or together with that soul, an animal. The body, be it of a living thing or of an animal, is always organic, for since every monad is in its own way a mirror of the universe and the universe is regulated in a perfectly orderly way, there must be order in the representer, and so also in the body through which it represents the universe.

64 So it is that every organic body of a living thing is a kind of divine machine, or natural automaton, infinitely surpassing all humanly constructed automata. This is because man-made machines are not machines in each of their smallest parts. For example, the tooth of a brass cogwheel has parts or pieces which are not themselves artefacts and so bear no special mark of the machine for which the cogwheel itself is designed. But nature's machines, which is to say living bodies, are machines down to their smallest parts, even to infinity. Herein lies the difference between nature and artifice, that is between divine artifice and our own. (*Theodicy*, sections 134, 146, 194, 403)

65 And the author of nature has been able to exercize this divine and infinitely marvellous artifice because each portion of matter is not just capable of infinite division, as the ancients recognized, but is actually subdivided without end, each part into smaller parts, each one of which has some movement of its own. Otherwise it would be impossible for each portion of matter to express the whole universe. (*Theodicy*, Preliminary Discourse, sections 70, 195)

66 Whence one sees that there is a whole world of created things – of living beings, of animals, of entelechies, of souls – in the least part of matter.

67 Every portion of matter may be thought of as a garden full of plants or like a pond full of fishes. But every branch of every plant, each limb of each animal, every drop of its liquid humours is another such garden, another such pond.

68 And although the earth and the air that are placed between the plants of the garden, and the water between the fishes in the pond, are themselves neither plants nor fishes, they do still contain such creatures, even though for the most part we cannot perceive them.

69 So there is nothing fallow, sterile or dead in the universe, no chaos, no confusion except merely apparent confusion, rather as when we see a pond at some distance and in it a confused and teeming movement of fishes without discerning the individual fish themselves. (*Theodicy*, Preface)

70 From this one sees that every living body has a dominant entelechy, which in the case of an animal is its soul. But the limbs of the living body are full of other living things, plants and animals, each one of which has its own dominant entelechy or soul.

71 It should not be supposed, as some who misunderstand my thought have done,

that every soul has a mass or portion of matter that is assigned to it for ever, and that it therefore possesses other living things that are destined to be forever at its service. For all bodies are in perpetual flux like rivers, and parts are continually entering and leaving them.

72 Hence the soul only changes its body little by little and gradually, so that it never loses all its organs at a stroke. There is often metamorphosis in animals, but there is never metempsychosis or the migration of souls. Nor are there souls that are entirely separated from bodies, or spirits quite without them. God alone is altogether detached from body.

73 This also ensures that there is neither any birth nor any death in the strict sense, which consists in the soul's separation from the body. What we call births are in truth cases of development and growth, just as what we call death is envelopment and diminution.

74 Philosophers have been much perplexed as to the origin of forms, entelechies or souls. But today we see from careful research into plants, insects and animals that natural organic bodies are never the products of chaos or putrefaction, but always arise from seeds, in which they are doubtlessly somehow preformed. So we may infer not just that their organic bodies were present before conception, but also that there must have been a soul in those bodies, in a word, the whole animal, and that by means of conception the animal simply became disposed to undergo a large transformation into an animal of a different kind. One sees something of the sort (apart from birth) when worms become flies, and caterpillars butterflies.

75 Animals, of which some are raised by means of conception to the rank of the higher animals, can be called spermatic. But those of them which remain of the same kind unchanged – and that is most of them – are born, multiply and die, like the higher animals. There are only a few, the elect, that are chosen to play a greater role.

76 Yet this is only half the truth. I am persuaded that if animals never have a natural beginning then they will never have a natural end either. So not only is there no new birth, but no complete destruction either, no death in the strict sense. These *a posteriori* reflections based on experience accord perfectly with the principles established above *a priori*. (*Theodicy*, section 90)

77 So we can say not only that the soul (a mirror of the indestructible universe) is indestructible, but also that the animal is so too, even though its machine [i.e. its body (AS)] often perishes in part and casts off and takes on particular organic elements.

78 These principles permit me to explain quite naturally the union or the conformity of the soul and the organic body. The soul obeys its own laws, as the

body obeys its. They agree in virtue of the harmony that is pre-established among all substances, since they are all representations of one and the same universe. (*Theodicy*, Preface, sections 340, 352, 353, 358)

79 Souls act according to the laws of final causation, through appetition, ends and means. Bodies obey the laws of efficient causation or of motion. These two realms, that of efficient and that of final causes, are in harmony with one another.

80 Descartes saw that souls cannot impart force to bodies because there is always the same quantity of force in matter. He did however suppose that the soul could alter the direction of bodies. That was because in his time the law of nature was unknown whereby the total directed force of matter is conserved. If he had been aware of that he would have stumbled upon my system of pre-established harmony. (*Theodicy*, Preface, sections 22, 59–61, 63, 66, 345–48, 354, 355)

81 According to this system all bodies act as if there were (*per impossibile*) no souls, and that souls act as if there were no bodies, and both act as if the one influenced the other.

82 As for minds, or rational souls, the same holds fundamentally of them as of all living things and animals, as we have said – to wit, that the animal and the soul begin with the world itself and end with the world's end. Nonetheless, rational animals have this peculiarity about them, namely that their smaller spermatic animals, as long as they remain just that, have ordinary or sensible souls. But as soon as those that are, as it were, elect attain to human nature by way of actual conception, their sensible souls are elevated to the rank of reason and to the prerogatives of minds. (*Theodicy*, sections 91, 397)

83 Among the other differences there are between ordinary souls and minds, some of which I have already remarked, there is also this: that while souls are quite generally living mirrors or images of the universe of created things, minds are even images of God Himself or of the very author of nature. They are capable of understanding the system of the universe and of imitating it in some measure through constructive exemplars, each mind being like a small divinity in its own sphere. (*Theodicy*, section 147)

84 This is what enables minds to enter into a kind of community with God. He stands to them not simply as an architect does to his machines, which is how He is related to other created things, but also as a prince to his subjects, even as a father to his children.

85 From which we may easily conclude that the assembly of all minds must constitute the City of God, that is, the most perfect state possible, under the most perfect of monarchs. (*Theodicy*, section 146; Abridgement, obj. 2)

86 This City of God, this truly universal monarchy, is a moral world within the natural world. It is what is most excellent and most divine among God's works. The glory of God consists in this, since it would be nothing were His goodness and greatness not recognized and adored by minds. It is also in regard to this divine city that His goodness is particularly exercised, whereas His power and His wisdom are everywhere manifest.

87 Just as above we have established the perfect harmony between the two natural realms, that of efficient and that of final causes, so now we should observe a further harmony, that between the physical order of nature and the moral order of grace, that is between God considered as architect of the machine of the universe and God considered as monarch of the divine city of minds. (*Theodicy*, sections 63, 74, 112, 118, 130, 247, 248)

88 By reason of this harmony things lead to grace even by the ways of nature. For example, it ensures that this earth shall be destroyed and renewed by natural processes at those times that the government of minds shall require it for the chastisement of some and the reward of others. (*Theodicy*, sections 18ff., 110, 244f., 340)

89 We can also say that God the architect satisfies God the legislator in all respects, and thus that our sins bring with them their punishment by the order of nature in virtue of the mechanical structure of things. Even so are our good deeds rewarded in mechanical ways as far as our bodies are concerned, although that cannot and should not happen immediately.

90 Finally, under this perfect government there shall be no good deed without its reward, no wicked one without its punishment, and everything shall serve the good of the righteous, that is, of those who are not discontent in this great state, who trust in providence after having done their duty and who properly emulate and love the author of all good, delighting in the contemplation of His perfection with true pure love, which finds pleasure in the happiness of those we love. It is this that encourages the wise and the virtuous to strive for everything that seems in conformity with God's presumptive or antecedent will, but nevertheless to content themselves with what He actually brings about by His secret, consequent or decisive, will. They recognize that if we were able to understand the order of the universe we should find that it surpasses all the desires of the wisest of men and that it is impossible to be made better than it is, not only taken as a whole, but with regard to ourselves in particular as long as we are as attached as we should be to the author of everything, not only as to the architect and efficient cause of our existence, but even as to our Lord and to the Final Cause, who should be the aim of all our endeavours and in whom alone our happiness can consist. (*Theodicy*, Preface, sections 134 *ad finem*, 278)

Select bibliography

The Monadology: editions and commentaries

Boutroux, Emile, *Leibniz: La Monadologie* (Paris, 1887).

Carr, Herbert Wildon, *The Monadology of Leibniz* (London, 1930).

Glockner, Hermann, *Gottfried Wilhelm Leibniz: Monadologie* (Stuttgart, 1954).

Lachelier, Henri, *Leibniz: La Monadologie* (Paris, 1881).

Latta, Robert, *Leibniz: The Monadology and other Philosophical Writings* (Oxford, 1898).

Rescher, Nicholas, *G. W. Leibniz's Monadology: An Edition for Students* (London, 1991).

Robinet, André (ed.) *G. W. Leibniz: Principes de la Nature et de la Grace fondés en raison et Principes de la Philosophie ou Monadologie* (Paris, 1954).

Other writings by Leibniz

Die Philosophischen Schriften von G. W. Leibniz, ed. C. I. Gerhardt (Hildesheim, 1996), vols I–VII.

Discourse on Metaphysics, trans. P. Lucas and L. Grint (Manchester, 1952).

G. W. Leibniz: Philosophical Essays, ed. and trans. R. Ariew and D. Garber (Indianapolis, 1989).

Gottfried Wilhelm Leibniz: Philosophical Writings, ed. G. H. R. Parkinson (London, 1973).

Leibniz Selections, ed. P. Wiener (New York, 1951).

Leibniz: Philosophical Papers and Letters, trans. L. E. Loemker (Amsterdam, 1970).

Leibnizens Mathematische Schriften, ed. C. I. Gerhardt (Berlin and Halle, 1875–90), vols I–VII.

Leibniz's 'New System' and Associated Contemporary Texts, ed. and trans. R. S. Woolhouse and R. Francks (Oxford, 1997).

New Essays on Human Understanding, ed. and trans. P. Remnant and J. Bennett (Cambridge, 1981).

Opuscules et Fragments Inédits de Leibniz, ed. L. Couturat (Paris, 1903).

The Leibniz–Arnauld Correspondence, ed. and trans. H. T. Mason (Manchester, 1967).

The Leibniz–Clarke Correspondence, ed. H. G. Alexander (Manchester, 1956).

Theodicy, trans. E. M. Huggard (London, 1952).

General

Adams, Robert M., *Leibniz: Determinist, Theist, Idealist* (Oxford, 1994).

Brown, Stuart, *Leibniz* (Brighton, 1984).

Cottingham, John, *The Rationalists* (Oxford, 1988).

Ishiguro, Hidé, *Leibniz's Philosophy of Logic and Language* (London, 1978).

Jolley, Nicholas, *Leibniz and Locke: A Study of the* New Essays on Human Understanding (Oxford, 1984).

MacDonald Ross, George, *Leibniz*, Pastmasters (Oxford, 1984).

Mates, Benson, *The Philosophy of Leibniz: Metaphysics and Language* (Oxford, 1986).

McRea, Robert, *Leibniz: Perception, Apperception and Thought* (Toronto, 1976).

Parkinson, G. H. R., *Logic and Reality in Leibniz's Metaphysics* (Oxford, 1965).

Rescher, Nicholas, *The Philosophy of Leibniz* (Englewood Cliffs, NJ, 1967).

Russell, Bertrand, *A Critical Exposition of the Philosophy of Leibniz* (London, 1901).

Rutherford, Donald, *Leibniz and the Rational Order of Nature* (Cambridge, 1995).

Sleigh, Robert C., *Leibniz and Arnauld: A Commentary on Their Correspondence* (Yale, 1990).

Wilson, Catherine, *Leibniz's Metaphysics: A Historical and Comparative Study* (Princeton, NJ, 1989).

Woolhouse, Roger, *Descartes, Leibniz, Spinoza: The Concept of Substance in Seventeenth Century Metaphysics* (London, 1993).

Collections of articles

Frankfurt, H. G. (ed.) *Leibniz: A Collection of Critical Essays* (New York, 1972).

Hooker, M. (ed.) *Leibniz: Critical and Interpretive Essays* (Minneapolis, 1982).

Jolley, Nicholas (ed.) *The Cambridge Companion to Leibniz* (Cambridge, 1995).

Kuhlstad, Mark (ed.) *Essays on the Philosophy of Leibniz*, Rice University Studies (Houston, 1977).

Okruhlik, K. and Brown, J. R. (eds) *The Natural Philosophy of Leibniz* (Reidel, 1986).

Woolhouse, R. S. (ed.) *Leibniz: Metaphysics and Philosophy of Science* (Oxford, 1981).

An invaluable reference work is the concordance to the Gerhardt edition, published as *Leibniz Lexicon: A Dual Concordance to Leibniz's* Philosophische Schriften, compiled by R. Finster *et al.* (Olms-Weidmann, 1988).

Index